SYMBOLISM IN TRIBAL RELIGION

Important Books of Similar Interest Published Recently

Encyclopaedia of Tribal Religion,
in 12 Volumes
Edited by Dr. Subhadra Channa

International Encyclopaedia of Anthropology,
in 12 Volumes
Edited by Dr. Subhadra Channa

Landmarks in Indian Anthropology,
in 74 Volumes
Edited and Written by Several World Authrities

Encyclopaedia of Sociology of Religion,
in 3 Volumes
Edited by V.G.Nayar and M.G.Nayar

Encyclopaedia of Sociology of Politics,
in 3 Volumes
Edited by R.Motwani and R.D.Saksena

THE BUDDHISTS.
Encyclopaedia of Buddhism, in 5 Volumes
Edited by Subodh Kapoor

THE HINDUS.
Encyclopaedia of Hinduism, in 5 Volumes
Edited by Subodh Kapoor

Encyclopaedia of Ethics and Logic, in 10 Volumes
Edited by Piet and Prasad

SYMBOLISM IN TRIBAL RELIGION

Edited by
DR. SUBHADRA CHANNA
President, Indian Anthropological Association

COSMO PUBLICATIONS
2002 INDIA

6. **Spatial Concepts of the Ainu of the Northwest Coast of Southern Sakhalin**

By Emiko Ohnuki-Tierney 173

7. **The Stranger as God: The Place of the Outsider in Japanese Folk Religion**

By Teigo Yosida 237

8. **Themes in Symbolism of Ndembu Hunting Ritual**

By Victor Turnel 265

9. **Spear Symbolism in Nuerland**

By E.E. Evas-Pritchard 291

Chapter-1

Symbolism in the Higher Rites

By W.E.H. Stanner

Chapter-1

I. Levels Of Awareness

The aborigines put no important restraints on what a European may see or do when they allow him to attend the celebration of their religious rites. Perhaps they may ask him to keep his knowledge of the more secret matters from the unauthorized, especially from the women and children, but beyond that there are no impediments. Nevertheless, he is likely to feel for a long time unable to pass beyond the anterooms of meaning, because the rites are made up of an infinitude to symbolisms, most of them obscure, for which the aborigines make no attempt to account and, if asked to, usually cannot. The usages are time-honoured and evidently well-loved, but their significance arouses no curiosity among the celebrants.

In the circumstances the "cake of custom" of which much was once heard in anthropology might seem to be a reality. But the facts would be misrepresented by any suggestion of mindless automatism, or blind or instinctual following out of a deadend tradition. Nor is there any need to postulate a collective unconscious. One is dealing with a dutiful submission to authority on solemn occasions, and with a rapt absorption in things that have emotional appeal and give aesthetic pleasure.

The young men who are being inducted into the rites are not warned against asking questions. There is no suggestion that they will be put under penalty if they do. A questioning or critical approach would be out of character with the occasion. Those whom I have examined on the matter simply say: "We looked, we stayed quiet, we did not ask." But there is more to it than that. The older men use many artifices to induce respect and fear. At various junctures the young men are admonished to comport themselves modestly and deferentially, and commanded to look carefully at what happens so that, when they too are men of authority and understanding, they will know what to do, and to require their sons to do, to "follow-up". A guardian is always close at hand to see that they conform to instructions. The form and matter of the rites are thus taught, and doubtless are remembered, in a somewhat rote fashion. The unquestioning attitude in this way is passed between overlapping generations.

What happens on such high occasions is also apprehended in a deeper fashion, and the interior life is shaped in a positive way. All the things seen and done have the authority of ancient, sacred ways (*mane mundak,* lit. "hand-fashion," "olden time"). They are also true things (*murin daitpir,* lit. "words," "lip"). More, they are good things of the utmost gravity (*nandji bata bata, nandji nala nala,* lit. "things," "excellent," "very heavy" or "very big"). These phrases are commonly used, and every circumstance of contex-beauty, drama, excitement, mystery-reinforces them. As well, both young and old, neophytes and instructors, have a lively dread of sanctions of irreverence. It would scarcely be possible to weigh the contributions made by these influences to the attitude of uninquiring acceptance exemplified by the old and emulated by the young. But clearly we are not dealing with a lifeless adhesion to a deadened routine.

It is not particularly difficult to bring the aborigines to see that many elements of the rites lack explanation. Their response varies from a naive and somewhat started surprise to a thoughtful reflection. A means of making them attend to the matter is to build on an example which they themselves see as symbolical. For example, the fact that the bullroarer, in their own words, "takes the place of" The Old Woman, or, as we might say, "stands for" her and "points beyond itself" to her. One may then ask if this is the case with other elements. The inquiry does not lead very far but it helps to adduce some significant details. One comes to two main conclusions. There is a conscious awareness that many elements of the rites designate things of nature. As a case in point, the rhythmic cries that punctuate dances, chants and songs are meant to simulate the calls of birds, the sounds of surf, tides and streams, and the winds. The fact is not at all obvious at first, for the cries do not necessarily refer to anything being celebrated in the rites, or stressed in the accompanying mythology. One is left with the impression that the ritual fashions are compound of old and new elements. The second conclusion in unavoidable: there are several levels of awareness of ritual symbolism. A few usages are recognized clearly as being symbolical; a few more, on the whole of minor importance, are demonstrable as such; but the vast majority are practised without clear recognition of the symbolical character. Direct questioning of the aborigines does little to clarify the matter, and if understanding is to pass this threshold then it must be by other means.

Many anthropologists, confronted by this situation, might feel that they must transpose the study to phenomena of the aboriginal unconscious. But the symbolisms are constituents of collective acts of mutuality, with a logical structure, a detectable range of meanings, and an aesthetic appeal as well as a premial place in the social development of individuals. These relations may appropriately be studied by the methods of anthropology. The fact that they are perpetuated apparently without the kinds of conscious awareness or rational consideration that might represent them to the aborigines as things requiring explanation is not in itself a sufficient reason for thinking them beyond the province of anthropological study.

In this article I propose to examine some of them as conventional signs with practical, logical and expressive functions in the symbolical systems of ritual.

2. The Geometric Idiom Of Ceremony

The religious rites involve anything from scores to hundreds of men at a place and time. They are all complex sequences of ritual forms in *unguided* coordination. There is no master of ceremony as such, only a concerting of familiar tasks. One is better able to understand what happens by beginning with the morphic aspect, the visual shape of what may be seen.

The celebrants of Murinbata rites arrange themselves in spatial patterns. These have a geometric idiom: arcs, circles or ovals, points and straight and curved lines. Each rite exhibit a somewhat different combination of the same elements. The compositions give an austere beauty to the inactive phases and an excited vitalism to the active phases. In both they are impressive essays in dynamic symmetry and asymmetry.

A knowledge of the patterns is part of the experience of every man; not, as far as I could determine, as the result of special instruction, but because everyone who passes through the rites becomes familiar with them. Certainly, at the celebrations, everyone appears to fall with an easy confidence into place, stance and posture, and to follow out the sequences of what has to be done to a set formulary.

The formulary is well understood. There is no difficulty in obtaining from informants, by the use of tokens or counters, clear rehearsals or reconstructions. The method of study is rewarding in that it reveals aspects of the rites that are all too easy to miss in direct observation. Some aborigines, without being solicited, will produce graphic sketches of the positions and movements to which the celebrants must conform. The sketches may resemble the patterns incised on bullroarers, a fact deeply significant in itself.

The spatial plans of the rites should not be allowed to pass as commonplaces of a just-so-kind. Each of the shapes has to serve as an arrangement of persons forming a conceptual class, each person and class having parts to play that require a sequence of sentiments, purposes and meanings to be expressed by action or inaction. The combination of shapes has to accord with the logic, the economy, and the aest-hetic canons of the ceremony. There is in each combination an undoubted structure—in the terms used in earlier articles, a structure of operations—with a kind of praxis by which the symbolisms indicate, represent and communicate the connected meanings which they express in a sequence, as do the ordered words of a sentence.

My use of the word "shape" may invite remark. I could not discover any linguistic concepts of the patterns or combinations used in different rites, but there are terms for each of the geometric elements that make them up. However, the word *ninipun* is often used to the total patterns, and it can here conveniently be given the meaning of "shape[1]." To use it comes very close to the aboriginal convention.

In the earlier article ("II. Sacramentalism, Rite and Myth") I put forward the hypothesis that familiar things of the social order provide shapes or *ninipun* by which religiously can be for-mulated in an understandable way. The same intellectual process seems to be revealed in the spatial configurations of ce-remony: familiar things of the physical environment provide shapes or *ninipun* for the arrangement of ritual conduct.

I have no direct testimony by the aborigines to cite as evi-dence that they wittingly imitate environmental things in their ritual use of geometric shapes, but the indirect evidence of intellectual and aesthetic influence is not unimpressive. (a) They are acute observers of their natural scene and little in it escapes notice, particularly the presence of shapely visual form or pattern. Anything that is symmetrically patterned attracts notice, and the same is true of marked asymmetry. (b) The word *dirmu* is applied to a wide range of phenomena: to (i) bodily decorations in dances and mimes, (ii) ancient cave-paintings, and (iii) the sp-iral, concentric and radial crystals of rock-minerals, the colour-markings of birds, the skin-patterns of reptiles. (c) The usages of the word *dirmu* make clear that it denotes visual form or pattern, and that it implies (i) the consequences of intent or purpose and (ii) the handiwork of beings, or the outcome of events, significant for man. The conception of non-intentional form or pattern seems foreign to the mentality. (d) The elements of *dirmu* are geometric shapes and it is to the totality of outward form or appearance resulting from a complex of such elements that the word *ninipun* is applied.

Things that to Europeans are "natural" forms are to the aborigines signs that *something happened* long ago, something mysterious, and heavily consequential for the human life that is continuous with the form-making events of The Dream Time. The past is the authority and the organon of the ontology. The "penetrating, possession-taking faculty" of aboriginal imagination sees in each shapely excellence of form a consequence which the mythology and totemism then make into a *Gestalt.* My hypothesis is that th egeometric forms enter the general system of symbolism as*conventional signs.* Their significance, which is always one of a completed and final action, is a kind of command for an exemplifying action by living men s the appropriate response. The exemplifying is consonant, on the plane of gesture, with the "following up" of The Dreaming on the plane of conscious intent: In our sense "natural" signs that become conventional signs, the given forms are in the aboriginal world a sort of authority gathered up into general symbolism for logical and expressive elaboration. As signs, they *designate* and *indicate* mysterious first things of the long ago, the mythical past; as symbols-that is, when elaborated by language, gesture and music within a system of conduct which is also a system of conceptualism-they *express* and *communicate* first things as last, permanent and continuous things.

An anthropologist encounters them as time—honoured elements of systems which are *already* formed even though, as I have suggested earlier, appearing at the same time to be developmental. In the circumstances, no hypothesis could be brought to "proof"; one can but raise probabilities. The logic of present conduct utilizing the geometric forms, and their rich expressive elaboration, are both evident in the actualities or rites, of which *Punj* is the outstanding example.

The principals at *Punj* cluster for the opening phase in a compact circle. Everyone faces towards the centre. The formation is one in which physical association is intimate. The men sit flank to flank, with knees often crossing, and with arms often flung around the shoulders of neighbours. The kinship and other social categories intermingle without any evident discrimination, except tat clansmen often sit close together and, likewise, pairs of men who later are to act boisterously towards each other under the licence of *Tjirmumuk*. While at song, the celebrants vie rather than complete. Some follow the melodic outline while others, without prearrangement, introduce a simple harmony. The men's face take on a glow of animation and tender intent. At the last exclamatory cry—*Karwadi, yoi!*—everone shouts as with one voice. An observer feels that he is in the presence of true congregation, a full sociality at a peak of intimacy, altruism and unison.

The oneset of *Tjirmumuk* brings a sudden session. The close circle explodes. The harmony of association disrupts. The men scatter into a new spatial pattern. The solemnity is replaced by ribaldry, the altruism by outward hostility, the solidarity by opposition, and the unison of common purpose by a jostle of similar purposes. But the spatial form is, in a sense, continuous with the old. The celebrants are still a kind of unity. They now act under another principle, from other sentiments, and with a different object. But the changes have the nature of transpositions. An observer has the sense of a negative affirmation of what was affirmed positively in the first phase. It is as tough the statement "everything that is *Karwadi* is sacred" now had the form "nothing that is not *Karwadi* is sacred."

The circle as a spatial form is suited by nature to the first phases of the rite. It permits an intimacy of face-to-face relations that no other formation can. It is as well appropriate to the logical datum of the rite: that there should be a unison of men in sentiment and object.

The physical gestures of touching, fondling and embracing between the celebrants express the sentiments after a sign-fashion that is universal to men everywhere. The aboriginal conventions differ only in the classes of persons to whom the signs are made, and in their symbolical conceptualization.

The conversational exchanges that go on during the intervals between songs exemplify the unison in the symbolism of language. They exhibit the qualities of good humour and tenderness that conventionally characterize relations between intimates, especially between brothers and between fathers and sons.

The meaning of the songs may be—and usually is—unknown since they, with the dances, come from tribes across the southern boundary of the Murinbata. But the manner of their singing—as with one voice, a harmony being added-reeiterates what may be seen on the spatial and gestural planes of symbolism.

Thus, the circle reduces to a minimum the social as well as the physical separation between those who make it up: for a time it makes inappropriate, indeed obliterates, all other social categories; it concentrates a unified totality around a centre. In these ways it makes possible a unison towards a dominating object. Four systems of symbolism-those of spatial configuration, gesture, language and music-are in congruence in this, the phase of congregation. On the facts, the form has a high practical, logical and expressive efficacy.

It was noted earlier that the credal formulation of *Punj* does not deal very explicitly with this phase, or with the second—*Tjirmumuk*-beyond the bare (and, as we shall see, partial) interpretation that the latter is "good fun." If the aborigines consciously appreciate any aspect of the geometric idiom, then it is probably the aesthetic aspect, for its appeal to them from that point of view has some suggestive illustrations. The circular motif has a high incidence in the graphic art. A study of the visual sign-system used in that context shows the circle with a range of meanings. It may be intended to show a camp, a water hole, a secret centre (such as *Punj*), a sacred totemic site, a yam, a woman's breast or womb, or the moon. The range defines a category, and the ultimate denotation of the sign is presumably the ground or principle of the category. But its nature or definition cannot be elicited by direct inquiry. One can only try to deduce it by observing and comparing the sequences through which the form passes in a sufficient set of contexts, each set occurring within a separable and identifiable process which is an entity in space and time. One such set of sequences may be seen in *Punj*.

The rupture of the circle by *Tjirmumuk* evidently is not—cannot be, if we accept what the celebrants say—intended as a denial of *Punj* in the respects in which that ceremony deals with things that are ancient sacred, true, and of the highest good and gravity. For the aboriginal testimony is that *Tjirmumuk* "belongs to *Karwadi.*" There is no discontinuity of place or persons. It is a matter of one phase of an entity turning into another, within the bounds of a continuous process. The same men who a moment ago were at one are now, in the same place, at odds. But in every other respect it is as though things had been turned upside down. To the reversals already noted we may add that where before there was song, there is now a babble of noise, sometimes simulating the noise of animals. In addition to being "good fun," the actions in *Tjirmumuk* are said by some aborigines to be "like the wild dogs." One unusually thoughtful man, trying to meet my repeated requests for an analogy-as I asked him, something that the custom "took the place of"-pointed to a covey of birds we could see and hear squabbling over a scarce food, and said: "Like that."

When the scission occurs, one may note that it is the social categories which, ignored in the first phase, are now stressed; *negatively* stressed, for it is the conflict, not the unity, among them that is expressed. The licence of *Tjirmumuk* is shown essentially between three pairs of classes of men: between (*nangun*), and the asymmetrical classes of (ii) classificatory mothers' brothers and sisters' sons (*kaka-muluk*), and (iii) classificatory fathers and sons (*nagulk-wakal).*[2]

Evidently we see again the process of familiar things of social life being drawn on to give shape to less expressible entities and relationships in another realm.

Tension and potential conflict are contitutively part of every aboriginal social relation, even within the patrilineal clan. In that mystical and perennial corporation, expediency as well as religious and moral sanctions are ranged strongly against division. But common—or at least not uncommon—experience is that siblings of the same womb do fight; that children defy and even strike their fathers; and that fathers reject their children. The fact that conflict is constitutively part of living is in logical accord with the fact that the principles of living are conjugate.[3] No single principle, or combination of principles, of social organization or conduct extends over all the desired objects of living, even for clan—members who, at least in dogma, are a combination, not a competitive association. That is, if they possess, they own or, share, under a tradition that clearly specifies rights *in rem, in personam* and *in animum* so that, again at least in dogma, no conflict should arise. But large fields for the expression of vitality, egotism and selfishness are still left open. These, together with the conjugacy of principles, make clan—unison in part an ideal and in part of a fiction. Beyond the clan they issue in an endless clash of interests. The three pairs of classes of actual or potential affines are those between which hostility is overlaid, or could be overlaid, by transacted or transactable interests in women.

The first phase of *Punj* uses a geometric imagery to express the relations of men in combination, at congregation, in unison, and-by the symbolism of many external signs-at one. The second phase destroys the geometric imagery to express the relations of men in association as distinct from combination; men at competition, divided, and—again by the symbolism of counterpart signs-at odds. In the first phase there is something like an element of bravura, a going beyond the mean of social life, which is mundane reality can have such unison only in aspiration. In the second phase, there is something like an element of caricature, a diminution of the mean, which is never one of animal anarchy.

As the rite proceeds the spatial forms have a somewhat different fashion. A linear motif is now added to them. The youths, being secluded at a concealed point some distance away, are brought in file of nudanu. Here they find their seniors crouched within the circular excavation, whether it be "nest" or "wallow," at the mime of the blow-fly. The excavation accentuates the crowding together of the celebrants and, visually at least intensify the significance or meaning of its referent. If the celebration is a large one, with many present, the singers form an arcuate line to one side of the circle. The usual position of the youths is between the arc and the circle.[4] At the dances and mimes which follow, the arc and the circle are retained, but the decorated men adopt one of two fundamental linear patterns. They emerge from hiding and, as a body, approach the circle either (i) in a sinuously curving line, or (ii) as a body less two men, who suddenly appear from concealment at another point, joining the main body by a zig-zag path, pausing in their mime at each change of direction, to make the characteristic quiver of body and shoulders which the Murinbata say is a simulation of birds ruffing their feathers.[5] Both styles issue in a dance before the assembled men enter the excavation.

The form of *Tjirmumuk* having been described sufficiently, we may look briefly at two other occasions when the circular-linear patterns are exhibited.

At night, when everyone in the camp (which has a circular form) is asleep, or is pretending to be, the young men are led to it in file, to sleep there unspoken to and unseen. The stealthy entry is the opposite of the sign-convention of *Tjirmumuk* at its camp-phase: the vociferous leap over the heads of everyone. The first tacitly restores a unity, the second dramatically typifies the tensions that are re-entering it.

When the time comes for thc initiated youths to be presented to their mothers, the camp assumes the form known as *mununuk* which, as I have said, connotes "waiting, with gifts prepared." The close kin of the youths sit in an arc of circle so that the concave side faces towards the two lines of men, one for each moiety, who stand with legs opened to make passages for the youths as they crawl towards and then away from their mothers.

I have found no way of fixing specifies social meanings on the spatial forms. They recur so frequently, however, in the aboriginal spatial and graphic symbolism that they seem a kind of "furniture of the mind"[6] (Fig. 1).

I lean to the view that the circle is a naturally-based conventional sign with probably the ultimate meanings of unity or continuity, the line the same type of sign with, probably, the ultimate meanings of action or change, and that the spatial, gestural, aesthetic, linguistic and religious symbolisms raise on them other meanings appropriate to each system.

3. The Problem Of Tjirmumuk

The upside-downness of *Tjirmumuk* may incline many to deny it any intrinsic connection with the sacral aspects of *Punj,* and to suppose that in Durkheim's terms it must be regarded as a profane activity.[7]

The custom is practised in two places, within the secrecy of njudanu, and at the open camp to which the celebrants return. At the first place it goes on, not *pro fanum*, but actually on the sacred ground of *Punj*. In the terms of *Durkheim's dual* categories there is no "break of continuity" (p. 39). The custom is preceded and followed by sacral actions, so that the continuity is immediate. Nothing overt or readily accessible to direct inquiry, suggests any "sort of logical chasm" (p. 40) to break the continuity, or any "absolute heterogeneity" (p. 38) between the successive activities such that the one set "radically excludes" (p.38) the other. When there is such a close and visible succession one cannot say with intellectual comfort that the activities "belong to two worlds between which there is nothing in common" (p.39), or that they "cannot even approach each other and keep their own nature at the same time" (p.40). The more closely the category of "the profane" is studied the less suitable it appears.[8]

Before considering the category of "the sacred" we may rule out certain order possibilities suggested by *Durkheim's* study. To all appearances, *Tjirmumuk* is not a magical rite "performing the contrary of the religious ceremony" (p.43). Some elements of Punj are magical, but none in the custom of licence. Nor does it suggest itself as "a swift revulsion" (p.40). On the contrary, there is much evidence of consciously symbolic intent and of consciously patterned conduct. A merely biopsychological explanation could not satisfy. And it does not appear the more intelligible it treated as an instance of "ritual promiscuity" (p. 216). The notion of a set formulary, i.e. ritual, of promiscuity actually doubles the explanatory problem. The three possibilities are to be rejected.

Durkheim's notion (after Robertson Smith) of "the sacred" as ambiguous and bipolar was based on a postulate that the religious life "gravitate(s) about two contrary poles between which there is the same opposition as between the pure and the impure, the saint and the sacrilegious, the divine and the diabolic." In short, that there are propitiously sacred and unpropitiously sacred things and, between them, an incompatibility "as all-exclusive as that between the sacred and the profane." We have already noted the elements of duality of

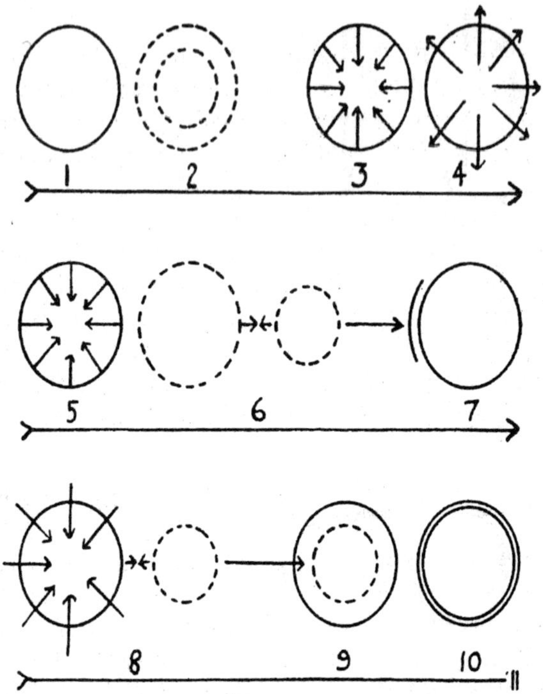

FIG1. Sequence of Spatial Forms.

NOTES

Figure 1 is in part a schematic and in part an actual representation of the sequence of spatial forms of *Punj*. (I) The initial situation: the undivided camp. (2) The diminution of the camp: mature men withdraw and the youths are segregated. (3) The song-circle assembles of Nudanu. (4) The scission by *Tjirmumuk*. (5) The song-circle reaggregates. (6) The ritual preparations are made in secret while the youths are segregated at Mambana. (7) The youths return to witness the rites. (8) The mature men at *Tjirmumuk* irrupt into the diminished circle, while the youths are isolated. (9) The youths enter the camp secretly. (10) The post-initiation camp with the youths, now men of understanding, in a new locus and status.

The "circles" are schematic in (2), (6) and (in respect of the youths) in (8), but are observable realities in the other cases.

Punj, and might well use Durkheim's terms, ambiguity and bipolarity. But a cardinal fact should here be underlined: Tjirm-umuk is as great a contrast with the ordinary life of everyday as it is with the imaginative life of Punj in its other mani-fes-tations. The contrasts are three-sides, not two-sided. Durkheim's dual categories do not between them "embrace all that exists." The *Tjirmumuk* and the Karwadi aspects of Punj both imply, refer to, and use a symbolic imagery drawn from a third realm, one that is neither sacred nor profane but merely mundane.

The celebrants return to the mundane world when they practise Tjirmumuk at the open camp, leaping over the heads of those who are waiting. The very men who, under the terms of the customs, exploded the close circle of *Punj,* now irrupt into the close circle of the camp. The geometric idiom is thus inverted. In both places they act in ways that seem as far removed as possible from the mundane conventions. The very condition of either demonstration is that there should be, on the one hand, a mean of common life and, on the other, a high order of aspiration and imagination, against which to make the demonstration. The custom does not profane-by desecrating, violating, degrading, vulgarizing, or secularizing—either the mean or the higher order. At Ijudanu it breaks up a solidary circle by using a symbolism of animal life to express the hostility underlying mundane relationships. At the open camp it uses the same symbolism, but with inverted geometric forms, to bring the hostility within the circle.

One can scarcely resist the conclusion that there is some kind of praxis and a development of correlated meanings underlying the arrangement of the signs. They are not unconscious; but one must not therefore be understood to say that they are conscious. That dichotomy is not necessarily relevant to the processes of symbolism.

4. Symbolizing ; Process And Types

The materials under study are by nature intricate, and the

anthropological analysis of symbolism is still in its very early stages. There is advantage in using as simple a conception of symbolism as possible. In what follows I prefer to speak, as far as practicable, of "symbolizing" rather than of symbolism in general or of particular symbols. The reasons for that choice may be stated summarily.

One has to dismember the wholeness of a rite to study it at all, but to study and analyse all the component elements of such a rite as *Punj* is beyond the capability of any single observer. For one must add to the spatial forms just discussed gestures and manual acts in definite sequences, mimes, dances, songs, melodies, bodily decorations, and many specific uses of language. What is selected for emphasis is selected in the light of its supposed significance, that is, because of a thesis.

The thesis of these papers has already been stated: that in the rite of *Punj* the Murinbata express outwardly a complex sense of their dependence on a ground and source beyond themselves. That sense, in my construction, is one of perennial good-with-suffering, of order-with—tragedy. It is a mystery which the Murinbata themselves say they do not understand. But in the words they use, and more understanding. They do so by putting into words a certain conception of what the rite refers to or "means." But the rite contains many expressions over a wider range than language and not inherently dependent on it. Language, in this case as myth, is but one of several means or vehicles of symbolizing. The spatial forms, the gestures and manual acts, the mimes and dances, the songs and melodies, the decorations and other components, are all symbolizing means. Each type of means has-or one may assume it has-an appropriate technique and syntactical system, and for each type of means there is, so to speak, a "language." One may reasonably assume also that the rite exhibit a measure of congruence, it perhaps not an integration, between the many "languages," though one may doubt if anyone will ever find it practicable to demonstrate the assumptions. In the circumstances, a discussion of symbolism-in-general must usually be too vague and of particular symbols usually too precise for the material as it presents itself in aboriginal Australia. I thus prefer to discuss the particular processes of symbolizing which are more observable and recordable.

The symbolizing of all types appears to me to be based somewhat arbitrarily-as I suggested in the discussion of spatial forms-on things interpreted as signs and arranged into patterns. The arrangement into patterns exemplifies the process of symbolizing. One encounters the already formed systems of symbolism. Now, I have chosen to discuss the spatial arrangements first because it appears to be through them that, to adopt Erwin Schrodinger's phrase, the aborigines most clearly "suck in the orderliness" of sign-patterns given in the spatial environment.[9] Arbitrary and conventional meanings are put upon the signs, which-being thus interpreted-are then elaborated by the principles governing that class or order of symbolism. The systems of symbolism are thus made up of anterior signs arbitrarily interpreted, transformed, and hallowed by tradition.

If there were an aboriginal word for "nature" then one might say that the spatial configurations are developments of signs drawn "from nature." But to do so would be meaningless, for there is no such word or conception. There is only The Dreaming, that which comprehends all and is adequate to all and, like the Deep of Babylonian mythodology, "of old time reckoned a thing of vast importance in the constitution of the world..."[10]

The mimes, melodies and songs are as important expressively-and therefore to the communication, sharing and teaching of meaning-as the spatial and gestural forms, or the manual acts which i have called "operations." In the light of this argument a primary task of study is to try to discover congruences between two or more formed systems of symbolism. Hence my earlier attempts to show, on the one hand, the homomorphism between *Punj* and the better-understood institution of sacrifice and, on the other, between the operational structures of the rite and the myth of *Punj*. I shall now examine the likeness between the operational structure of the rite and the sequences of spatial forms. There too a certain measure of congruence is exhibited.

5. A Repeated Theme And Congruent Symbolizing

We saw, without drawing on the mythopoeic thought of the murinbata, that the observable acts of *Punj* exemplify a kind of drama on the theme of withdrawal, destruction, transformation and return. The associated myth then showed itself to be, not the pathological "disease of language" of which Max Muller spoke but a credal formulation of the sama drama. The structural patterns of both sequences of acts were found to be generally conformable.

The acts or operations at *Punj* were abstracted from the larger whole of the rite and necessarily included the spatial forms through which they were done.d The forms further abstracted, show that they too exemplify the drama.

The processes of the rite begin, not at Ijudanu, but at the open camp. Yet an examination starting with the assembly of the celebrants at the secret place reveals something like the familiar sequences going on in a somewhat involuted way within a narrower compass and at the same time within a wider compass. There seem to be three interconnected (by the scattering) and then transformed (by the licence of *Tjirmumuk*) before reaggregation (the restoration of the song-circle). (b) The new assembly is again dispersed (by the detachment of the youths under a guardian, their isolation at a hidden place, the secret decoration of the dancers, and often the concealment of the mime-dancers) before being drawn together again in a new unity with a radically different structure. A ground-circle is now flanked by an arc and is either filled by masked or decorated men (i.e. in new personalities) or is being penetrated from outside by men performing the contrasted movements which have been described. That formations then dissolves into a somewhat formless unity distinct from the initial assembly. (c) The full unity of the whole camp (a circle) is broken by the withdrawal of all mature and young men. Each night, while still reduced, it is transformed into a different character by the custom of *Tjirmumuk* and by the symbolical denial that the youths really visit it or sleep there. It is fully reconstituted again-and then with a *developed* character-only after the termination of the rite, when the initiates assume their new status.

Act, myth and spatial forms belong to distinct orders. We are thus not "discovering" the same phenomenon under different names. What we find by analysis is a set of congruences between components of a whole which are expressed according to the technique and system appropriate to each mode of symbolizing. A familiar distinction may now be made.

The spatial forms are, in the terms suggested by Mrs. Langer,[11] *presentational* symbolisms. They have somewhat indeterminate meanings imposed on them and, as signs, somewhat indeterminate referents. They have about them something of the character and quality of images or pictures that may be either still or moving. But they are symbolisms because they are vehicles for the conception and expression of the meanings of things, events, or conditions. The process of rite which makes use of them is thus a symbolizing process, one of spatial arrangement.

On the other hand, the acts or operations of both the rite and the myth are *discursive* symbolisms. They express mental conceptions which are fairly definite or definite. There is clearly a range from high indefiniteness to definiteness. An example of indefiniteness is that part of the rite at which the young men are taken to the spot where The Old Woman is to become manifest. The old men in this way make a gestural and manual sign towards The Mother by takings or compelling the young men to that place. It is *like* offering them. But the sign does not" mean" an" offering." The aborigines describe what they do have no clear intellectual conception about it. It is not, therefore, a formed symbolism. On the other hand, there is a clear conception of the blood smeared on the initiates, since it is represented as the blood of the The Mother and thus symbolizes her. One is scarcely more, if at all, than a presentational symbolism; the other is a clear discursive symbolism.

It will be plain in these papers that I depart from the views of some other anthropologists who have discussed religious symbolism. My friend and colleague, the late Professor S.F. Nadel, argued that "uncomprehended symbols" are not really symbols at all since they indicate nothing to the actors. Thus, they have no interest for the anthropologist.[12] In the sense that "uncomprehended" means "unaccompanied by intellectual conceptions" I am not in disagreement. But one can rarely be sure of the uncomprehension or unaccompaniment. One cannot justifiably infer either from implicitness of wordlessness. A methodial search for congruences between ritual. facts of different orders may show that an implicit and apparently uncomprehended symbolism of one order is formulated explicitly in another order. On the other hand, Professor Monica Wilson appears to argue[13] that, in order to avoid "symbolic guessing," the anthropologist should limit himself to a people's own translations and interpretations of their symbolism. This advice, if followed in aboriginal studies, would prevent anthropology from going very far beyond just-so descriptions. But in *every* field of anthropological study, a going beyond the facts of observation-a "guessing" about them-is intrinsic to the act of study, and not even theoretically separable from it.

Ritual symbolisms extend over *all* the orders of facts that are separable as components of human conduct. The symbolisms of the *other* orders are not inherently dependent on the symbolisms of language, though they may receive their clearest expression *in* language. We may see that this is so by referring to the most fundamental categories of the Murinbata language, which are themselves symbolical, though somewhat indefinitely so.

6. The Build of The Dreaming

The Murinbata language designate nine or more classes of entitles (Table). Each class is known by a name that may be used done or as a prefix to the name of any member of the class. In common speech, the prefixes are sometimes omitted although grammatical speech requires them to be used.[14]

The classes are not noun-classes in the ordinary sense used to aboriginal languages. As far as I have been able to determine, there are no grammatical consequences or correlations. It seems best to regard them as existence-classes, i.e. as existential or ontological conceptions, which divide all significant entities in the world into classes which are mutually exclusive.

Table
Existence-Class.

Name of Class	*Content of Class.*
1. *kadu* ..	Human beings, male and female. Human spirits other than 6(i), but probably including *ngarit ngarit* (spirit-children), *ngjapan* (souls), and possibly including *mir* (freed souls?).15 Subclass: (i) *kadu-Punj* : youths undergoing initiation.
2. *da..* ..	Camps and resting-places. Localities. Subclass: (i) *da-Punj* : places known to be, or to have been *ngudanu* and *mambana*. (ii) *ngoiguminggi* : totemic sites.

3. *nandji* .. Most natural substances and objects, e.g. stone, minerals, wax, wood. The inedible parts of animals (bones, hair), and plants (leaves, bark). Artifacts, e.g. utensils, implements, ornaments, ritual objects. Certain natural phenomena, e.g. fire, mist, clouds, winds, the heavenly bodies. Urine and human milk.
Dances.
Subclass:
  (i) *nandji-Market :* any members of Classes (3) and (4) with an exchange-value in intertribal trade.
  (ii) *nandji-Punj :* any members of Classes (3) and (4) of high ritual significance.

4. *ijo* .. .. Offensive weapons, e.g. spears, fighting clubs, boomerangs.
Thunder and lighting.

5. *mi* .. .. Vegetable foodstuffs.
Faces.
Subclass:
  (i) *mi-Punj :* any vegetable food forbidden to initiates.

6. *ku* .. .. The flesh, fat and blood of animals (birds, beasts and fish) and of men.
Honey.
Subclass:
  (i) *kukarait :* human ghosts.
  (ii) *ku-Punj :* any flesh food forbidden to initiates.

7. *murin* .. Speech and language
Words,[15] songs,[16] stories and myths, gossip and news.

8. *kura* .. Fresh or drinkable water.
Rain
Subclass :
  (i) *kura-mutjingga :* springs and spring-water.
  (ii) *kura-Punj :* ritually dangerous waters.

9. *lalinggin*.. Salt-water.
The sea.

* There are severalclasses of spirits which the aborigines do not classify either as *kadu or ku.*The distinctions are to e dealt with in a later aritcle.

† I have no evidence of a secret language used by initiates only, although among th eMarithiel, a people following a different regional culture to the north-east of the Murinbata, intiates were required to use a special set of words for all food species.

‡ There is not Murinbata word for "song" as such, though there is fo rth eact of singing. i have not heard the secret songs referred to as *murin-Punj,* but their secrecy, and the condign sanctions of betrayal, are commong matters of talk amogn the initiated.

It is possible (though I think unlikely) that there may be more than nine classes. Some may be unnamed, or it may simply be that I failed to discover them. But those mentioned are readily ascertainable and, with a few minor qualifications, are quite clear in their uses and meanings. The class *tjo* could perhaps be regarded as a subclass of *nandji,* and *lalingin* as a subclass of *kura;* on both matters the aboriginal testimony is a little uncertain. But, with those exceptions, each class is exclusive of every other.

Any attempt to understand the aboriginal philosophy of life and religion must take the classes into primary account. They are of so fundamental a nature that to try to go "beneath" or "behind" them by direct inquiry usually only bewilders the aborigines.[15] The most fruitful interpretation to be put on them is thus a matter of difficulty. I have come to no final conclusions, but some general truths seem probable.

(1) They apparently embody the character and significance of things that constitute and co-exist pernnially in the world, and are thus symbolical. Each class is a distinct and incomparable set of existences, with a type of individuality which the aborigines generalize. Inference is the only means of discovering the principles of generalization.

(2) On the evidence of the mythology, the classes as such are not part of the conception of "the totemistic dispensation" to which reference was made. As far as the aboriginal outlook can be gauged in this way, they seem understandable as conditions of the dispensation. That is, they already *were* when particular ancestors put these *nandji* and these *tjo* in the *noigumingi* of some clans or dreaming-places and not of others; or found these *ku* and *mi* to be good and not those; or by their exploits named, or shaped the physical properties, of places or *da* where some ancestors went into the ground and the waters, and others flew into the sky. Much of the kind suggests the inference that the classes as such are logically anterior, denoting conditions while the dispensation observed. Thus, they do not of themselves bring relation and moral order into the world of multitudinous existences in co-existence: that was done by the ancestors through totemism; what the classes do is to serve as a ground of that dispensation. They are in this sense primary data of life and thought underlying the prolegomena-the discourse on The Dreaming-to the main aboriginal system of belief.

(3) The list of includes all the exterior or sensible objects of life which the aborigines strived to attain or avoid. Within each class things are valued, negatively as well as positively. The language of the systems of valuation is very simple-a few adjectives expressing crude linear scales-but the systems themselves are multiple. The value-contexts are technical, magical, religious and social, all having negative and positive dimensions. Thus, it is a matter of common experience to see natural objects flung aside with indifference and a disdainful remark *"nandji-wiya!"* (lit. "thing," "bad"=unusable, in this context); or food dismissed as *"mi-wiyal"* (lit. "thing," "bad" = unusable, 'bad-tasting"); or waterholes pointed out as *"kura-wiya"* (*"dangerous"*); or to become aware of the hush that falls on a camp at night when an untoward sound in the darkness suggests are presence of *kukarait*. But Murinbata usage suggests

that the classes are not simply of *entities*. They are also, at least in part, groupings of *functions* in that the entities have a determinate place in the scheme of life, and of *powers,* in that the entities have efficacies of one kind or another. At the same time they are *generic* concepts of a kind.

(4) Some of the things, considered as entities, have *dirmu* and many have *ninipun,* but these aspects are not developed significantly to make groupings within or between the classes. The idea of *ninipun* is best developed, and then primarily in relation to the eight sub-sections of the class of *kadu.* These are thought to be bi-sexual groups, each having its own bodily conformation generalized (in English) as a "skin." The idea is used, but only in a vague and general way, outside that class. The principle of sex is used to a very limited extent outside the *kadu* class. For example, the red ochres (which are *nandji*) have sex-names (*nogan,* "male," *mirni,* "female") according to their brightness, the female ochres being the brighter. The same terms are used for the sex of animals (*ku*). But the classes are not further differentiated, except by secondary classifications: by utility, physical properties `(weight, size, colour), age, value-in-exchange, magical efficacy whether benign or malign, and ritual importance.

(5) The factual reference of each class is proximate rather than primary. Certainly, each of them names and groups objects; but not *as* mere objects. Every class is a sort of dualism, sometimes a multiple dualism, that state some principle or principles of the thing's being-there, so that the primary reference is really to pattern "within" or "behind" the factual reference. The pattern is relational, and one capable judging by the lists-of holding contraries together in unity; but to extract the contraries which are related whether as functions or powers, does not seem practicable.

Class (1) bridges the visible and the invisible; (2) unifies the Here-and-Now with The Dream Time; (3) deals jointly with the corporeal and the incorporeal, the disgusting and the pleasurable, the benign and the harmful, the tangible and the intangible; (4) brackets the human and the cosmic; (5) and (6) makes classes-a unity of some kind-out of the stuff of sustenance and the vileness of its process in the one case, and out of that which is most corruptible and that which is most sweet in the other case. Perhaps (7), (8) and (9) suggest more clearly functions or powers only through the pattern, the relation of the terms, and not through an isolation of the terms themselves, whatever they may be.

(6) The contexts of use suggest that, if we are to understand the classes at all, it is as having a three hold reference. (a) They categorize the kinds of *stuff* that make up the external objects of living. (b) The stuff on *pattern* or *constitutive form* of perennial stability at the events of The Dream Time. (c) Each of the patterns has its own *import* for men. My earlier observations that both the rite and the myth of *Punj* are "dense with import," are thus reinforced; for the very language through which the more mundane things of life are dealt with is itself dense with symbolical import, although it may be somewhat indeterminate.

(7) There are whole realms of aboriginal experience and life that lie outside the stuff, pattern and import of the class, or any combination of them. For they do not embrace the inward or ideal or eternal objects of life, and they assume the actions of men towards or away from those objects.

The analysis has shown that the primary object of *Punj* is to make youth understand a mystery. But for the myth-and the other commentary offered by the aborigines we should not have been able to draw any such conclusion from the rite itself. The *apercu* given expression in the myth leaps beyond the import of anything that makes up the rite. The myth is not the only one to suggest that alternatives existed in The Dream Time but, as I have already stated, it seems to be the only truly sorrowful myth.

Several things are to be noted. The leap forward, the "going beyond," is as much in the realm of life-striving as it is in the affective and cognitive realms of experience. It takes the form of a story which seems new and unprecedented, but the symbolizing of mystery is commensurate with all the other *concurrent* orders of symbolizing. That is, the *spoken* drama of tragedy and suffering is commensurate with the *acted* drama. And this in turn is commensurate□simultaneous in time, congruent in structural form, and evidently common in meaning-with the spatial configurations through which that drama is acted out.

It is as though that inner paradigm of which I spoke earlier-the *ninipun* or shapely pattern of setting apart, destruction, transformation and return—being immanent in the whole ritual culture of the Murinbata, if not more widely still, were being given, in the myth, its full import through a brilliant *apercu,* a new illumination. As though the immanent were being made outward, and being transcended while remaining itself. And this in spite of the fact that boundaries between distinct orders of symbolizing are crossed.

(8) The problem of interpreting the classes is made much more difficult by a view that they first have to be made intelligible empirically and scientifically. It is hard-and, for any own part, I would say impossible-to equate or delimit or satisfy any of the classes by empirical fact as we grasp it. But if one does not begin with the assumption that there is only *one* mode of intelligibility then the difficulties diminish. The classes, like the myth and rite which they subserve, belong to the same order to reality as poetry, art and music. On this, let me repeat and endorse what professor James has said.[16] Myth rite, poetry, art and music, "each according to its own technique, externalizes and express a feeling, a mood, an inner quality of life, an emotional impulse and interpretation of reality..." Goethe, in his conversation with Heinrich Luden, states our first principle: "What the poet has created must be taken *as* he has created it;

as he made his world, so it is."

(9) The course of study must evidently proceed from symbolic through repeated pattern to constituent stuff. But the significance of the entities-among them the most outstanding being such fundamental things as blood, fire, water, earth, winds, songs, holes, leaves, red ochre, fat, weapons, and spirit-children-in part depends on the human actions taken about them. In the myths, which are the main evidence on which to draw, the actions are assumed as often as stated. The act-structure of myths requires the study of an immense number of discrete activities towards and away from the entities: campaign, hunting, tracking, dividing and quarrelling over the fruits of the chase, love making, plotting, fighting, acts of deception, murder, sorcery and the like. The symbolism of the things is certainly wrapped up with the symbolism of the activities into which they enter, and the classes give us *part* only of the furniture of the aboriginal mind. A full understanding of the religious symbolism is to be attained only by a thorough morphemic analysis of the whole language. That study is beyond my technical competence. But until the analysis is made we have not penetrated the true inwardness of the stuff of symbolism. All we have done is to attain a rough idea of its pattern and import. The "build" of The Dreaming is the product of an intimate interrelationship between all three.

Perhaps we have shown, however, that the fact that many of the dominant symbolisms are not put clearly into words does not condition their velence. It conditions only the capacity to express clear conceptions in words and sentences so that for the most part they remain beyond the symbolism of language. But *not* beyond the symbolisms which are independent of spoken language. The Murinbata have no words for, say, "sine curve" and "leftward-moving spiral," but the celebrants of the rite trace out such evolutions year after year. These and other forms are so clear, dominant, and persuasive in their minds that, as they trace them out, the aborigines seem to be saying (as R.R. Marett once put it): "How, if not thus?" They are drawing on a rich stock of conventional signs known and used skillfully without any necessity of verbal symbolism. An observer has to stifle his own mind not to see in them the expression of aesthetic insight and a rhythmic symmetry of design. It is impossible to dismiss them as "uncomprehended."

7. The Dominant Symbolism

The telling of Murinbata myths often but by no means always ends with the exclamatory word *Demninoi!* A plural form is about as common as the singular: it then becomes *Pirimninoi* (sometimes pronounced as *Peremninoi*). Both are verbs in the third person and evidently in the past tense. The usage suggests a reflexive verb, but this remains uncertain. No other forms-if there ever were any-survive.[17]

English-speaking aborigines phrase the meaning of demnioni as "changing the body" or "turning" from man (kadu) to animal (ku). It appears to have certain connotations, at least further suggestions, among them "spreading out," "flying away," and "going into the water." There are distinct words for such activities, but they are seldom used in the myths, *demninoi* evidently being able to suggest them. The central meaning of that word seems to be "metamorphosis," one that is instant, a voluntary exercise of choice, and at the same time a necessity of overwhelming circumstance. It is nearly a metapirical conception.

One man, trying to clarify the meaning for me, referred to the Murinbata belief that a hunted animal, in order to save its life, may change itself instantly into something else. He said: *"ku-daitpir bamgadu ku-ninipun dinida...damul manaka panya-tka nyinida nandji-burur wada demninoi."* Literally, "ani-mal or flesh+true—I saw—animal or flesh+shape or body (i.e. having the body or outward form of an animal)—being there—spear—as soon as, at the same time as-I threw—that which is there—inanimate thing+antbed—now, instantly—changed mysteriously."

In other words, "I saw a veritable animal; I threw a spear; instantly and mysteriously, it changed into an ant—bed." He put the story forward as an instance of personal experience.

The demninoi in this explanation could not be replaced, my informant said, by any other word and still have the same sense. For example, by dinim, which means approximately "became" in the ordinary English sense and, in Murinbata, is used when a man becomes a wise man (*wanangal*) as the result of a mystical experience. Or by*banambitj*, which means something like "made itself" or "was responsible for its own existence," the word being used for self-subsistent spirits (*kadu banambitj*) which are distinguished from the spirits of dead human persons. Or by *yiinambata*, which means the mystical process by which a totemic ancestor—at the instant of, and also by the act demninoi—made a spirit site or *noigumingi*.

The conception of a metamorphosis of animals into humans or humans into animals is of course at the very centre of aboriginal symbolism throughout Australia. The facts that the myth of The Old Woman does not stress, or apparently even mention, the *demninoi* motif and that the transformation of youths during the rite of *Punj* is not consciously likened to that type of transformation, are therefore interesting and in need of explanation. At the same time there is undoubtedly a certain likeness—the kind of likeness that constitutes metaphor—between (*a*) the sequences of mythical events leading up to the "changing of body" and "spreading out," etc., and (*b*) the sequences acted-out in the rite or narrated in the myth of *Punj*. Obviously, a more careful study is needed of the apparent reduction or elision of so dominant a motif, or its possible concealment in metaphor.

It is to be remembered that we are dealing with a *moment* in the development or practise of a religious cultus. The *Karwadi* exemplifies a leap forward from older religious habitudes. By "cult" one means precisely a going-beyond what was before. In such a cult a hitherto common value may be made sacred, or one that is already sacred made holy.

Evidently it is the second step that has been taken in the rite and myth under study. In such a process a kind of chiaroscuro results : the blaze of the holy casts many shadows dimming much that before may have had the highest significance, even blotting it out, since there is nothing so dead as last year's cult. In linguistic symbolism we are dealing with intellectual conceptions making use of familiar imageries. in the linguistic symbolism of cults of the second kind, we may suppose that we shall meet with conceptions that are enhanced in much the same measure as the religious value. The motive of the *Karwadi* cult has been suggested as a discovery, or an illumination, of something in the condition of human life that excites sorrow by its sad inevitability. The particular symbolism through which this is expressed in the myth of The Old Woman appears to be made up of enhanced tropes or embellished metaphors of a conception arranged and expressed differently, but still recognizably, in other myths. The myth of Old Crow tells how men learned to die. The myth of The Rainbow Serpent tells—among other things—how the very condition of humanness, the possession of fire, was at the expense of the death of the father's father of one moiety of men and the mother's father of the other. The myth of *Karwadi* tells, in terms of sorrowful mystery, how young life had to be saved from its guardian. There is no evidence on which to base a chronology of the three myths, but the second certainly antedates the third. The myth of the Rainbow Serpent stresses the *demninoi* motif; the myth of The Old Woman does not elide but trans-figures it, by changing some elements, by rearranging others and embelishing the same general pattern. In one, the death of a dualistic father one generation removed is the condition of the survival of all humanness. In the other, the death of The Mother is the condition of the perpetuation of human life through its children. The latter is a metaphor of the former, but intensified: the locus of good-with-tragedy is unified in the image of a single instead of a dual personage, and one that is a generation nearer.[18] And the element of sadness within, the evident in the telling of, the myth of The Old Woman has no counterpart, to my knowledge, in the myth of The Rainbow Serpent. We seem thus to meet a consonant development of insight, linguistic expression, and emotion.

It might seem, however, that the congruence of pattern between the myth and the rite under study argues against rather than for the thesis of cultistic development. The relation may be stated more exactly. It is one of *analogous* elements arranged with *similarity* of form or pattern and having a *commonness* of import manifest in different *types* of symbolism. Having examined a rite associated with a myth, I propose in the next article to examine (*a*) a myth *not* associated with a rite and (*b*) a rite *not* associated with a myth. If a pattern can be found constant between all three, then its dominance seems well established, and we shall be better able to ask what evidence should be discoverable if in fact a development of symbolizing has taken place around a continuous form. In (*a*) the structure of the myth of The Rainbow Serpent will be studied, and in (*b*) that of a funerary rite which one brought all the clans together to give a man's soul its quittance. Taken together, they seem to me establish that aboriginal man, "the victim of transience in himself and in the forms among which he dwells, is yet endowed with the power to create forms which endure." And more, has the power to adapt the work of his imaginative mind to the unfolding of history.

References

1. See *Occania,* Vol. XXX, No. 4, p. 270, for other meanings.
2. In the Murinbata system of kinship, affinity and marriage the class of wives' fathers *(kapi)* is a subclass of the class of mothers' brothers *(kaka)*, such that any kaka who is not a uterine brother of a man's own mother may become kapi. Since there is frequently an exchange of sisters in marriage, the wife of kapi is

distinguished from the class of fathers' sisters *(pipi)* by the (untranslatable) suffix nginar. A man's own father's sister's cannot be pipi nginar in any circumstances. A brother of pipi nginar is distinguished from the class of fathers *(yile)* by being termed ngaguluk. This term was adopted from the Djamindjung and, being affected by Murinbata phonetics, is sometimes pronounced ngawuluk.

3. See 'On Aboriginal Religion' II. *Oceania,* Vol. XXX, No. 4, pp. 245-278; especially pp. 266 ff.
4. My earlier statement that they "are taken into the centre of the circle, told to kneel, and to imitate the action of the others" is in error. They are taken to the centre of the arc, told to sit, and to "follow up," i.e. on future occasions, the actions of the mime.
5. I could discover no evidence that the Murinbata, like the Warramunga of north-central Australia, think of this gesture as setting free spirit-children or any kind of life-principle. Otherwise, they given only technical and aesthetic explanations of the customs. The Murinbata ideology associates *ngarit-ngarit* or spirit-children only with green leaves. The dancers ties to their shoulders, and carry in both hands, bundles of leaves which have been starched crisp so that the quivering of the shoulders will give out a pleasing sound.
6. I adopt the phrase from W.H.R. Rivers, "The Symbolism of Rebirth," Folk Lore, Vol. XXXIII, No. I. Rivers was discussing the problem of universal symbolism, a matter that does not enter into my examination.
7. *All references are to the 1915 edition of* The Elementary Forms of The Religious Life.
8. In an as yet unpublished article, I have questioned both the logical adequacy and the empirical warrant of the dual categories. Durkheim gave various meanings to "the profane": among them, minor sacredness, non-sacredness, dangerous non-sacredness, anti-sacredness, and simple commonness. His system requires, among other additions, the recognition of a third category, that of the common or mundane. His analysis appears to rest implicitly on such a category. Consider, for example, his many references to "ordinary things," things of common use," "the ordinary plane of life," etc., etc. But he gave the category no

place in the "bipartite division of the whole universe, known and unknown, into two classes which embrace all that exists, but which radically exclude each other."

9. Quoted by F.W. Dillistone in Christianity and Symbolism, London, 1955, p. 36.
10. F.E. Coggin, The First Story of Genesis as Literature, 1932. One might adapt to the aboriginal use of the phrase "The Dreaming" the author's remark that "any name for the material which goes to the making of the world would have been deficient had the Deep not been included...", pp. 4-5.
11. Susanne K. Langer, Philosophy in New Key, 1942. My use of "discursive" symbolism is also from this source.
12. S.F. Nadel, Nupe, Religion, 1954, p. 108.
13. Monica Wilson, Rituals of Kinship Among the Nyakyusa, 1957, p. 6.
14. Aborigines often complain that their children speak ungrammatically, pronounce words incorrectly, and use slang.
15. I mentioned earlier the embarrassment of my informants at the disclosure that Europeans are (at least, were) given the same prefix (ku) as the class of beasts and honey. On the same occasion I was defeated-by, among other things, the merriment of my informants-in an attempt to get their explanation of the inclusion of food and faces in the same class (*mi*). No, they said, it did not imply that anyone ever ate faces; how could this conceivably be so? It was just a matter of *murin,* of language; perhaps faces *looked* a little like *mi;* now that I had mentioned the matter, it did seem amsuing; but it was not a thing of any importance. The more intelligent men developed a marked interest in my morphemic inquiries, and had some interesting things to say about how words might have been "built up" in The Dream Time, but the discussions were never of any use in clarifying the existence-classes.
16. E.O. James, *Myth and Ritual in the Ancient Near East,* 1958, p. 309. Though developed mainly with reference to other cultures, Professor James's thesis holds true of the aboriginal material in all essentials. Myth and rite "give verbal and symbolic form and meaning to the emotional urge and rhythmic relations of life as a living reality, recounting and enacting events on which the very existence of mankind has been believed to depend, and

proclaiming and making efficacious an aspect and an apprehension of truth and reality transcending historical occurrences and empirical reasoning and cosmological and eschatological speculations."

17. I heard one possible exception, the form *pennginoi-nu,* which could be the Ist peers. sing. fut. but there was some head-shaking about it.
18. The dualism is not wholly removed for the myth records her remarks to grand-children.

---

* Oceania vol. xxxi

Chapter-2

Magic: Colour Symbolism

By Wilfrid Bonser

Chapter-2

The Significance of Colour in Ancient and Medieval Magic: with some modern Comparisons.

Colour is a significant factor in folk-medicine. It may be important that (*a*) a thing should be all of one colour, (*b*) of a specific colour, and (*c*) piebald or variegated, especially in the case of clothing. This last is usually the case when the rites have become complicated. The same principles seem to hold in most races.

(a) *One-colour Magic.*-Two examples of one-colour magic occur in Anglo-Saxon leechdoms. "For flying venom...on a Friday churn butter which has been milked from a neat or hind all of one colour"[1]: and again, "The woman who cannot bring her child to maturity, let her take the milk of a cow of one colour in her hand, and sip it up with her mouth."[2]

Pliny says of the agatre, "the stone that is of an uniform colour, renders athletes invincible."[3]

Dioskorides give a cure to be effected by hanging round the neck of the sufferer two stones, to be found in the maw of a swallow, "unum quidem colore varium alterúm purum et unicolorem."[4]

Similarly, in an Irish charm against shingles, nine drops of blood from the tail of a male cat, which is all black and has no whiteness on it, are a necessary ingredient.[5]

The following legend of Newington church, near Chatham, is also relevant. The Evil One deterred the building of it; and on the first night after the bell was hung it was removed and thrown down a neighbouring well. The villagers had resort to a witch, who said it must be drawn out by twelve jet black oxen. When the bell nearer the top, it suddenly fell to the bottom again. It was then found that one of the oxen had a few white haris in the left of one of its front feet. Another all-black ox was then obtained, and the bell was successfully raised and fixed, nor did the Evil One again interfere.[6]

(b) *Specific Colours.*-The difficulty of identifying the specific colours of the ancients is due to the uncertainty as to the meaning of the words used. In contrast with the Greeks, the Anglo-Saxons had words for most colours. Nine colours occur together in the famous charm[7] in which the nine specially magical herbs "avail against nine spirits of evil, against nine venoms, and against nine winged onsets, against the red venom, against the foul venom, against the purple venom, against the yellow venom, against the green venom, against the white venom, against the livid venom, against the blue venom, against the brown venom, against the crimson venom."

The individual colours were often associated for magical purposes with those things which obviousness suggested: *e.g.*, red with blood, yellow with jaundice and the liver, the spotted leaves of lungwort with diseases of the lungs, and so on.

Plants with red blossoms, berries or roots were used for cases of hemorrhage. Examples are the red seed of palony and the red root of astragalus.[8] There is one instance of this—in Sextus Placitus—which does not quite conform to type. Here the fruit of the morbeam, or mulberry, is to be taken (with the thumb and ring finger of one left hand) *before* it has become red.[9] The passage occurs in the Anglo-Saxon version, but not in the original Latin. As the idea appears to be to stop red (*i.e.* blood) from coming, so something which might have become red is used before it turns red; and it is also prevented from becoming red. This connection persisted until modern times, for the *unripe* fruit of the mulberry is prescribed by Colbourne for "spitting of blood."[10]

It is not always red flowers that are prescribed in cases of hemorrhage. In the whole of the Herbarium of Apuleius, I can only find one red—and that not a blood-red—flower used for this purpose. This is betony, which is to be used to stop blood both from the nose and from the mouth.[11]

The use of a red fillet for tying herbs round the head in cases of headache[12] is less obvious, but is perhaps explainable in that red is the colour for expelling demons. It is also prescribed, in the case of lunatic, that clove—wort should be tied round the man's neck with a red thread : if done in April or early October, when the moon is on the wane, "soon will be healed."[13]

Pliny says the Magi attributed many very wonderful properties to the anemone-a plant with a scarlet flower. As a remedy for certain and quartan fevers "the flower must be wrapped up in a red cloth and kept in the shade, in order to be attached to the person when wanted."[14]

Red is still considered obnoxious to evil spirits: *e.g.*, the red berries of the rowan are used, as in medieval times, to keep away witches.

Red flannel was worn round the neck for sore throat and whooping cough the flannel gave the necessary warmth, but the colour was considered important for magical reasons. This is evidently a sympathetic connection between the redness produced by the inflammation and the redness of the material applied.

In Assyrian medicine there is an incantation for a sick (*i.e.*, bloodshot) eye. "Ritual for this: red wool, white wool, separately shalt thou spin:...the thread of red wool shalt thou tie on his eye which is sick, the thread of white wool shalt thou tie on his eye which is whole, and he shall recover."[15] Many other Assyrian examples of the magic of red things could be given.

The most celebrated case of the sympathetic use of red in the Middle Ages is John is Gaddesden's cure of Edward II.'s son when suffering from small-pox. "Feci omnia circa lectum esse rubea," he says, "et est bona cura, et curavi eum in sequenti sine vestigiis variolarum."[16] John of Gaddesden was, however, unaware of the scientific explanation of the use of red light in the treatment of small-pox, although he may have known by experience of its utility.

The connection between the colour red and small-pox has survived in the practice of wearing a red ribbon round the arm after vaccination.

The symbolic use of red paint in connection with small-pox is found in India at the present day. The chief deity of the Marias, Matadevi, is small-pox. She is represented by "a stone set up by the side of the road and dappled with red paint."[17]

In Southern India, when an outbreak of small-pox threatens a village, the inhabitants make a horse of clay, painted white and with scarlet trappings, which they take in procession with the image of the goddess, who is named Sowaramma, the riding goddess. They leave the horse under a tree outside the village; in order that the goddess may ride away on it. If no horse is provided, she will remain in the village. All offerings to the goddess are scarlet in colour: cooked rice, for instance, when offered is dyed red with saffron and chunam.

The following black magic is still practised in Southern India: it is also a remedy for, and to ward off, diseases. A small pot, full of scarlet-coloured water (again produced by a mixture of saffron and chunam), is thrown down and broken so that the water is split, where three roads meet. Coins are also put in and whose picks them up is supposed to have the disease transferred to him.

Red water (with rice in it) is used at all festivals. It is waved in front of a child on its birthday. At the *holi* festival in honour of Kali, god of love, which is held a fortnight before the beginning of the spring, rose-coloured water, called *wasanta*, ("spring"), is squirted over everybody.[18]

"To dream of eating anything red brings disease" runs an Aino proverb.[19]

Verses from the Koran, written on paper and enclosed in a smaller leather case, are worn in Egypt at the present day as charms, both by men and animals. For women and children the case may be of any colour, but for the important creatures—the men and the donkeys—the colour is always red.[20]

As regards yellow, flowers of this colour were given for jaundice and disorders of the liver: yellow-wort (chlora perfoliata)[21] and flea bane are[22] examples.

Lady Wilde says that "homeopathic adepts among the Irish doctors always employ yellow medicines for the jaundice, as saffron, turmeric, sulphur, or even yellow soap."[23]

Frazer mentions a ceremony among the ancient Hindoos for banishing jaundice into thee yellow birds—the parrot, the thrush and the yellow wagtail—by means of yellow porridge.[24]

Pliny says: "I find it stated that in the most ancient time, yellow was held in the highest esteem, but was reserved exclusively for the nuptial veils[25] of females, for which reason it is perhaps that we do not find it included among the principal colours, these being used in common by males and females: indeed it is the circumstance of their being used by both sexes that gives them their rank as principal colours."[26]

Colours, especially in a fixed order, were of great importance in iatro–chemistry. The pseudo Basil Valentine (16-17c.) holds that antimony contains all the colours, namely "black, red, green, blue, yellow, and more other mixt colours than can be believed, all which may be separated apart, and known particularly, and singularly applied to use." It is, therefore, a panacea for all ailments. "But as all the colours of all metals and precious stones are clearly found in antimony; so also all the powers and virtues of medicine are no less shewed in it, than the colours aforesaid."[27]

In ancient India, plants of certain colours were believed to have magical qualities. "The plants that are brown," runs a passage in the Atharva–veda, "and those "that are white, the red ones and the *speckled* ones [of which more anon], the sable, and the black plants, all these do we invoke."[28]

Similarly, the sacred magic colours of the Zuni Indians of New Mexico are "yellow, blue, red, white, *spotted,* and black." They have names for other colours, but only these have magic power.[29]

(c) *Piebald.*—Finally, with regard to the employment of the variegated, speckled, or piebald in connection with magic, the more complicated the magic, usually the more this obtains.

Perhaps the example from Basil Valentine, just quoted, applies to this section as well as to that of specific colours, especially as it is late and complicated.

Turning to Egypt in the days when she was the home of "mysteries," one finds that Isis, in the Demotic Magical Papyrus, is called "mistress of magic, the great "sorcerer of all the gods"[30] If my thesis holds, one would, therefore, expect to find her attired accordingly. Plutarch says: "Now as to the robes: those of Isis [are] variegated in their dyes...while the [robe] of Osiris has neither shade nor variegation."[31] This is remarkable since, in representations, the gods of ancient Egypt are attired in self-coloured garments, without any pattern.

Another late Egyptian charm is as follows "You take a band of linen of sixteen threads, four of white, four of green, four of blue, four of red, and make them into one band...and you bind it to the body of the boy who has the vessel, and it will work magic quickly."[32]

Lucan tells us that before the battle of Pharsalia, Sextus Pompeius consulted the witch Erichtho as to the event of the ensuing fight. She works magic spells for him, but first arrays herself in a dress of many colours.[33]

The Pied Piper of Hamelin performs his magic in a parti-coloured robe.

Two examples from the Bible are suggestive: one is Joseph's "coat of many colours,"[34] which was taken from him by his brethren as being too precious to be endangered. The other is the dress of the High Priest. The ephod "was made of richly variegated stuff of four colours." The breastplate was to be in part of the same material as the ephod, and was to be "of gold, of blue, and of purple, and of scarlet, and of fine twisted linen"[35] it also bore the twelve different coloured stones on its front face. The breatplate is especially important in this connection since it was used for purposes of divination.

The dragon-god among the Aino appears as a man "dressed altogether in speckled raiment."[36]

Piebald horses are often connected with workers of magic. A man on a piebald horse can always given an infallible remedy for whooping-cough.[37] Marko, the "King Arthur" of Sarbian legend, possessed a magic steed named Sharatz ("piebald"), which was endowed with extraordinary powers. Rustem's Raksch was of a saffron colour, spotted with red. In Japan "three-coloured cats are more powerful in magic than other."[38]

To return to medicine in its most degenerate period. Marcellus Empiricus prescribes in one case the use of a silver needle with threads of nine different colours.[39]

The magic of the Finns is full of the use of variegated things—usually stones.[40] The Sampo, for instance, has a variegated lid, and is made in a smithy erected beside a "stone all streaked with colours."[42] The "speckled stones" used by the Tuatha De Danaan of ancient Ireland may also be mentioned in this connection.

References

1. "Leechbook of Bald," Book 1, 45, v.
2. "Lacnunga," 104.
3. Pliny : "Nat. Hist.," xxxvii, 54.
4. Dioskorides, "Parabillium" (1598), Book 1, 7.
5. R. Marlay Blake: "Folk-lore, with some Account of the ancient Gaelic Leeches" (*Journal of Country Louth Archaeological Society,* iv, 3, Dec. 1917).
6. Told me by Mr. Henry Davis, a native of Chatham. Though the church is medieval, the legend is still current.
7. "Lacnunga," 45.
8. Pliny: "Nat. Hist.," xxvi, 82.
9. Sextus Placitus: "Medicina de quadrupedibus," I. 5
10. Colbourne: "Plain English Dispensatory," 1753, p. 70.
11. Apuleius: I, 7 and 13.
12. "Leechbook of Bald," Book 3, 1.
13. Apuleius, "Herbarium," X. 2.
14. Pliny, "Nat. Hist.," xxi, 94.
15. Thompson, "Assyrian Medical Texts," 15 (*Proc. Royal Soc. of Medicine,* vol. 17, pt. 4. Feb. 1924).
16. John of Gaddesden: "Rosa Anglica," fol. 51, recto, col. 2.
17. Holdich: "The Mardian Hills and the Lower Indravati in the Bustar Dependency" (*Proc. Royal Geogr. Soc.,* N.S.I, 1879), p. 380.
18. I am indebted for these Indian examples to Mr. M.H. Krishniengar, of Mysore University.
19. Chamberlain: "Aino Folk-Tales" (Folk-Lore Society), 1888, p. 57.
20. I am indebted for this to Miss M.A. Murray.
21. Apuleius: "Herbarium," xxxv, 1.
22. Dioskorides: Book 3, 126.
23. Lady Wilde: "Ancient Cures, Charms and Usages of Ireland," 1890, p. 19.
24. Frazer: "Magic Art," vol. 1, p. 79.
25. Flamineum (=orange-yellow?).
26. Pliny: "Nat. Hist.," xxi, 22.
27. Basil Valentine: his "Triumphant Chariot of Antimony," London, 1678, pp. 59-60.
28. Atharva-veda: viii, 7—"Hyron to all Magic and Medicinal Plants."
29. Culin: "Magic of Colour" (*Brooklyn Museum Quarterly* for April, 1925), p. 102.

5. R. Marlay Blake: "Folk-lore, with some Account of the ancient Gaelic Leeches" (*Journal of Country Louth Archaeological Society,* iv, 3, Dec. 1917).
6. Told me by Mr. Henry Davis, a native of Chatham. Though the church is medieval, the legend is still current.
7. "Lacnunga," 45.
8. Pliny: "Nat. Hist.," xxvi, 82.
9. Sextus Placitus: "Medicina de quadrupedibus," I. 5
10. Colbourne: "Plain English Dispensatory," 1753, p. 70.
11. Apuleius: I, 7 and 13.
12. "Leechbook of Bald," Book 3, 1.
13. Apuleius, "Herbarium," X. 2.
14. Pliny, "Nat. Hist.," xxi, 94.
15. Thompson, "Assyrian Medical Texts," 15 (*Proc. Royal Soc. of Medicine,* vol. 17, pt. 4. Feb. 1924).
16. John of Gaddesden: "Rosa Anglica," fol. 51, recto, col. 2.
17. Holdich: "The Mardian Hills and the Lower Indravati in the Bustar Dependency" (*Proc. Royal Geogr. Soc.,* N.S.I, 1879), p. 380.
18. I am indebted for these Indian examples to Mr. M.H. Krishniengar, of Mysore University.
19. Chamberlain: "Aino Folk-Tales" (Folk-Lore Society), 1888, p. 57.
20. I am indebted for this to Miss M.A. Murray.
21. Apuleius: "Herbarium," xxxv, 1.
22. Dioskorides: Book 3, 126.
23. Lady Wilde: "Ancient Cures, Charms and Usages of Ireland," 1890, p. 19.
24. Frazer: "Magic Art," vol. 1, p. 79.
25. Flamineum (=orange-yellow?).
26. Pliny: "Nat. Hist.," xxi, 22.
27. Basil Valentine: his "Triumphant Chariot of Antimony," London, 1678, pp. 59-60.
28. Atharva-veda: viii, 7—"Hyron to all Magic and Medicinal Plants."
29. Culin: "Magic of Colour" (*Brooklyn Museum Quarterly* for April, 1925), p. 102.
30. "Demotic Magical Papyrus," transl. Griffith and Thompson, col. ix (19).
31. Plutarch: "De Iside et Osiride," lxxvii, 1.
32. "Demotic Magical Papyrus, p. 39, col. iv (33).
33. Lucan: "Pharsalia," vi, 653, *et seq.*

34. According to the usual translation. The original Hebrew signifies "patches."
35. Exodus: xxviii, 15.
36. Chamberlain: "Aino Folk-Tales" (Folk-Lore Society), 1888, p. 13.
37. Whately's "Remains." The cure of whooping-cough is also often connected with the colour scarlet.
38. N.W. Thomas: *Folk-Lore,* 12, 1901, p. 70.
39. Marcellus: "De medicamentis," cap. 29.
40. *Cf.* "Loitsurunoja,"
41. 2a; 10a; 226a; 232b, etc.
42. "Kalovala," Rune 10.

---

* *Man* Nos. 117-118. 1925

Chapter-3

African Symbolism

By Edwin W. Smith

Chapter-3

I

I esteem it an honour to be invited by the Council of the Royal Anthropological Institute to deliver the fourth lecture of this series. In the first of them Professor Radcliffe-Browne expounded the thesis that a religion, independent of its truth or falsity, has an effective function as part of the complex system by which human beings are enabled to live together in an orderly arrangement of social relations. Professor Raymond Firth showed how religious beliefs and practices are related to the attempts of individuals to secure coherence in their universe of relations, both physical and social. Professor E.O. James carried inquiry a stage further by considering religion in terms of reality, value and validity. Historical truth, he said is only one aspect of Reality. "At a deeper level of experience there are recurrent situations of profound emotional significance which can only find expression in symbolic representation." I propose to offer you some remarks on symbolism, drawing material from the field with which I am most familiar—Africa, to wit.

II

I will deal first with the general question: What is the nature and what are the functions of symbols?

Etymologically the word denotes a throwing together. The German equivalent *Sinnbild* suggests that a symbol contains and conveys a picture of meaning. The semanticists say that a symbols is an outstretched finger pointing to a referent (Walpole, 1941, p. 104). Coleridge (1825, p. 173) takes it to be an actual part chosen to represent the whole. From the behaviourist point of view Charles Morris (1946, p. 355) considers that a symbol acts as substitute for some other sign with which it is synonymous. Dr. Nadel appears to agree with this: symbol, he says, "are substitutes, capable of 'initiating' a particular behaviour in the absence of the stimuli normally producing it" (1951, p.297), For Freudians "symbolism" denotes the process whereby one idea is used (mostly unwittingly) as a substitute for an unconscious idea; in other words, a symbol is the veiled, masked expression of a thought in a fantastic form which contains an analogy (Jones, 1951, p.130; Pfister, 1913, p. 274). On the other hand, Suzanne Langer (1942, p. 60) asserts that symbols are not proxy for their objects, but are "vehicles for the conception of objects". "The human mind", say white head (1928, p.9), "is functioning symbolically when some components of its experience elicit consciousness, beliefs, emotions and usages respecting other components of experience." An American sociologists, Kimball young (1946, p. 565), puts it in this way; a symbol is something "which stands for, represents, or serves to recall a meaningful experience, and which directs mental and actional associations."

A symbol is thus definable in relation to something else that is called its referent, object or designatum. We may summarize the varius views by saying that a symbol points to a referent; pictures the referent's meaning; is an instrument for comprehending a referent; is a part which represents the whole, or is a surrogate for the whole, searing to recall to mind an absent referent. Symbols, says an authoritative writer on Mysticism are "the clothing which the spiritual borrows from the material plane" (Underhill, 1923, p. 95). The visible stands for the invisible; the material for the immaterial; the palpable, the graspable, for what cannot be seized by the sensory organs.

A French writer(Monod, 1950, p. 13) calls a symbol *signed visible d'une invisible realite;* but there is a fundamental difference between the two kinds of signal. A sign relates to and announces something which is known to exist: thus, a red light is semiotic it tells that the road is closed to traffic; wet streets are a sign that it has rained or is raining. A symbol, on the other hand, indicates something which indeed exists, or is postulated to exist, but which is dimly or partially apprehended or it in itself incomprehensible: it is the best description possible of a relatively unknown fact.[1] Symbols bring home to men's hearths and bosoms what is inaccessible to the understanding.

All words, all articulate utterances, are symbols. And a symbol may be a material object; it may be an animal, a person, a rite, a ritual, an institution, or, as Dr. Fortes says, "a complex of a material object together with the ideas, beliefs attitudes and conventional actions associated with it." And he adds the important point: "It always carries a strong emotional charge and has the value of a direct moral imperative" (1945, p. 136 n.).

The material symbol may have no intrinsic value or significance in itself; indeed its symbolic value may be in inverse proportion to its intrinsic value; and it may bear no apparent resemblance to its referent. The piece of coloured bunting which you can buy for a few pence and which we call the Union Jack, stands in the eyes of a patriotic Briton for all the values of the British Empire: values for the sake of which he would lay down his life although he may have but the dimmest notion of what those values are. It is its historical associations, not its form and colour, that give it meaning. On the other hand a wedding ring, both through its shape and the value attached to its constituent metal, carries a suggestion and a promise of a precious never-ending affection.

Some noises and some marks and some objects mean nothing in particular; other mean a very great deal. Their meaningfulness depends upon an interpreting mind. The cuneiform impressed upon an Assyrian tile, the hieroglyphics on an Egyptian papyrus, mean less to me than the Lord's Prayer printed in Choctaw; but some people can read the symbols. They know the language and they know the script; and to this extent the symbols are rational. But a true symbol can never be fully explained,[2] for in part at least it is the product of the imagination—"reason in its most exalted mood" —its appeal is to the feelings, tits meaning is graspe by intuition. You can understand a people's symbols, only in so far as you enter sympathetically into their daily experience and see the world through their eyes.

"Expression," says Whitehead (1927, p. 117) "is the one fundamental sacrament. It is the outward and visible sign of an inward and spiritual grace." the relation between "sign" and "grace" enshrines a mystery. Inspite of all that has been said on the subject, the process seems inscrutable by which light and sound waves impinging upon my eyes and ears are transmuted into something which appears to be of an entirely different nature—percepts and concepts; so that, by means of those physical vibrations. I am enabled to interpret the thought and intention of the person from whom they originate. Shakespeare, speaking 350 years ago with the voice of a Hamlet and a Prospero, can still arouse thought and emotion in ourselves through the spoken or printed symbols. Leonardo da Vinci and Michelangelo can do the same through visible symbols—paintings and sculptures. The Flag which flew day and night over the ruined Residency at Lucknow had the same mysterious power to evoke emotion and stimulate noble action. This response to the stimulus of symbols is not peculiar to any ethnic group: it appears to be universal. There would seem to be a innate tendency to symolization everywhere. Certain symbols, such as Light and Darkness, Heaven and Earth, crop up among many peoples, ancient and modern, so much so that they may be called racial symbols. Their wide extension provides a problem for anthropologist and psychologist—a problem which Jung seeks to solve by his hypothesis of a collective unconscious.

The human mind everywhere works by nothing likeness and difference and by classifying things accordingly. It delights in drawing analogy; this thing, it says, it like another in some known respects, so probably it is like it in other respects which are not known. I assume an element of identity in the two things. Analogy thus argues from the part to the whole. Occulists would object to my using the word "probably", for in their doctrine the correspondence between appearance and reality, the seen and the unseen worlds, is implicit and complete. Their axiom is *Quod superius sicut quod inferius.* Analogy, they say, is the Key to all the secrets of nature. The argument from analogy may be pushed to absurd lienghts, and lead sadly astray, but while it cannot offer proof it has its value as a mode of advancing knowledge. Psychologists employ analogy when they speak of "psychic energy." We are analogizing when we speak of "a mother country," "a fatherland," "child race." Many peoples, including Africans draw the analogy between a fruitful mother an the teeming earth. Evidently we have in analogy the root of much, if not of all, symbolism: the analogue becomes the symbol. Mother, father, child, are universal symbols. "In the widest sense", says McDougall (1950, p. 106), "every instance in which the perception of some part, some aspect, or some quality of an object provokes the reaction appropriate to the object as a whole every such reaction is an instance of this function, the use of symbols." Analogy, and the symbolism based upon it, are not infallible, in the sense that they may arouse emotions and beliefs which further knowledge shows to be fallacious.

Men, whether civilized or uncivilized, speak more than one language. There is a language which science aims at talking though it does not always succeed (social anthropology in particular): precise in its vocabulary, univocal,geometrically fixed; to use the somewhat disdainful words of a literary artist, "a botanical collection of colorless, scentless,dried weeds, each individual symbol poorly tethered to some single object or idea" (Raleigh, 1918, p. 41). Over against this thee is the language spoken, at various levels, by common folk and poets: pictorial, analogical, equivocal, ambiguous, chameleon-like in its variability. This language may be visuals well as oral, appealing to us both by eye-gate and by ear-gate. It may, that is to say, express ideas through material, non-verbal, symbols. The florist's advice is. "Say it with flowers." It is to this pictorial language that metaphor, simile, allegory, types, archetypes, rituals, dramatizations belong.

This language even science is compelled to talk when it wishes to communicate its findings to ordinary laymen. It is compelled to substanmtialize its concepts. If the physicist is to convey his ideas he must drape their inscrutable nakedness in garments borrowed from the world of sense. Thus, i) Sir James Jeans attempted to expound in mathematical terms the movement of the ultimate particles of matter, he would utterly fail, so far as I am concerned; but when he likens the movements to the movements of kangaroos hopping about in a field, I get a notion of his meaning. So when Sir Arthur Eddington (1929, p. 342) says that stepping on a plank is really like stepping on a swarm of flies he gets some glimmering of the modern theory of matter across to my infantile mind. I and like the child Sir James Jeans speaks about (1942, p. 9)—the child who when beginning to earn agebra never takes kindly to X,Y,Z; he is only satisfied when you tell him they are numbers of apples or pears. The child—which is myself and most of humankind—wants some thing concrete on which he can lay hold. Therein lies the philosophy of symbolism.

And when physicists communicate on a technical level, their mathematical formulae are symbolical. They have gone far, marvelously far, in their exploration of the nature of things, but Sir James Jeans acknowledges that "our studies can never put us into contact with reality: we can never penetrate beyond the impression that reality implants in our minds." "Yet, " says he, "partial aspects of the truth can be made comprehensible through pictorial representations or parables"(1942, p. 16). Such symbols may be related to objective facts no more closely than letters are related to sounds or notes of a score to musical tones. As Eddington says (19229, p. 338): "We have to build the spiritual world out of symbols taken from our own personality as we build the scientific world out of the metrical symbols of the mathematicin."

Symbolism is the natural idiom of the artist. What has been said of painting may be said of symbolism in general: its aim is to make the invisible visible.

And philosophy does not disdain it. "The soul never thinks without an image", said Aristotle. When in his speculations Plato reached the limits of ratiocination, he (as Lowes Dickinson finely says) shakes the wings of his imagination and flies inot another world. He clothes his gospel in the exquisite form of a myth (Dickinson, 1950, p. 52). When he would expound the process of attaining the absolute Good which is above knowledge, or truth, or being, he says: "Picture men in an underground cave..." (Plato, *Republic,* vii).

Religion, it is said, is a form of human art (Firth, 1951, p. 250). Its method is certainly analogous to that of art. As a Turner seeks to transfer his vision by means of pigment on to canvas, and to some degree not satisfying to himself does so; and as a Dante gives his dream a local habitation in the *terzina* and through it lives the drama of his soul; even so religion habitually expresses itself in symbolic form. The Christian creeds were in a ancient times named Symbols. They brought together in summary form the various articles of the Faith; they served as badges and rallying-points of the Churth; they also attempted to express in finite human terms the truths of religious experience which no human mind can fully apprehend and no human vocabulary can adequately expound.

Religion in all its aspects—cognitive, affective, conactive—has its foundation in some form of direct experience (Bartlett, 1950, p 5). The experience comes by an intuitive leap of the mind, so vivid, so compelling, that he to whom it comes believes that it springs not from within but from without. To communicate such a cardinal experience (the adjective is H.G

Wells's) is never easy. The mystics of all ages—Christian and non-Christian—agree at this point. What they see with the inner eye they seek to convey by means of pictures drawn from the world of everyday life, and that, as Sir Frederick Bartlett says, is never every successful, "as everybody finds who tries to paint a poem or describe a symphony" (150, p.13). Experience is always richer than thought and no dogma can fully express the secret s of the inner life. The figures and images—the symbols—with which the dogmatic theologian works are suggestive of truth but are not preise truth. Dogma should be taken for what it really is, not scientific formulation of spiritual reality but figurative and therefore approximate expression of a spiritual content whole value lies in being experienced (Galloway, 1914, pp. 167 sq.).

He who experiences religion may use verbal symbols to communicate it to others an these symbols may sooner or later crystallize into a creed. He may express himself in action which becomes a ritual. He may embody his emotion in a material object which serves to focus and fix the attention. In any case his exposition is symbolic: it is an attempt to utter the unutterable. By sensory activity somewhat is repre-sented which lies beyond sense. The symbol is not the reality, but it may be a clue to the apprehension of reality.

To say that religion has its foundation in personal experience is not to say that every individual adherent of a religious system has undergone a definite religious experience. The symbol expressing the experience may originate in the mind of an individual, but it becomes the possession of a group. Their acceptance of it may appear merely conventional, but its regular use leads them to grasp at second handsome what of the values of that experience through the emotive effect which the ritual or the myth or the creed or material symbol exerts upon them. Regular attendance at public worship does influence attitudes even when it does not lead to that complete transformation which we call conversion. Every ambulance man and nurse who wears a Red Cross does not enter into the full experience which the Cross does not enter into the full experience which the Cross symbolises, yet the badge means something to them—means quite a lot; it represents an ideal of humanitarian service which influences conduct. I have know rough backwoods, to whom the religion of the Cross meant apparently nothing, who yet would fasten two sticks together crosswise and plant them on the grave of a comrade.

Some devout religious thinkers have reached the conclusion that it is impossible to describe ultimate reality, the Absolute in human terms. This attitude is characteristic of certain strains of Hindu philosophy. In the strict vedanta teaching Brahman the One reality, is impersonal, actionless, beyond thought or speech; no qualities could be ascribed to Brahman; neither sacrifices nor prayers could be offered to Brahman. Not worship but absorption into Reality was the disciple's aim. From the point of view of the common man this is metaphysics not religion and does not meet his needs. To meet those needs it was conceded that Brahman might be worshiped in his avatars—his representations or incarnations. Even worship of the images of Vishnu was permitted, each of them instinct with his essence. The evidence of man's need of the concrete in religion is thrust every day upon the visitor to India. And even the mystics who dwelt in the most rarefied atmosphere of contemplation had their symbol—the ejaculated syllable OM! This symbol was to them the means of knowledge: "one knows through it all that has to be known" (Macnicol, *Brihadaranyaka Upanishad* V.I, Every man, p. 102).

The conviction has seized many Christian and Muslim mystics that, since it is only the limited that can be presented in a figure, all symbols that the human mind can conceive must fail to portray the Infinite.

Here we encounter what has been called "the antinomy of religious feeling" (Hoffding, 1906, p. 163). There is on one hand a disposition to rest in the assurance that one Power, beyond our apprehension, changeless amid all change, controls the universe: "God is great and we knew Him not!" Yet even those to whom this sense of a remote Providence brings comfort may at times feel it is net enough: they want something nearer and more human than the Absolute; they want to realize that in the midgst of turmoil and struggle they have a fellow-struggle by their side, one who knows from his own experience what it is to suffer and meet resistance. They can never rest content until the infinite and exalted is presented it eh form of the finite.

Dante, that master of symbolism, at the end of his pilgrimage tried in vain to tell the Vision that came to him of the Supreme Good, the ineffable Glory of God. It came to him as light.

O luce eterna, the sola in to sidi,
sola t'intendi, e., da the intelletta
ed intendente te, ami ed arridi!

With the profundity of that Light he saw a circle—*mi parve pinta della nostra effige*— the featured countenance of humanity. No more than a geometrician can square the circle could Dante express in finite terms his vision of the Godhead; but what he saw in the heart of it brought comfort to his exiled and harassed soul. It was the symbol of

I'amor che move il sole el'altre stelle
(*Paradiso,*xxxiii, 124, 145).

It is a far fry from Dante to the Africans yet is it fanciful to hear in the African's ancestor cult an echo of the universal cry for a God near at hand? "We *pata* ('adore') those whom we had seen with our eyes, their death and their life among us"—so Zulus said to Dr. Callaway.

Gautama the Buddha rejected all metaphors as inadequate to express the Highest; and his followers of the Mahayana sect reacted by worshiping him as the god of gods. "Of all the great religious teachers of the world," it has been said, "Christ is the most unashamedly anthropomorphic...The whole basis of Christ's practical religious teaching is just one great anthropomorphic thought" (Streeter, p. 142). He spoke not without parable. He conversed with Galilean peasants in the home-speech, drawing His symbols from kitchen and field, from domestic and social life. He spoke of God as father; of men as potential sons of God and brothers. His followers have never been quite sure where in His teaching the figurative ends and the literal begins; and the uncertainty, a philosopher suggests, has given rise to most of the grave doubts and conflicts which have arisen in the Church (Hoffding, 1906, p. 309).

Religion draws its symbols not only from human personality but also from the material world. In spite of all argument that nothing "exists" save what is perceived through the senses, it is convinced that beyond the world of sense-data there is another world —a world of values. "The severe schools", said Sir Thomas Browne (1642, p. 16), "shall never laugh me out of the Philosophy of Hermes, that this visible world is but a picture of the invisible, wherein,as in a Pourtraict, things are to truly, but in equivocal shapes, and as they countrerfeit some more real substance in that invisible fabrick."

My heart leaps up when I behold
A rainbow in the sky.

So may a physicist's heart leap,but as a scientist he is bound to describe the rainbow as a band of ethereal vibrations of various wave-lenghts. It should make the same impression on his mind as a table of wave-lengths. But I dare think it does not. Unless he is a peter Bell he sees and admires the beauty of the bow's form and colour—things which his scientific conscience warns him are not in the waves. But he sees them: "no complete view (of the world) can be obtained so long as we separate our consciousness from the world of which it is a part" (Eddington, 1929, p. 328 sqq.). The entities of physics (as I have already said) are of a symbolic nature; so, it may be said, are the entities of religion; but at least to some scientists the symbol is a partial aspect of an ulterior existence, and to the religious mind (as to the artist) the symbol points to the actual existence of something beyond itself—the symbol has its referent in reality, and is a means of apprehending that reality. So when the African observes the rainbow he calls it "the Bow of God"; it is not God; it is a symbol, a manifestation of the Supreme Power. "For", says St. Paul, "from the first making of the world, those things of God which the eye is unable to see, that is, His eternal power and existence, are fully made clear, He having given the knowledge of them through the things which are made..." *(Romans,* i. 20, Basic).

Baron von Hugel reminds us that religion comes first to a child by way of the senses, through some external symbol, some picture or status. The appeal is directed through the senses to the imaginative faculty first. The external sensible, readily picturable facts of religion correspond to and feed the child's imagination as readily as the mother's milk corresponds to and feeds its body. "Religion is here above all a Fact and Thing" (1923, i, 51). The youth and adult pass through other stages of religious development; but they never outlive their need of symbols. We are so constituted that our minds demand some graspable raft in this boundless ocean of mystery upon which we float. The most rigid Puritan who ever banned the wedding ring and Christmas plum-pudding did not rid himself entirely of symbolism: he exhibited in his dress what Dr. Nadel calls "diacritical symbols."

Adoration of the Almighty pours itself out in the symbolical language of poetry, as in the words of Scripture set to music by C.H.H. Parry:

"Behold He is great and we know Him not; neither can the number of His years be searched out. The Lord's seat is in heaven. Clouds and darkness are round about Him. He decketch Himself with light as with a garment and spreadth out the heavens like a curtain. He layeth the beams of his chambers in the waters and walketh upon the wings of the wind."

So, from the simple ritual of the African barbarian to the gorgeous ceremonial of a Pontifical High Mass in St. Peter's, symbolism is the natural language of religion. But not of religion only. "Social life", says Durkheim (pp. 230 sqq.), "in all its aspects and in every period of its history, is made possible only by a vast symbolism." The symbol not only serves as a ralling center for any sort of group; it makes social unity obvious to the members; it clarifies the sentiment society has of itself; and it also creates that sentiment. Without symbols social sentiments could have only a precarious existence, for the symbol constantly brings the sentiments to mind and arouses them. They are not mere lables but an ingegral part of the collective life. "Symbolism," says Raymond Firth, "serves as a behicle for the expression of values which are significant for the social relations of the people" (1951, p. 177).

"Without symbolism", says Cassirer, "the life of man would be like that of the prisoners in the cave of Plotos famous simile. Man's life would be confined within the limits of his biological needs and his practical interests; it could find no access to the 'ideal world' which is opened to him from different sides by religion, art, philosophy, science." Instead of defining man as *animal rationale* Cassirer would define him as *animal symbolicum* (1945, pp. 26, 41). Thomas Carlyle in his rhetorical manner put it in this way: "Is not all that man does symbolical?—a revelation to the sense of the mystic God-given force that is in him. Not a hut he builds but is the visible embodiment of thought. It is in and through symbols that man consciously or unconsciously lives, works and has his being (1894, p. 135 sq.).

Symbology should lead us to a better understanding of the life of any people—particularly of their religion, always remembering Dr. Marett's dictum: "it is not the outward symbolism but the inward sense that can alone provide the basis of an intelligent judgment concerning the value of a religious act" (1927, p. 396). But the pathway of a symboligist is beset with many snares and pitfalls.

He must beware of the slippery slope of etymology which leads to destruction. If you would know the fantasticalities into which it is possible to fall, you can hardly do better than read some chapters of Harold Bailey's *The Lost Language of Symbolism.* Therein you may learn that the Zulus are a branch of the Bantus, a name comparable to the British names of Bunty and Bundy; and that, moreover, the word "Zulu" is probably cognate with "Zulu", a place name in Cornwall.[3]

We have to bear in mind the admonition of a distinguished psychologist: "There is no branch of psychological interpretation more liable to wild and generalized speculation than this branch of the interpretation of symbols...Any explanation which turn supon symbolic representation can be accepted as valid only in so far as it keeps clearly to the principle that a symbol must be interpreted strictly by reference to the mental life and personal history of the individual who uses the symbol, or to the characteristic responses of the group to whom the symbol may be said to belong" (Bartlett. 1923, pp. 247sq.).

There is no inherent connexion between verbal symbols and their referents. The meaning of words is given by what Malinowski called "the context of situation"[4], and this is equally true of non-verbal symbols. The signification of a material object depends upon its context. An earthenware pot as it leaves the hands of an African woman is definable in terms of the use to which it is put: it may be a "cooking-pot", it may be a "water-pot." Place a pot on the apex of a hut, it is no longer a mere pot but a sign that the Mwila who resides beneath it has killed a man in battle or a ferocious wild beast. The pot in that position may also be interpreted as a symbol in that it points to a courage that is outside the range of ordinary men. It is the Ila equivalent of the Victoria or George Cross. If the pot is cracked, it means to the Kavirondo Bantu that the owner is afflicted with *luswa,* is ceremonially unclean. By a natural association of ideas, a pot may represent a young woman, for (a) both are of domestic use, and (b) both are potential containers. If a man comes to you and says: "I am come to talk about a pot," you know that he has his eye on your daughter as a wife for his nephew. Breaking a pot may be an incident in funeral rites, probably the symbol of death. To Rattray's Nankanse a pot might become a *bagere,* the shrine of an ancestor, and may even be identified with the ancestor. Among the same people "setting a pot" is an important hunting-rite apparently for the purpose of fending off, or conciliating, the spirits of the animals that have been killed (Rattray, 1932, i, 215, 171 sq). The significance of an object depends then upon its context of situation.

Interpretation of social data is never easy—the hazards are so many. On the one hand there is the subtle danger of seeing symbolism where there is none. A person of imaginative temperament is tempted to read it into everything. On the other hand, a matter-of-fact person is liable to interpret literally what is matephorical. Symbolism largely employes analogy and two observers may seize upon different elements of the analogy and thereby reach disparate interpretations of the same symbol. Among the Balla, bride and bridegroom sit side by side, they hand each other a morsel of food and eat together, as part of the marriage ceremony. I interpret this act on the principle that eating together indicates comradeship on terms of equality and conclude that here is an affirmation that ideally at leat marriage is the union of two equals in a bond of mutual serive. Dr. Glucknman notices that the Lozi bride and bridegroom eat the porridge off a stone and sees therein a symbol of a hope that the marriage may endure as a stone endures (Colson & Gluckman, 1949, p. 80). Malinowski interprets the funeral rites of savage societies as expressing the dogma of continuity afterdeath: "The whoel conduct of the group," he affirms, "expresses the hope of a salvation and immortality"

(1925, p. 58). Raymond Firth, on the contrary, sees in the ritual a symbol of finality. In essence, the community says to the relatives: "Your boy is dead; he is now buried. Wail for him in one final outburst, before us all. We expect it of you, an dwe demand it of you. Then to-morrow you will return to a normal social existence" (1951, p. 63).

Another potential source of misinterpretation lies in the fluidity of symbolism. Ideas move more rapidly than their expression in word and deed. Owing to man's innate conservatism, his psychic inertia, the ritual may perdure when the dogma is obsolete. Our language reflects many outworn beliefs. We still talk of "influence" but it is without reference to the floowing of an ethereal fluid from the stars. The modern mind is baffled by the vivid symbolism of medieval mystics who expressed themselves in terms of a conception of the material universe that is now out of date. We still keep to some ancient spatial images, as when we speak of "ascending into heaven" or "descending into hell", while giving them a differnt symbolic meaning. As scientists discard outworn hypotheses, so advance in civilization involves casting off what Carlyle called "the tatters and rags of superannuated worn-out symbols." We do not abolish hypotheses and symbols but we substitute new ones to keep step with fresh enlightenment. We place flowers on graves instead of the victuals which, no doubt, our ancestors, like Africans, placed there. What was a live symbol, pregnant with significance, may become dead, like the monoliths of Stonehenge or the figures in Egyptian tombs. Or we may keep the old symbols and give them a new meaning. To the Roman citizen the Cross was a symbol of the utmost degradation, an obscene object never to be mentioned in polite society; to the Christian it is a living symbol, pointing to something that is unutterable—the love of God which passes all knowledge. So a symbol may have more than one meaning; one for you, and one for me. In the thought of the early Christians, the figure of a fish was a symbol of Christ. To the modern psycho-analyst a fish is a dream symbol of represssed sexuality. That I suppose, is what Dr. Brtlett meant when he said that "the success of the attempt to treat the significance of symbols as matter for scientific investigation depends to a large degree upon the study of individual and group differences."

Of the origin of symbols we can assert nothing. They may have sprung from the individùal mind, conscious or unconscious, or from a collective unconscious. Individudals have symbolisms that are proper to themselves. But in general, symbols, whether verbal or non-verbal, pertain to groups. This is not to say that every member of a group is aware of the meaning of the symbol. The observer may ask for an explanation and be blandly told: "It is our custom," or " We doas oru fathers did"; or he may be given an interpretation introduced by such a formula as *Nkukuti,* "i.e., "that is what it means." That may or may not be the communally accepted meaning, but only an individual opinion. It is never safe to accept without ample confirmation what one man says of the ritual in which he participates.

Furthermore, let us note that frequently what appears to be symbolic, and is so interpreted by one individual, may to other people be something more than an index pointing to an object other than itself. As we have already seen, sybols carry strong emotional charges: they have evocative, incitive, stimulative power. Durkheim (p.230 sq.) lays stress upon this dynamical aspect of symbolism. when the participant in a ritual experiences an exaltation of spirit, anincrease of psychie energy, an enhanced confidence or sense of security, these effects may appear to emanate from the riote itself or from the material object which is the focus of the ritual. It is not difficult to enter into his feeling. Ayone who has lived long in a foreign land knows well the exaltation produced by the first sight of the Union Jack when he lands on these shores. Not understanding the psychological processes involved he may easily assing the effects to the symbol itself as their efficient cause.

We shall see before we have finished that Africans believe that in material objects, in words spoken, in actions performed, there resides some mystical energy that is efficacious in the production of certain definite results. That is to say, what appears to be a symbol is in reality atalisman, a vehicle of mystical energy. The disinction is subtle, tenuous, but real.

The confusion of symbol with talisman is not unknown in Christendom; which is why, I suppose, Evellyn Underhill (1923, p. 189) says that "religion on its ceremontial side is always largely magical." So it may appear. In the Christian sacraments, as in talismans, attention is focussed on material objects; and psychological processes operate in the use of both. To many Christians, the water of baptism, the bread and wine of Holy Communion, are purely symbolical —"a visible form of an invisible grace," as Augustine said. Others believe that just as a poet conveys his meaning through his words and the sound of his words—i.e., through a movement of inorganic particles—so God communicates Himself to the soul of the worthy recipient through these material objects—His "visible word" (to quote Augustine again). Archbishop Temple (1935, p 492) sees in the sacraments a clue to the undestanding of the relation of spirit to matter in the universe. Sacrament is not magic: but according to this view, sacrament is endowed with the virtue and potency which magic claims falsely to offer. I have no doubt that many people, whose minds are still dominated by what talians call *la religione vecchia,* take the same view of the sacraments as the Africans take of their talismans—things which in themselves have causal efficacy. Talismans might be taken as in some sense proleptical of the sacraments.

One more remark before I leave these generalities. I borrow the words of one who is a psycho-analyst as well as an anthropologist.

"Now both the Old Testament and anthropology show that man's early development was far from being regulated by dogma, but proceeded by a system of trial and error, always guided in the long run towards higher things, but groping its way by means of symbolic beliefs of all kinds and by ritual practices expressing and gradually crystallizing these beliefs. Nor can any one who has lived with primitive peoples,as the writer has, have an doubt as to the vivid nature of these beliefs and practices or of their immense value as indispensable vehicles of the nascent comprehension by mankind of the truths later expressed by dogma" (Layard, p. 92).

III

Let us then turn to the Africans.

They are fond of playing with words. They have a remarkable gift of drawing analogies. They are adepts in the use of metaphor. They habitually think and speak in pictures.

"The discovery of likeness in the midst of differences and of difference in the midst of likeness is the keenest pleasure of the intellect" (Raleigh, 1918,p. 61). The young African finds that pleasure in composing and asking riddles.[5] "*Kako*", says an Ila urchin, "Heres one for you!" and he expects the conventional reply: *Kakeza,*" "let it come!" "let it come!" "A house without a door," "says he, and presently after some cogitation the correct answer is given: "An egg!" "A pool in the midst of reeds" says another; and the reply comes: "The eye!" "My hen has laid among throne" is a Swahili riddle; the answer to which is "a pineapple". This youthful propensity for tracing similarities continues throughout life.

The proverbs, maxims, wise-saws, which are an open door into the African mind, point to an ability for conveying abstract ideas effectively and picturesquely by means of concrete facts. "The potter's wife eats from a potsherd" (Ganda). "No elephant feels the burden of its trunk" (Xhosa and Ila). "Boboons laugh at each other's eye-sockets"; "a red fig does not lack worms inside" (Thonga). It is noteworthy that in such sayings metaphor is more common than simile. The African does not say" "wealth is *like* dew"; he says: "wealth *is* dew"; "death *is* sleep"; "the heart of man *is* a bee"; "anger *is* stable". This characteristic is apparent not only in proverbs, which are more or less sterotypes, but also in aphorisms thrown off in every-day speech, as when an old chief turned to me after I had sat with him all one long laborious day in his court and said: "*Bwami mbuzhike,* chieftainship is slavery". So Cullen Young's Tumbuka say: "*Umfumu unkuwoko,* chieftainship is a hand"—the (open) hand symbolizing generosity (1931, p. 268).

It has been said that one should handle the little word "is" as carefully as a stick of dynamite (Chase, 938, p. 57) and the warning is equally applicable to the copula in Buntu languages. Old Shaloba was not identifying chieftainship with slavery; he was saying that in certain respects his position as chief was similar to the position of a slavery; he was saying that in certain respects his position as chief was similar to the position of a slave: he was asserting not identification but similitude. The confusion of these two concepts is a frequent source of minister predation.

The metaphorical language offers many a semantic problem to the anthropologist. H eust continually ask: What is the referent of this verbal symbol? I would illustrate this necessity by reference to Dr. Evans-Pritchard's study of Nuer prayers. These are spontaneous meaningful utterances addressed to God which do not require any special method of interpretation but only adequate translation. Literally rendered one prayer reads: "Let the breath of the people be very cold." But the primary meaning of the words *vic* and *koc* ("breath." and "cold") is not the right meaning in this context; the man is asking God that in their inner selves the people may be free from anxiety. Another prayer run: "May we tread on wild rice." The reference here is to a tender pasture grass on which small calves feed and which is soft to the feet of man. What is asked of God is a path through life free from harm, a mind atease. As is the case with many other Africans, the analogy is drawn between sleep and peace. (Fifty years ago, the most frequent greeting I received when traveling in Central Africa was: "*natural,* Let us sleep!"—a reflection of the insecurity in which the people were living). The commonest of phrases in let us sleep!", i.e., "Let us be at peace, not only in relation to other men, but with ourselves." When greeting his fellows a Nuer will say: "*ci tol?* have you smoke?" Smoke rising from the hearth is, like sleep, a symbol of contentment, tranquility, deliverance from evil. The Nuer regard the misfortunes from which they wish to be delivered as due to "faults' *(dueri)* and hold therefore that they can be avoided by the man who possesses *cuong,* that is to say, the man who is right in his dealings with God and man. "These two ideas of being in the right and of deliverance from evil are", concludes Dr. Evans-Pritchard, "basic to their' religious thought and complementary " (1952). This should give pause to those who imaging that Africans in their prayers seek only for material blessings.

In the symbolism of the Africans there is much that emphasizes their conviction that desirable ends of a material nature are also, and intrinsically, ends of a spiritual or mystical nature. Their ideal of a good life includes tangible values—abundant crops, plenty of children, health; and the health is moral as well as physical. The ritual practices seem to symbolize this close connexion, announting to identity, between what is palpable and what is spiritual. When BaSotho cry aloud "*Pula!* ("rain") they are not only asking that rain may fall: it is an aspiration for peace, for domestic and natural well-being in all respects.

African idiom abounds in euphemism. They do not like to say straight out that a person is dead. "He has changed his abode", the BaSotho say, or "He has returned home" (Casalia, 1861, p.318). The Zulus (Krige, 1937, p. 171) never announced that their chief was dead "*Uyadunguzela",* they would declare, "He is brooding" (or hibernating).

Africans, as a rule, are decorous in social intercourse and, especially in mixed company, seek to avoid offensive expressions. They shrink from calling a spade a spade, or even an agricultural implement. They exercise a penchant for allusive locution. This applies, not only as among ourselves when speaking of natural functions of the body but also on other occasions when delicacy calls for roundabout speech. When a Tallensi becomes a father he announces the fact to his parents-in-law in this form: "Your daughter has brone a calabash"—if it is a girl; "a staff", if it is a boy (Fortes, 1945, p. 61). Indeed in African symbolism, a pot or a calabash or water stands for femininity a spear or rod for masculinity. In Busutoland the birth of a son is announced by beating the father with a stick; the birth of a daughter by drenching him with water (Ashton, 1951, p. 29). These are symbols which psycho-analysts will recognize.

The same kind of circumlocution occurs in proposals of marriage. In Kavirondo a man proposes to a divorcee in such terms as these: "You are living here by yourself, but we need women to build the fire for us.". If she is well-disposed she may reply: "Look at your fingers"—in other words, "count your cattle." He follows by saying: "If a man tightens the strings of his lyre he knows what he is going to play" (Wagner, 1950, p. 439).

Usually the proposal to a maiden is made through a mediator. He opens the matter by saying to her parents: "I have come to talk about the handle of a hoe." All the subsequent conversation is in terms of that implement; and finally if favourably impressed the parents will admit: "Yes. perhaps the handle of a hoe may be here", and the mediator returns to report that the omens are favourable.[6]

Similar periphrasis is used often by the diviner when consulted by a client. "Go and burn black ants," be may say, meaning "Go and dig up so-and-so's bones and burn them" (Wagner, 1950, p. 289). The Sotho diviner's recitations to his huckle-bones (*lithoko tsa maoa)* are as enigmatic as the ancient Delphic oracle and open to as many various interpretations; e.g., "White ox, I die, I die for the land", (Ashton, 1951, p. 297).

As in Hebrew and Greek, so in Bantu, intellectual ideas are expressed largely by roots of concrete significance and the passions by words indicating primarily the organs of the body. When a concrete object has the same name as an abstract idea, the object may be regarded as a symbol of the idea. It is always fascinating to trace these extensions of meaning. The idea of reincarnation which is wide-spread in Africa is expressed in the Ga language by the word *gblamo,* the name of a vine which twines round and round a post (Field, 1937, p. 197). Similarly in Ila, the symbol of the lineage is *lunungu,* the long succulent branching stem of the pumpkin and melon. In Sotho *letlokoa,* "a straw" connotes "vanity", and "a yellow heart" *(pelo ae tsetla)* is "jealousy". Perseverance and firmness in danger are expressed in terms of the liver. "I am eatenr by my *letsoalo* ('midriff')" is the Sotho way of saying: "I am stung by remorse."

Dr. Field is probably right in tracing to this region of metaphor the birthplace of many imaginary beings that dance their way through African phantasy.[7]Some mysterious operations of Nature become objectified, or even personified, even as haunting fears are figured by some of ourselves as Germlins and as psychologists personify as the Censor the discriminatory, inhibitory processes of the unconscious. An example of this reification, or personification, is offered by Chibumba, the female creature which the Balla believe to be the generative agent in the womb, forming the foetus and causing the pangs of childbirth by its violent efforts to retain its product. Chibumba might be taken as a symbol of the Life-force in one of its aspects.[8]

Many Africans draw a distinction between the right and left sides of the body: the right is a symbol and seat of strength and virility, the left of weakness and femininity. A candidate for chieftainship may be rejected on the ground that he is left-handed. BaSotho say that if a woman lies on her right side during and immediately after the sexual act she should produce male children; if on the left, then female (Ashton, 1951, p. 27). An inferior person should not stand on the right of a superior for it would take away the superior's strength. For the same reason you do not pass on a person's right hand. African mothers are keen observers of their daughters' suitors and of the girls whom their sons want s wives. If a Mandingo young man puts his left foot foremost in crossing and obstacle, a mother may say to her daughter: "Marry that man. He will always be a feeble character: his wife will lead him by the nose" *Africa,* XVI, p. 52).

Are we already reaching the limit of symbolism and entering the region of what is called "magic"? It looks like it if a man can draw strength from another by standing on his right side. A European is baffled in his search for interpretations. When Africans speak as they do of heart and liver and other organs, are they employing figurative language? Or do they mean that by turning yellow a man's heart exudes jealousy? Does the hardening of his liver induce patience? Have we here an intuition of the modern discovery that endocrine secretions, such as thyrosin, become a factor of temperament by sensitizing certain propensities? Or is it that patience hardens the liver and jealousy yellows the heart? Or again, is there a mystical identification of the physical organs and the affects? Or can we not be content to say that heart and liver are symbols?

I cannot dwell at length on the fascinating subject of names, which also like the heart and other organs, are to be regarded as elements of the complex personality. Names are symbolical in so far as they are not mere labels but point to the owner's status or characteristics. The real or sacred name has religious significance when it is the name of the ancestor who is the living person's guardian or tutelary spirit; along the Balla it is the name of the ancestor who is actually reincarnated in him: since he has returned to earth he naturally resumes his old name and status. The name given at initiation is symbolical of his new position in the tribe; he is a new man therefore has a new name.

That names point to qualities is seen most clearly in the praise-titles: the *izibongo* of the Zulus, the *lithoko* of the BaSotho.

These are made up of single words or short phrases, or they may be expanded into poems in which the singer *(umbongi)* stretches his fancy in search of metaphors to describe the greatness of his chief. Thus of Dingane, Chief of the Zulus:

Bird of the morning!
Thou art the purple dawn
Thou art beautiful as an isle in the Umsinyati,
Thou art the great shade of the Zulus.
Ravager of provinces,
Deep abyss which engulfest all! (Shooter, 1857, p. 312).

It used to be the custom for warriors to extol their own prowess, as did a MoSotho named Cucutle:

I am Cucutle
I am the black warrrio,
I am the white thunder
Which growls after rain (Casalis, 1861 p. 333).

Note here the metaphorically on which I commented before. Cucutle does not say: "I am *like* the white thunder": he says" "I *am* the white thunder."

It is by a study of such praise-titles given to the Supreme Power in the universe that we can learn much of the African's theology. They know that (as the Ngomble say)[9] the Power is *Endandala,* "the Unexplainable," but when they speak of the Power as "the Moulder", "the Constructor", "the Giver," "the Kindly-disposed", "the Great Mother," "the Greatest of

Friends", all such epithet are symbolical: attempts to conceptualize in familiar human terms what is incomprehensible. Some God-names sound strangely to Europeans who do not appreciate the African poet's liking for metony my and synecdoche. For instance, the cattle-loving Nuer salute as Tutgar the most majestic long-horned beast of the herd; and this epithet (meaning literally "omnipresent strength") is also given to Kwoth, the Supreme Being (Evans-Pritchard, 1951). The God-names which refer to celestial phenomena—sun, thunder. lightning, rain—are no more to be taken literally than the poetic description of the rainbow as "God's necklace." I cannot but think that Dr. Meek is mistaken when, writing of certain Nigerian tribes, he says that Hyel, the Supreme Being, "is the firmament, the sun, the moon, the stars" (1931, i, 221). Some Balla would say during a rain-storm "God (Leza) is falling", but I never met a man of that tribe who would say that God and rain were identical.. These celestial phenomena are symbols and undoubtedly in the minds of many Africans (as Dr. Evans-Pritchard says of the Nuer) more than symbols: they are modes and manifestations of Deity. Africans have a profound sense that the Supreme Being, who is not localized, for whom no sanctuaries are built, for whom no cult is organized and of whom no images are shaped, is involved in these phenomena and in human life.

Descending from these high levels, we may glance at the symbolical value of colours and numbers.

A Zulu girl indites her love-letters in the form of beadwork, the patterns and colours of which express her sentiment. White beads symbolize love; black, disappointment, hope deferred; green, sickly feeling; pink, poverty; red, yearning; blue, happiness; yellow, wealth in cattle. A single string of white and pink beads reads: "My heart is full of love, but you have no cattle to marry me with " (Krige, 1936, p. 132). It is curious that among dark skinned folk black stands universally for impurity,misfortune, wretchedness, while white stands for purity, prosperity, happiness. Among the Mashona a bride-groom is given a pure-white egg to indicate that the bride is *virgo intacta* (Bullock, 1950, p. 62). The priests of Ga temples always wear white robes; and among the same people the victor in litigation is smeared with white clay as a symbol of his innocence and of congratulation (Field, 1937, p. 7, 163). Where haruspication is practised, a whitish spleen indicates that the patient will recover, a red spleen indicates persistent danger, and a black spleen indicates death. Some Kavirondo Bantu distinguish two Gods: *Wale omuwanga,* the White God, is benevolent; *Wele gumali,* the Black God, is malevolent (Wagner, 1950, p. 175). *Ukuba nesinyama,* "to have blackness", is the Zulu equivalent of "to be impure"; the term would be applied to menstruating and pregnant women, to attendants at a funeral, and especially to those who have handled the corpse. The process of purification includes taking certain "white" medicines (Krige, 1936, p. 82).

Some occasions demand the sacrifice of pure white goats, sheep and fowls; but more often it is a pure black beast, without a single white hair, that is called for. For instance, among the exogenous Mashona, if two people marry who are of the same clan though distantly related, the fault may be adjusted by offering a black bull to propitiate the ancestors (Bullock, 1950, p. 87). In such cases, I suppose, the blackness of the animals smbolizes the sin which has to be expiated. When , as is common, a black beast is slaughtered during the "rain-making" ceremonies, the blackness typifies the desired black rain bearing clouds. It is not purely symbolical. It is intended to produce an effect; the symbol passes into a talisman.

The attitude towards numbers is often ambivalent. The Vugusu regard seven as many enlightened Europeans regard thirteen. Among them a father will never admit having seven children; a raiding party will never bring home seven cattle; if they count people, instead of saying "*varano na vavili;* seven persons" they say "*varano na musafu muvi,* bad luck persons" (Wagner, 1950, p. 210). Zulus would regard it as a reflection on the girl's chastity and a deadly insult if parents of a suitor offered seven cattle as bride-wealth; only for a divorced woman would that number be acceptable (Krige, 1936, p. 132). The meaning of many of their symbols has been forgotten by the Akan but, says Mrs. Meyerowit, the symbolism of numbers is intact. Among them the number seven is not bodeful but sacrosanct: it stands for the State which is made up of seven clans representing seven planets, the deity of each one of which rules a day in the seven-day week. An axe with three points is the Akan Omanhene's most ancient emblem; he is proclaimed king by being lightly seated on his stool three times. The act symbolizes his connesion with Nyame, the Creator and ruler of the universe which consists of sky, each and the underworld. So, according to Mrs. Meyerowitz each of the cardinal numbers carries a mystic significance.[10]

Just as the seal of a medieval emancipated English borough was the symbol of its corporate union and in Britain to-day the crown is a symbol of kingship, the great Seal a symbol of legislative power, the Lord Chancellors Purse a symbol of the nation's wealth, even so in Africa there are objects and actions which convey a meaning that is not inherent in themselves.

Here we may note the distinction that is drawn (as by Dr. Nadel, 1951, pp. 262 sqq. Morris, 1946, pp. 190 sq.) between natural and artificial symbols. In the former the correspondence between the symbol and the thing it stands for is at once apparent. Iconic symbols, such as portaits and models, exhibit perceptible similarity in various degrees. Certain objects have a physiognomic character residing in their "look" and expressing emotional states. The Zulu girls's love-letters are an example. Artificial or extrinsic symbols, on the other hand, are constructed and invested with meaning by some arbitrary and merely conventional rule. Diacritical symbols, natural or artificial, indicate that a certain behaviour may be expected both of the persons displaying them and of those to whom they are displayed. In their interpretation the fallacy must be avoided of thinking of them in mechanistic terms as external stimuli producing automatic responses. Social nomenclature, such as the classificatory kinship terms, falls into this category. So also do objects which define and express social relations, status and rank.

Mrs. Meyerowitz illustrates an applique cloth of one of the Akan chiefs which is divided into 25 fields each containing some symbol of royalty. The Akan Queen-Mother also has her insignia. She is regarded as a daughter of the moon and her people desire her to be as calm and peaceful as her "mother", her body as delicate and beautiful. Silver, representing moon-light, is her metal; she wears silver jewellery and silver ornaments adorn her ceremonial robes. The king, as divine, has mystical connection with the sun, and gold, the colour of the sun, is his metal. His was the Golden Stool as the Silver Stool was that of the Queen-Mother.

It is not only among the Akan that diacritical symbols are found: they are the vogue all over Africa, even in tribes that have not the highly developed hierarchy and artistic skill that characterize some of the Sudanic Negroes. Even among the Balla the communal heads were distinguished by leopard skins, ivory bracelets and the *impande* shell. Nyakyusa headmen are each given a horn, a tail and a spear as emblems of their office. The spear is the symbol of the headman's manood and strength. The other objects—as is so frequently the case with regalia—as more than symbols they embody *amanga,* "mystical power." The *amanga* of the horn will enhance his prestige by increasing the number of this adherents; the *amanga* of the tail will enable him to dream of threatening dangers (Wilson, 1951, pp. 25, 95,n.).[11] The scepter of the Sotho chief handed down from Moshesh to his successors, is a club fashioned from a rhinoceros horn. It also has occult properties symbolized by the enormous strength of the rhinoceros. So long as the chief held it in his hand he was invincible on the field of battle (Laydevant, *Africa,* XVIII, pp. 41 sqq.).

Fire is a not uncommon symbol of perennity or continuity. In Ruanda, the fire which was lighted for the founder of the dynasty was sedulously maintained for his successors all through the centuries (Kagame, *Africa,* XVII, pp. 41 sqq.) Among the Shilluk the death of a Reth (king) temporarily breaks the link between the people and Nyikang, the founder of the royal house, and this break is marked by extinguishing all fires; the lighting of new fires symbolizes the restoration of the continuity (Howel & Thomson, 1946). The Nyakyusa have a similar custom. "The fire is the fire of lordship (*unoto botwa)"* they say. "The old chieftainship is coming to an end, the new has come" (Wilson, 1951, pp. 26 sq.).

Animals, as might be expected, enter largely into African symbolism. In the folk-tales the characteristics of beasts are not only set forth for entertainment; they are held up for emulation and detestation. The hare, for exmaple, stands as a symbol of the what Baila call *mano,* the quality of cunning which wins its way against superior physical strength. Evil qualities are associated with repulsive appearance: the hyena is the epitome of gluttony. Many tribes regard the chameleon as a symbol of death: the snake as a symbol of life (Abrahamson, 1951, pp. 17 etc.).

The regalia of Akan chiefs, their robes, their ornaments, their umbrellas, the officials staffs and raiment of their retinue, all have a meaning, or may be supposed to have had a meaning at some time. Thus the lion, cast in gold, which figures on the royal umbrella and on the staff of the *okyeame* (spokesman), is an obvious emblem of power. The leopard is fierce and the kings, stool is placed on a leopard skin to symbolize his daring and fierce character. Moreover, on the principle of *pars pro toto,* some of the leopard's fierceness is conveyed to the king through this contact with the skin. The Queen Mother's stool rests appropriately on a sheepskin. The elephant, an embodiment of transcendent strength, suggests to the Akan more than the river Tano which it represents: they say : "The great spirit *(sunsum)* that is everywhere—it is he we call elephant." This may remind us nthat Christian Yoruba speak of Christ as *Erintunde, "Erintunde,* "the Elephant returned, for just as every human spirit returns to be reborn so the mighty power of God, manifested in Christ, has come to be possessed by men. An interesting example of the new extension of old symbols (Parrinder, 1952).

Among the Akan each animal totem is thought to represent the qualities and embody the ideals which members of the clan must live up to. Thus, the parrot, the totem of the Anana clan, symblizes eloquence and persuasiveness; the crow of the Asona clan, wisdom; and the buffalo of the Konna clan (for some recondite reason) stands for conscientiousness (Meyerowitz, 1951, pp 29 sqq.). It cannot be said that this form of symbolism is common—it would seem to be a rationalization to explain why animals are chosen as totems. The Bakwena of South Africa do not hold up the crocodile an an exemplar.

Diacritical symbols are by no means confined to the aristocracy. As among the Kavirondo Bantu, the garments worn by girls and women often indicate their status; the length of the tassels hanging from the belt of a female depends upon whether she is unmarried or has borne children or has passed the menopause (Wagner, 1950, p. 307). When she is about to be married a Zulu woman begins to build her chignon *(isicholo)* which is the symbol of full female maturity. The much treasured head-ring *(ikehla)* was sewn on the heads of Zulu warriors who had completed their active service and were allowed to marry: to tear it from a man's head or even to touch it was an insult of the gravest description (Krige, 1936, pp. 370 sq.). The rod *(ekisuli)* placed by Kavirondo Bantu on the apex of a hut is a symbol of manhood, particularly of a man's procreative power. It indicates that the roof of a hut is a man's prerogative; if a woman climbed up there is would be taken as a sign that she wished for a divorce (Wagner, 1950,p. 385). Among Tallens, the stirring-stick used in making porridge is the symbol of woman hood, as is a bow of manhood; for man and wife to fight each other with these weapons is a heinous sin—an unnatural warfare of the sexes.

Pictures, we are often told, are the books of the illiterate; and many of the objects we call symbols are pictographs with a didactic, or at least suggestive, intent. Some of the gold weights of Ashanti are called "Proverb weights" because they iconize, and so call to mind, valuable truths of experience. Thus a weight showing two human figures carries the meaning: "I who am lying on my back cannot see the Sky God *(Nyame),* how do you expect to, who are lying on your belly?" (Rattray, 1923, p. 312).[12]

For another iconic symbolism we may take a glance into the hut which is the center of the ceremonial of the Buyeye society in Sukumaland. The hut itself is a symbol of the earth and upon its walls and roof the sun, moon and stars are depicted. Time is represented by a grinding-stone and copper bangles, the maternal ancestors by a pot-ladle. Pegs driven into the ground stand for knowledge, a pad of twisted grass for the strength and unity of the society, and earthenware pot for its prosperity. A small circular termite hill outside the hut symbolizes the communal spirit of the society (Cory, 1946, pp. 160 sqq.). This is the mulieu for the initiation into this fraternity of snake-charmers.

I am not competent to enter into a technical discussion of African art in general. My chief concern here is in regard to its symbolical elements. I agree with Dr. Raymond Firth who, in his excellent treatment of the subject (1951, pp. 155 sqq.) says:

"By no means all primitive art is symbolic. Much of its is simply descriptive...Many motifs employed by the primitive artist are simple line arrangements of a geometrical order, with no allusive significance. Or they are conventionalized representations of natural or cultural objects, the reference being a direct one to them without any further significance."

I have no doubt that a large proportion of the carvings and moldings and paintings and textile designs which attract us by their beauty are expressions of the art is' joy in creation and no more. Yet symbolism is there; and perhaps it is only our ignorance of what the artist is trying to express that blinds us to the meaning of his creations.

Many of the statuettes, with disproportioned and distorted limbs and other exaggerated features, are portraits of ancestors, like the famous figure of Shamba Bolongongo brought home from the Congo by Emile Torday (1925, pp. 148 sqq.). This might be taken as a symbol of eternal serenity. Other statuettes are so-called "fetishes", supposed to be temporary dwellings of ancestral spirits. Their function is to focus the attention of worshippers. They are shrines.

Other works of art have a "magical" significance. For example, the Dogon of French West Africa believe that since a man killed in battle or hunting is not able to undergo rites of purification, the *nyama (force vital)* of the men or animals he has killed will attach itself to his should (*kikinu say)* and give him no rest, and also be harmful to the living members of the community. To ovbiate this calamity they paint on a rock figures representing him and the arrow with which he was killed, and then bring his shaven locks into contact with the pictures. By this means the *nyama* is conveyed to, and fixed in, the designs, so that it is no longer a danger to dead and living (Dieterlen, 1941, p. 189).[13]

African artists might say with Picasso (who drew inspiration from the Congo) "Je de'teste la nature." The dancing costumes and the masks which are donned on many ceremonial occasions are often masterpieces of the macabre. They seem to be intended to inspire a sense of mystery and of terror. What exactly they symbolize is difficult to determine. Perhaps we might get a clue from Ruskin's chapter on "Crotesque Renainssance" in *The STones of Venice.* I may be quite wrong but as I look at some of these hidcous figures I feel that the artist has some serious purpose in view. This face, malign,cynical, evil—this is life as he sees it and as he wishes observers to see it, to revolt against it and to seek something better. "It has not," says Ruskin, "been sufficiently considered how evident, throughout the system of creation, is the purpose of God that we should often be affected by Fear; not the sudden, selfish and contemptible fear of immediate danger,but he fear which arises out of the contemplation of great powers in destructive operations and generally from the perception of the presence of death" (1874, Vol. III, ch. 11, 41). Am I very far from being right in imagining that some such intuition moves the African artist and is expressed by the masqueraders, when they celebrate the dead?

Much more might be said about material symbols. Let me, before passing on to ritual, say another word about shrines. According to the O.E.D. a shrine is "that which encloses, enshrines, or screens or in which something dwells; a place where worship is offered or devotions are paid to a saint or deity". Such a definition covers the statuettes commonly labelled "fetishes" and also many other objects associated with the religious cults of Africans. It may be a human relic (skeleton, Jawbone, etc.), a tree or grove of trees, a clay mound, a stone, a cave; and with them goes an altar in the form of a receptacle to receive the offerings. Shrines are graded according to the range of the divinitys powers. The family altar of the Balla is an unmarked spot at the foot of the central pole of the hut and other spots just within the doorway: it is there that the mother and father offer their prayers and gifts to their respective ancestors. This corresponds to the space at the back of the hut whih the head of every Zulu household reserves for the ancestors and where he makes his offereing and says his prayers. If he moves to a new residenc ehe induces the spirits to amccompany him, buy first sacrificinga bullock and then dragging a branch of a certain tree along the path to their new home (Krige, 1936, p. 46). The Balla also have village shrines: miniature huts built over graves of former headmen; and each commune has a common shrine, consisting of s grove of trees that has grown around the grave of a long-departed Chief Although not organized administratively into one whole, all the Ila communaes have a bond of union in their devotion to a divinity named Bulongo, for whom temporary shrines are built on occasion. The Supreme Being, Leza, has no shrine. Where there is highly organized tribal system, the shrines are more elaborate, such as public temples in parts of West Africa, on which the artistry of the people is lavished and which harbour symbols representing the attributes or the powers of the gods (Parrinder, 1949, p. 72). All shrones have one common feature: the shrine is not itself an object of worship but points beyond itself; it localizes, bodilizes, makes easier to realize, the presence of ancestors and gods. In this sense they are religious symbols.

Some shrines and altars are more than symbols: they are vehicles of mystical energy. Take for example the *kutogolo* and *jabye* of the Dogon—personal altars made by a father for his young son. These people believe that at death a person's "soul" *(kikinu say)* joins the collectivity of ancestors while his *nyama* (viral force) is set free and seeks a new support. It may find thatsupport in thefoetus of the man's grandson, in the constitution of which it shares with the father's *nyama*. The ancestor is the child's counterpart *(nani)* in the spirit-world, since both participate in the same *nyama*. That vitalforce needs constant replenishment, so that it may grow and remain pure. After modelling the *kutogola* in clay, the father puts it into contact with his son's head and then consecrates it with a bloody sacrifice, sprinkling the *kutogolo* with the blood of a fowl and throwing upon it the fowl's heart and liver. Part of the liver, which contains fowl's *nyama,* is eaten by the boy. By this rite the boy and the *kutogolo* are brought into close connection; thereafter every sacrifice upon the *kutogolo* strengthens the boy's vitalforce. In making the *jabye,* the father incorporates with the clay parings of the boy's finger and toe nails and drops of his blood. An annual sacrifice is made on the *jabye* and also whenever the boy, or grown man, needs strengthening ina a particular crisis. If is be omitted the owner will fall ill or suffer a reverse of fortune (Dieterlen, 1941, pp.74 sqq.). It may be that in these rites we have a clue to the understanding of the value which Africans assign to their shrines and altars: these not only symbolize a spiritual presence but embody a mystical force strengthened by the blood of sacrified animals.

Be that as it may, the shrine has very considerable value as a social symbol. Africans, it has been well said, feel their unity and perceive their common interests in symbols. Attachment to these more than anything else gives society cohesion and persistence. Reflect the system and endow it with mystical values which evoke acceptance that goes far beyond obedience exacted by the secular sanction of force (Fortes and Evans-Pritchard, 1940, intro.). It is probable that the shrine as a unifying factor is of greater importane in tribes organized in a segmentary system than in tribes with a centralized administration under a chief or king. That is to say, we should expect the shrine to pay a greater part among the Tallensi and Nuer and Tonga than among the Akam Zulu, Tswana and Lozi.

The ancestral cult of the Tallensi centres upon the *bogar,* the shrine, which may be a tree, or a grove of trees or a cave in a hillside. The *bogar* of a clan, the *bogar* of each lineage which is a sub-division of the clan, the *bogar* of each segment of the lineage, and the shrine of a single household, each and every one is the dwelling of ancestors and so close is its identification with the ancestor in the minds of people that it maybe invoked as *yaab,*" ancestor." It symbolizes the unity of the clan, the lineage and the household and its differentiation from other groups. The *bogar* of the clan symbolizes the idea of the ancestors in general; one might even say, with Dr. Fortes, that it symbolizes the concept of ancestry. Further, the *bogar* is a symbol of the whole social order, conceived as brought into being by the ancstors and kept in being under their spiritual aegis.

When clansmen sacrifice together and participate in eating the sacrificial animals they express and pledge their mutual amity and dependence. You cannot sacrifice propitiously with an enemy—mat would anger the ancestors. Initiation into the cult binds the individual, by the most solemn covenant known by these Africans, to uphold the social order bequeathed to the living by the ancestors. Anti-social acts are sins against the ancestors. An adulterous wife is haled to the shrine and made to confess in the presence of the spirits. Her sin endangers the life of husband and child by bringing upon the family the wrath of the ancestors, for her infidelity may make a breach in the continuity of the patriarchal line (Fortes, 1945, p. 98, etc.: 1949, p. , 328 sqq.). Much that Dr. Fortes writes about the Tallensi may be said of Africans in general.

I have no doubt that religious-minded men of the ancient Greek world regarded Zeus and Apollo, not as fictions or creations of art, but as living deities. To us they appear symbolizations of spiritual ideas and as such have psychic reality —as Shakespeare's Ariel has. Any one who has watched the rituals will not doubt that Africans believe implicitly both in the existence of the ancestors and in their intervention in affairs. The psychologist, who does not share that belief, may yet recognize its social value and regard it as a cultural and standardized projection on to the mystical plane of the tangle of attachments, reciprocities, tensions and submerged antagonisms that bind parents and children to one another in life; even as a humanist may regard theo-symbolism as no more than a social construct wherein "God" exists as a human idea, presumably fulfilling some conceptual and emotional needs of man, but without separate existence as an exterior entity. According to these views, the symbol has a subjective not an objective referent. (Jung & Kerenyi, 1951, p. 145; Fortes, 1949, p. 234; Firth, 1951, p. 247). In these matters I prefer to stand with the Africans.

All over African you will find actions which have a meaning

beyond themselves. Even the simplest may be symbolical—shaving for example. The final act in a Nuer marriage is the shaving of the bridge's head by a member of the groom's family; this, with her arrayal in new clothes by her in-laws, symbolizes her new status as a member of their family; she has thrown off the old and taken on the new (Evans-Pritchard, 1948, p. 39). Bathing the body is a universal symbol of inner purification. A lustration is often more than a symbol: it is an efficiatious act, producing the effect desired. The seducer of a girl among the Ga of the Gold Coast is heavily fined and both of them plunge into the sea to wash away their sin. Eating and drinking together is almost, but not write, a universal symbol of amity and reconciliation. If they wish to be particular friends in future two or three youths of Kavirondo, who have passed through the initiation rites together, partake of a common meal ceremonially: the dish of eleusine porridge becomes the symbol and pledge of their comradeship (Wagner, 1950, p. 372). When two Zulus have quarreled seriously, reconciliation is brought about by a ceremony named *ukuthelelana amanzi*. "To pour water for one another". They wash in medicated water, confess their faults, and finally sit together on one mat and drink beer from the same vessel (Krige, 1936, p. 59). African marriage has a twofold aspect: it is a compact between two families, the seal of which is the transfer of goods from the mans to the woman's family; it is also the union of two individuals, and this, as I said before, is often symbolized by the bride and groom eating together ritually. An exception, to the general rule is found among the Dogon who believe that impurity is contagious; food and drink taken in common establish contact between the *nyama* of one person and the *nyama* of another and enable impurity to flow from one to the other (Dieterlen, 1941, p.74 sqq.).

The African's career maybe likened to passing through a series of rooms, the doors of which open and close as he makes his progress. Each state is marked by a *rite de passage*—

rites which abound in vivid symbolism. There is birth and a naming ceremony; there is initiation into maturity and membership of the tribe; there is marriage; there are death and burial; and, to complete the cycle, what Zulus call*ukubuyisa,* the bringing of the spirit home.

To describe the symbolism of all these rites would fill a book. Let it suffice to refer briefly to two events, first to the dramatization of a new birth often performed in initiation ceremonies. Such dramatization is essentially symbolical for it presents to eye and ear, and to the emotions, a figuration of a spiritual or social fact; the entrance into maturity, with all the rights and obligations there to attached. Boys are individually or as groups secluded as if shut up in the womb, the instruction given is preparatory to a new life, the hardships they endure represent the pangs of travail, and at the end they may have to creep between the legs of the efficient, as if making a new entry into the world; the camp and all its paraphernalia are burnt, and the initiates are given new clothes and new names; they are reborn. The old women of a Ga family treat an initiate as a corpse, washing him and cutting his nails: then they dress him magnificently and give him a hearty meal. The boy is dead; a grown man takes his place (Field, 1937, p. 194). The Zulu father solemnly gives his son an assegai as a symbol of his new status.

Dead symbols figure in our marriage customs—dead in no longer having a meaning to us: the throwing of rice, for example. The symbolization in African marriage is apparent to an intelligent observer, whether or no the participant are conscious of it. The symbals, whether are what Jung designates "uniting symbols", picturing the synthetic union of disparate contending parties. One group is losing a daughter to the other: the incipient antagonism thereby set up meets a corresponding reaction in the other group. This conflict and the subsequent establishment of harmonious relations are symbolized in various actions. The bridge's family make it clear that she is of inestimable value and far beyond the merits of the other family. When the groom's people bring the bride-wealth cattle, her father assumers a wrathful demeansour; the other males of her family oppose the entry of the cattle into their byre; a sham fight and mutual vituperation follow. When, accompanied by the bridesmaids, the girl pays a first visit to her future home the two parties sit face to face and hurl insults to and from obssenities which could not be uttered on other occasions without rousing the deepest resentment are now shouted with impunity. The girl's chastity is attacked. This may continue all one long night. There are other sham fights, which serve one great purpose: to show that the girl is worth fighting for. The bridegroom probably keeps out of sight. It the bridesmaids see him they may drive him to distraction by their singing of derisive songs. The bride offers—or pretends to offer—resistance up to the last moment: she will not do this, she will not do that, until persuaded by gifts. As Dr. Wagner observes of the Kavirondo Bantu, to make a success of the new relationship a balane must be a achieved between the two families: each side must be made to fell that the other side is its equal. The primary significance of the exchagne of gifts (other than the bride-wealth) is a demonstration of equality in economic and social stauts (Wagner, 1950, p. 430 sqq.). We can see then that the actions in the course of a marriage are not purely symbolical; they achieve an end; they are efficacious.

I can not enter at length into the vast question of tabu, of which Dr. Fortes has taught us to see the symbolical meaning. Irrational and even nonsensical as many tabus appear to be, they are not to be dismissed lightly. We have not finished with them when we described them as "negative magic" or "negative *mana*. They point to constitutional infirmities in man which need controlling and mastering: their function is reformative and educative. The totemic proscriptions, the food tabus and the other inhibitions regulating social behaviour, are all simple and definite imperatives sysmblizing fundamental imperatives and paramount moral values upon which society is founded but which do not originate in society. "The very fact that they are trivial and can be easily remembered and kept without hardship by young and old make them the more effective social symbols." their observance is a matter of conscience and belief. "Ritual idas and values and morphology of the society are interrelated as and body. Though Tale religion springs directly out of the social structure, it is led by streams whose sources lie beneath and beyond the social structure" (Fortes, 1945, p. 142). That structure is the vehicle and instrument of religious and moral values, not their orgin. The tabus reflect a conviction that there is a moral order in the universe and that man's well-beign depends upon obedience to that order as men see it.

African mythology expresses speculative thought in symbolical guise. As Baumann has shows (1936, p. 1) by the analysis of 2,500 myths and folk-tales it is concerned chiefly with a creative principle (generally identical with the High God) and the first man conceived, formed or called forth by this creative power. Among the mythologems we an recognize some of the archetypes which, on Jung's hypothesis, are primordial images which in here in the collective unconscious and which (Like cool springs and hot geysers gushing forth from a subterranean ocean underlying allthe continents) emerge into the individual unconscious and conscious in personified or symbolical picture form in myths, fairy tales and dreams (Jacobi, 1951, pp. 56 sqq.). Three of these archetypes—Sky, Earth and Wise Old Man—which figure largely in African myths, may be exhibited diagrammatically as a triangle, with th eSkyas apex and Earth and Old Man (transformed into king or chief) as the base. These may be taken as symbols; the Sky stands for the Supreme Power; the Earth for the germinative processes of the soil; and the Chief or King as repreentative of the people whom he rules. The diagram suggests the intimate relationship of these three constitutents of the African's universe. And to complete the diagram we should insert on the left side between earth and sky such beings as Tano, the Akan river-god, who figure as the offspring of the Sky. In a corresponding position on the other side of the triangle must be placed the hierarchy of ancestors who are the link between God and Man.

In the old civilizations of the Near East "the depth and intimacy of man's relationship with nature found expression in the ancient symbol of the mother goddess" (Frankfort, 1946, p. 371). She was hailed as "wide-bosomed earth, the ever-suroundation of all", "mother of all", "mother of the gods, wife of starry Heaven", "She feeds all creatures that are in the world, all that go upon the godly land, and all that are in the paths of the sea, and all that fly; all these are fed of her store" (Hesiod. *Theogony,* 116, *Homeric Hymns,* XXX, pp. 87, 457). So it is in some parts of Africa. For the Igbo of Nigeria she is Ale, nearest and dearest among the deities; the Ibibio speak her name Eka Abassi in hushed accents: "she it is who dwells on the other side of the wall" (Talbot, 1915, p. 8); the Yoruba know her as Odudua; the Akan as Asase Ya—her sacred day is Thursday and on that day no farmer will till or break the soil (Rattray, 1927, p. 215). As in Greek mythology Ouranos and Gaia were husband and wife, and in Egyptian mythology Geb and Nut were wife and husband, so the African Earth-Mother is widely known as the spouse of the Sky, whose seminal showers fructify her, so that she gives brith to gods and men and all things.[14] I found a similar idea among the Baila.

The Earth-goddess does not make an appearane among the Tallensi but they stand in awe of the earth, symbol of the forces that promote the common welfare of mankind. When they refer to earth (Teng) in its material aspect they use a neutral pronoun, *ka*; but in reference to earth's mystical aspect, the pronoun is personal, *u*. Alongside the cult of ancestors is the earth cult, each aximla lineage having its *tendaana,* priest of the earth. The cults intermingle; while the sowing festival dramatizes man's dependence on the fertility of the soil and on rain, and the dependence of these on the mystical power of the earth, the harvest festival is dominated by the cult of the ancestors and dramatizes man's gratitude for crops and children granted by earth and the ancestors. Earth and the ancestors are linked indissolubly. The shrines rest on the earth n which th eancestors were buried and which wouldbe derelict without the descendants of the ancestors whose dwelling is the shrines. Wild naimals roaming the surface of the land symbolize at once the mystical "livingness" of the earth and the mystical force of the ancestors, their power and efficacy in the lives of the descendants. Certain reptiles are "tabus of the earth": to kill a python or a crocodile within a settlement is almost as bad as murder. There is a strong ethical element in this earth-cult for the earth forbids the shedding of blood: the cult makes for peace (Fortes, 1945, p. 176). If anyone fights and spills blood on the ground, raises a war-cry without cause, sells anothers person, he must purify the land by an offering of a cow or sheep. A *tendaana* said to Rattray: "The land owns the people, that is why a sacrifice is made to her" (Rattray, 1932, pl 347).

Rattray found a dual leadership among the Nankanse, who are neighbours of the Tallensi: the *Rendatana* and a secular ruler. The latter said to him: "The people belong to me; the land belongs to the *tendaana.*" The *tendaana* is trustee of the land as representing the original inhabitants who as ancestors are still the real owners. The secular ruler descends from a conquering group of invaders who recognized that if the land was to be fruitful the goodwill of these spirit owners must be secured and hence approached them through their actual representative, the *tendaana*, the land-priest (Rattray, 1932, p. xv).

This ideas of spiritual ownership, which makes the living occupants tenants of unseen landlords, seems to be fairly widespread in Frica (Richards, 1932, pp. 154, sqq.): I found it among the Balla.

So far as I know the earth-goddess, the great Mother, is not worshipped by the Bantu. Perhaps there is a vestige of her in the Ceres of the Zulus, Nomkhubulwana, in whose honour young girls dance in springtime. But everywhere there is the same reverence for the earth, in which the ancestors are buried and which for living agricultural and pastoral peoples is the source of their material well-being. The strong sentiment built up about it, making alienation of the soid almost a sacrilege, has never been fully realized by Europeans. As a rule, the two functions of territorial ruler and land– priest have coalesced in the person of the chief or king . One epithet of a Tswana chief is *Mosadi wa morafe,* "Wife of the nation", i.e., the provider, as if he summed up all productivity in himself. While this is so, there is some evidence among the Bantu of a distinction between the two offices.

The Bemba in Northern Rhodesia were conquering invaders; and it would seem that at first they resorted to the ancestors of the old inhabitants for blessing on the land they forcefully occupied. To some extent they still do so, but in course of time the ancestors of the Chitimukulu, the Paramount Chief, have mostly supplanted the ancestors of the conquered, and he has become land-priest as well as ruler. The fortunes of the soil and of the nation depend upon him. His sexual power imparts vigour and warmth to the land. Senility in him is a menance to the whole people. Were he allowed to sink into feeble old age and into a natural death, the streams would dry up, crops would fail, children would cease to be born, the game would disappear. The unfortunate Chitmukkulus were therefore throttled, when their virility diminished.

The same identification of nation, land and kingship is seen among the Lozi of Northern Rhodesia. The king's most specific title is *Litunga,* "earth". He is approached with elaborate etiquette as a semi-divine being. The kingship enshrines the virtue (*mala*) of all past kings, of God, of the land, and of the nation. The royal graves, the homes of his ancestors, are the center of a cult which symbolizes the unity of the nation, made up of many subject tribes. These tombs have a mystical power *(mata)* which symbolizes the power of all past kings, of the land and nation. Before his accession the king is taken to the grave of Mbuyamwambwa, the daughter and wife of God (as in Hesiod Gaia is both spouse and daughter of Ouranos), so that her power may enter into him.

"One common characteristic of shrines of the earth", says Dr. Gluckman," is that they are believed to have on the one hand specific power over small neighbourhoods and over local communities, and on the other hand that they have no boundaries so that their spirits may influence wide areas or the territory of a whole nation. In the latter circumstances they sometimes form an inter-locked cult. This is marked in the structure of the earth shrines of the Tallensi and the royal graves of the Lozi, and appears to be the case of the sacred graves of the Kamba. The shrines appears thus to symbolize both small variations in the fertility and health of different communities and areas in different years and also to symbolize sectional and general interests in fertility and health over small and large regions of social life."

The Lozi have a dual system that is reminiscent of the Tallensi. The king is owner of the land; the *ngambela* (often entitled "Prime Minister") is the owner of the nation; nay, the king *is* the land; the *ngambela* is the commonality (Colson & Gluckman, 1949, pp. 19 sqq.).

Complete merging of the two offices appears in other divine kings. The Shilluk *rewth* is considered by his subjects the dynamical center of the universe: the well-being of all things depends upon his course of life. The line of divinity runs through him to Nyikang, the first king, and back to Juok, the original source of all power. Nyikang is the Mythological personification of the timeless kingship which itself symbolizes the national structure and changeless moral order. The *reth* is the central figure of tribal religion as well as the symbol of political unity. If he shows signs of senility or physical imperfection he must be ceremonially removed by killing and a successor appointed.[15]

The divine right of kings was never more positively stated than by the dynastic poets of the kingdom of Ruanda. They multiply metaphors in extolling the king's power over nature. The king is the Bull that fecundates the realm. He gathers the clouds, he causes rain to fall, the lightning to flash, the thunder to roll, all by the grace of God who made him king and infused mystical power into him at the moment of conception. As every Hamite sets apart an official bull to be the symbol of its master, so God enthrones the king to be his symbol. Indeed the king is God made accessible to our prayers. God created kings with a view to increase the cows.

Le souverain que voici boit le lait trait par Dieu,
Et nours buvons le Jait qu's son tour il trait pour nous.

So runs a French rendering of two lines of these remarkable poems.[16]

What I have said about land, nation and chief exemplifies the truth of Whitehead's dictum: "the object of symbolism is the enhancement of the importance of what is symbolized" (1928, p. 74). To clinch the matter let us glance at the Swazi ceremonial of Incwala so graphically described by Mrs. Kuper. It is enacted yearly, in connexion with eating the first fruits, and is intended to maintain and increase the vigour of the king. His mystical power is, one with the powers of nature: upon him depends the rainfall, the fertility of the soil, the success of harvest; and his growth in power is the nation's growth in power. The time for holding the Incwala is fixed by reference to both sun and moon. It must begin when the moon is "dark" so that as the moon waxes the king may waxe with it in strength. The sun must have reached his southernmost position; that is, according to Swazi fancy, when the sun is resting in his hut and is about to leap out to start his journey anew: The King races with the sun." The gathering of the people, all dressed in their finery, demonstrates and cements the unity of the tribe. The dancers first assume the shape of a crescent and then that of a circle. This is not pure symbol: they represent the waxing moon; and their vigorous dancing imparts such vigour to the king that he too may wax in fullness of power. "Medicines", the vehicles of mystical force, are administered to the king. Men are sent to wade into the sea to catch foam at the top of the waves, which is the strength of ocean; other men bring water from a river in spate. As the Swazi say: "The waters of the world are fetched to give strength and purity to the king." At a certain point the king secluded in his ceremonial booth, spits "medicine" to the east and to the west, and as he does so the people shout: "He stabs it!" It means that he is strengthening the earth. He is hailed as "Our Bull!", for just as a bull fecundates the herd so he fecundates the soil. The king, seated naked upon a black ox, is washes with sacred water in which "medicines" have been placed. One of these is a drug given to bulls and men to stimulate their procreative power. The finest bull in the herds is slaughterd and the parts which contain its power are made into "medicines" for the king. Another "medicine" is *lusekwane,* a tree which grows with amazing rapidity and whose leaves retain their verdancy for many months. Branches of this tree and a shrub that is distinguished by its hardness are piled about the king's hut so that their qualities may pass into him. By the fifth day he has acquired sufficient strength to eat the first fruits; and the people too can then eat of them. The king now appears before his people in the guise of Silo, a monster of fearful shape. Each item of his clothing bears a meaning. The bright green, razor edged grass and evergreen shoots which cover his body are not only symbols of life, they impart their freshness to the king. His shield is smeared with *mukwane* fat, a medicament so potent that only the king, this mother and his chief wife are strong enough to tolerate it, and it makes them still more powerful.

The final day is one of purification. A huge pyre is built and the king sets it alight by rubbing two sticks together. All articles used during the Incwala are thrown into the flames. "The filth of the king and of all his people," the Swazi say, "lies here on the fire," The fire is cathartic in effect. It is also an offering to the ancestors. If they are pleased with the Incwala they will send rain. Now the nation gives itself up to revelry. The king is strong; the earth is strong; the nation is strong (Kuper, 1944,pp. 230 sqq.).

The king of the neighboring Zulus also underwent rejuvenating processes at the time of the annual First Fruits (*umkosi).)* He was not only the symbol of social cohesion: he was its artificer (Gluckman. 1940, pp. 25 sqq.).

IV

From what has been said it is evident that Africans make use of pure symbols—symbols, that is, which point to, represent, call to mind, something other than themselves. Some objects and many actions, however, which appear at first glance to be symbolic are not indicative, nor representative, but coercive, creative, productive. Others appears to combine both functions; they are both symbolic and efficacious; lustrations not only suggest purification, they purify. The shrine is not only a reminder of the ancestors' presence; it is the residence of ancestors and has a mystical power in virtue of their dwelling therein. The symbol melts into the talisman; or the talisman melts into the symbol. It is often difficult to determine which is which. We are thus led to the consideration of occult forces, automatic in action or activated by persons.

The frequent confusion of symbol with talisman may be illustrated by reference to language. The semanticists, who rightly inveigh against "verbal magic," point to the dual function of words: the symbolic and the emotive. The symbolic use is to record or to communicate; the emotive use is to express or excite feelings and attitudes. The two functions may occur together but in principle are distinct. Their subtle interweaving is the main reason why the difference is not always recognized (Ogden

& Richards, 1940, pp. 1949 sqq.) We are all familiar with the evocative virtue of words. The transition if easy to the idea that words have themselves causal efficacy.

"Comment changer le monde ?" asks one of Antole France's characters. "Par La parole, mon enfant", is the answer. "Rien n'est plus pussant que la parole...La parole, comme la fronde de David, abat les violents et fait tomber les forts. C'est I'armer invincible" (*Monsieur Berger a Paris,* p. 257).

"And though a tongue may shoot forth bolts undue

To stir men's spleen and gall their in most soul,

Yet words may salve the wound that words have made."[17]

Africans, like ourselves, know the power of words, evocative, persuasive, compelling. What our poets affirm metap-horically, they accept as literal truth: words are projectiles charged with explosive substance and driven by mystic force.

Verbal abuse (the BaIla call it *kutuka)* is vehemently resented and may even result in the enslavement of the abuser, not simply because it is an offence against personal dignity but because it produces some physical or metaphysical harm to the abused. There are occasions—as in the so-called "joking relationships"—when abusive and obscene language of the most vitriolic kind is not only tolerated but enjoined; it is an approved pattern of behaviour. It all depends upon the motive. Intention is the explosive with which the projectile is charged.

The curse is a particularised and intensified form of abuse. It has a malefic potency of its own, imparted by the ill-will of the curser. Nothing sounds terrible in the ears of an African as the curse of his mother. She resorts to it only when everything else fails to win him from his evil ways. She may reinforce her words by a gesture, or the gesture may carry her unspoken thought. An Ila woman strips off her scantly garment before her incorrigible son: that is *chikuto:* the most awful curse conceiveable. It strikes with damning effect. Go where he may, do what he may, he cannot escape: it will hound him to violent, ignominious death. The Greeks would have said that he was pursued by the Erinnyes.

Threatening, whether in words or in gesture (such as the pointing of a forefinger) are to be avoided: *predicate c' est produire.* You do not express admiration for a pretty child: your fair words may be taken to express a concealed malice. It is in thought that mystical force resides.

It is here that we discover the secret of witchcraft as Africans believe in it and dread it. In sorcery man or woman employs certain substance sbelieved to a contain occult force which can be liberated by the utterance of a spell. Witchcraft, on the other hand, consists in the emission of psychic energy from a malevolent disposition, with intent to cause misfortune and death to a particular person or group. It may be pictured as, or identified with, an organ of the body, real or mythical: the Azande name it *mangu,* the Mende *hona,* the Tetela, *aloka.* The malice, jealousy, hatred, is thrust from the mind like a beam of electrons from radar transmitter: the analogy is very close when, as may happen, the beam rebounds back on the witch. The Zande word for shooting with bow and arrow—no—also signifies" to bewitch" (Evans-Pritchard, 1937, p. 37). The Ila expression for the witch's effluence is derived from the verb *zua,* "to push, thrust": *inzuikizhi* is "that by means of which one thrusts out in somebody's direction." The warlock and witch work in an atmosphere laden with envy and malice: the circumfluent-feeling strengthens his or her power to do evil. Scientists are inclined to treat with scron the idea that the human brain can emit electric charges which may be picked up by a receiving brain. They are not so sure that telepathy is a fantasy. Telergy, telekinesis, present no difficulty to Africans.

Africans are intuitively or inductively aware of what modern physical science teaches: there is more in things than appears to the senses. They are more capable of abstract thinking than is sometimes recognized: witness the facility which their language affords the Bantu of expressing qualities by means of the nominal prefix *bu:muntu* is "a person"; *buntu* is the inness of a person, personality, virtue *(virtus)*.[18] So in things there is an essence which may or may not be manifested in their appearance but is certainly known by its effects. Plants and roots have their therapeutical qualities. An Ibgo doctor knows the difference between *ogwu,* the visible and tangible root or leaf, and *ire,* the essential effective element of the *ogwu.* He himself possesses *ire* as a congenital quality, as also does a woodcarver of pre-eminent skill and an orator who is eloquent beyond his fellows. The Ila doctor distinguishes between *musamo,* the medicine which he handles, and *bwanga,* its active principle. The Nkundu doctor likens the *elima* of his medicines to the power of a electric fish to give you a shock. The occult power is manifest and operative in animals and men and in ritual acts.[19] It is this potentiality that differentiates a talisman from a symbol. Up to a point the African is correct in his observations and in his intuitions. There *is* a latent energy in things. The African goes astray by pushing his analogies too far—as my old friend Mungaila did when he slipped on my wrist a bracelet containing a powerful *bwanga* and said that while I wore it everybody would love me!

This sort of thing is usually described as "magic," and"magic" and "religion" are distinguished as two disparate things. Yet many anthropologists recognize that the distinction is difficult to maintain and is indeed artificial (Fifrth, 1938, p. 152). I think that in this context the word "magic" might now be given a decent burial and that we should rather speak of various levels or stages or phases of religion. That is the practice of the latest students of Comparative Religion such as Dr. John Murphy (1949, p. 76, etc.). Where others have written "magic", I have preferred to write "dynamism." I did not invent the term. Van Gennep (while retaining "magic" for the technique of religion) adopted "dynamism" for the impersonalist theory of *mana* in contrast to the personalist theory of animism, These two theories constituting the belief-system of religion (1909, p. 17). Dr. Marett took dynamism to be that elementary stage of religion in which to the sacred and divine are attributed the impersonal nature of a fore (1914, p. xxxii). In Africa the there phases of religion dynamism, spiritism and theism—exist side by side or interwoven in one whole.

Conclusion

Professor Whitehead once hazarded the opinion that modern civilized people exhibit a revulsion from symbolism: "Hard-headed men want facts and not symbols." Yet, he added, however you may endeavour to expel symbolism, it ever returns. "It is inherent in the very texture of human life." While this lecture was making, the place and power of symbolism in our national life were magnificently and unmistakably revealed. In the majestic pageant of King George's funeral procession the symbols of sovereignty, the crown, the Sceptre, and the Orb, brought home to multitudes the meaning of kingship; the martial splendour bespoke the power of Britain; the music, sad and triumphant, expressed the nation's faith; and the final word's "our dear brother" proclaimed the oneness of king and people in a common humanity. The King himself was acclaimed "the symbol of the people's unity"; and the Queen "the symbol of the life of the nation and Commonwealth—the temporal embodiment of an undying idea" (*The Times,* 8.2.52).

Some observers noted and regretted the absence from that magnificent procession of the democratic symbols of Parliament and Cabinet. This anachronism calls to mind another of Whitehead's dicta—one that is very relevant to our subject. "The art of free society consists first in the maintenance of the symbolic code; and secondly in fearlessness of revision, to secure that the code serves those purposes which satisfy an enlightened reason. Those societies which cannot combine reverence to their symbols with freedom of revision, must ultimately decay either from anarchy, or from the slow atrophy of a life stifled by useless shadows" (Whitehead, 1928, p.104). Symbols are not something adventitious.They are grounded in, they spring from, are supported by, an intellectual structure. A crisis comes when that structure is undermined by the advent of new knowledge. Until new symbols expressing new convictions are born and generally adopted there is mental chaos and a slackening of moral restraint.

The political, social and material transformations that are taking place so rapidly in African are necessarily accompanied by ideological changes which involve psychological crisis for many Africans. The introduction of modern scientific knowledge and of Christianity cuts at the roots of much of their old religion. Many of the feature of dynamism, with its erroneous assumptions and irrational practices, are seen to be inimical to progress. "Did you ever hear leaders like George Bernard Shaw suggest that they attained success through the medium of a few words written upon a piece of parchment?" In those words an African leader challenges his educated fellow-countrymen. In some respects the ancestor cult fosters inertia. Symbols they will, and must, have. Will they throw overboard all the old symbolism and the value which it enshrined? Will they discover new unitive symbols? Will they take over and reshape our European symbols? Will African Christians follow the example of the dearly Church and adopt, and read new meanings into, the old pagan symbols? Much depends upon the answers that are given to such questions...But *that*—that is another story.

Postscript

Since this lecture was put into print a book written by a eminent neurologist has come into my hands—*Mind, Perception and - Science* (Oxford, Blackwell, 1951) by W. Russell Brain, President of the Royal College of Physicians of London. I find support therein for some things which I tried to say in the first part of the lecture. One of the functions of the mind, says Sir Russell,[20] is symbolical representation. Knowledge of the physical work is knowledge by means of conceptual symbols derived from perception by a process of inference. "Need we believe that a nervous system evolved to facilitate action upon the physical world is capable of providing conceptual symbols adequate for the whole of reality? He is a bold man who could claim that to-day" (p.71). "...as soon as we realize that science is only language (i.e, a form of symbolical representation) and that many aspects of the 'invisible fabrick' of life can be better understood in other languages, and even in symbols other than words, we have opened the door to a great liberation of the spirit" (p87). He quotes with approval Suzanne Langer's words: "the limits of language are not the last limits of experience and things inaccessible to language may have their own forms of conception, that is to say, their own symbolic devices."

Reference

Abrahamson, H.,	1951	*The Origin of Death.*
Adam, Leonhard	1949	*Primitive Art.*
Ashton, Hugh	1951	*The Basuto.*
BAILEY, H.	1951	*The Lost Language of Symbolism.*
BARTLETT, SIR F.	1923	*Psychology and Primitive Culture.*
——	1950	*Religion as Experience, Belief, Action.*
BAUMANN, H.	1936	*Schopfung und Urzeit des menschen i m Mythus der Afrikanischen Volker,*
——	1950	"yama, die Rachemacht" in *Mythe, Mensch und Umwelt,* edited by A.E. Jesen.
BRELSFORD, W.V.	1944	"Aspects of Bemba chieftainship." *Communications of the Rhodes-Livingstone Institue,* No.2.
BROWNE, SIR T.		1642 *Religio Medici* (Temple edn.).
BULLOCK, C.	1950	*The Mashona and the Matebele.*
CARLYLE, T.	1894	Edn. *Sartor Resartus.*
CASALIS, E.	1861	*The Basutos.*
CASSIRER, E.	1945	*An Essay on Man.*
CHASE, S.	1938	*The Tyranny of Words.*
COLERIDGE, S.T.	1825	*Aids to Reflection.*
COLSON, E. AND GLUCKMAN, M. (ed.)	1949	*Seven Tribes of British Central Afraica.*

CORY. H.	1946	"The Buyeye" in *Arica,* xvi.
DICKINSON, G.L.	1931	*Plato and his Dialogues* (Pelican, 1950).
DIETERLEN, G.	1941	*Les Ames des Dogons.*
DURKHEIM, E.	1910	*The Elementary Forms of the Religious Life.*
EDDINGTON,SIR A.S.	1929	*The Nature of the Physical World.*
EVANS-PRINTCHARD, E.	1937	*Witchcraft, Oracles and Magic among the Azande.*
———	1948	"Nuer marriage ceremonies" in *Africa,* xviii.
———	1948	*The Divine Kingship of the Shilluk.*
———	1951	"Some Features of Nuer Religion" in *J.R.A.I.,* LXXXI.
———	1952	"A note on Nuer Prayers " *Man,* 1952, 140.
FIELD, M.J.	1937	*Religion and Medicine of the Ga people.*
—.	1940	*Social Organization of the Ga People*
FIRTH, RAYMOND	1938	*Human Types.*
———	1951	*Elements of Social Organization.*
fORTES,M.	1945	*The Dynamics of Kinship among the Tallensi.*
———	1949	*The Web of Kinship among the Tallensi.*
FORTES, M., and EVANS-PRITCHARD, E. (ed)	1940	*African Political Systems.*
FRANKFORT, H., and others	1946	*The Intellectual Advanture of Ancient Man.*
GALLOWAY, G.	1914	*The Philosophy of Religion.*
GLUCKMAN, M.	1938	"Social aspects of First Fruits ceremonies among the South-eastern bantu," in *Africa,* xi, No. 1.
———	1940	"Analysis of a social situation in modern Zululand," in *Bantu Studies,* xiv.
———	1941	*Economy of th eCentralbarotse Plain.*
———	1943	*Essays on Lozi Land and Royal Property.*
GRIAULE, M.	1938	Masques Dogons.
———	?	"Philosophie et religion des Noirs" in *Le Monde NOir,* Presence Africaine, numero special 8-9.
HESIOD HOFFDING, H.		*The Homeric Hymns,* translated by H.G. Eveyn White (Loeb).
HOFFDING, H.	1906	*The philosophy of Religion.*
HOLLOWAY, J	1951	Language and Intelligence.

HOWELL, P.P., and THOMSON, W.P.G.	1946	"The death of a Reth of the Shilluk and the instanllation of his succesor" in *Sudan Notes and Records*, xxvii,
HUGEL, BARON VON	1923	*The Mystical Element of Religion.*
JACOBI, J.	1951	*The Psychology of C.G. Jung.*
JEANS, SIR J.	1942	*Physics and Philosophy.*
JONES, E.	1951	*Essays in applied Psycho-analysis*, vol. ii.
JOYCE, GC.	1908	"Analogy" in *Encyclopaedia of Religion and Ethics.*
JUNG, C.G.	1923	*Psychological Types.*
——	1939	*The Integration of the Personality.*
JUNG, C.G., and KERENYI, C.	1951	*Introduction to a science of Mythology.*
JUNOD, H.A.	1912	*The Life of a South African Tribe.*
JUNDOD, H.P.	1938	*Bantu Heritage.*
KAGAME, Abbe A.	2947	"Un Poeme du Rwanda" in *Africa*, xvii.
KRIGE, E.J.	1936	*The Social System of the Zulus*
KUPER, Hilda	1944	"A Ritual of Kingship among the Swazi" in *Africa, xiv.*
——	1947	*An African Aristocracy.*
Langer, S.K.	1942	*Philosophy in a New Key.*
Layard, J.	1944	*The Lady of the Hare.*
Laydevant, F.	1948	"Le Sceptre des Chefs Basuto " in *Africa*, xviii.
Levi, Eliphaz	1906	*II Rituale dell'alta Magia.*
Malinowski, B.	1925	"Magic, Science and Religion" in *Science, Religion and Reality*, edited by Joseph Needham.
——	1930	"The Problem of Meaning in Prinmitive Languages", supplement i. in *The meaning of Meaning* by Ogden & Richards.
Machicol, N. (ed.)	1938	*Hindu Scriptures..*
Marett, R.R.	1914	*The Threshold of Religion*
——	1927	General aspects of Ashanti Religon" in Rattray's *Religion and Art in Ashanti*, chap. xxxiii.
McDougall, W.	150	*The Energies of Men.*
Meek, C.K.	1931	*Tribal Studies in Northern Nigeria.*
Meyerowitz, Eva	1951	*The Sacred State of the Akan.*
Monod, T.	1950	Introductio, *Le Monde Noir*, Presence Africaine, numero special 8-9.
Morris, C.	1946	*Signs, Language and Behaviour.*
Murphy, J.	1949	*The Origins and History of Religions.*

Nadel, S.F. 1951 *The Foundations of Social Anthropology.*

Ogden, C.K., and Richards, I.A. 1930 *The Meaning of Meaning.*

Paprinder, G. 1949 *West African Religion.*

—— 1951 *West African Psychology.*

—— 1952 *Religion in an African City.*

Pfister, O. 1913 *The Psychoanalytic Method.*

Plato *The Republic* (Jowett).

Raleigh, Sir W. 1918 *Style*

Rattary, R.S. 1923 *Ashanti.*

—— 1927 *Religion and Art in Ashanti.*

—— 1932 *The Tribes of the Ashanti Hinterland.*

Richards, A. 1932 *Hunger and Work in a Savage Tribe.*

—— 1939 *land, labour an ddiet in Northern Rhodesia.*

Ruskin, J. 1912 (pop.edn.) *The Stones of Venice.*

Shooter, J. 1857 *The Kafirs of Natal.*

Smith, E.W. (ed.) 1950 *African Ideas of God.*

Smith, E.W., and Dale, A.M. 1920 *The Ila-speaking Peoples of Northern Rhodesia*

Streeter, B.H. 1926 Reality.

Talbot, D.A. 1915 *Women's Mysteriers of a Primitive People*

Torday, E. 1925 *Women's Mysteries of a Primitive People.*

Torday, E. 1925 *On the Trail of the Bushongo.*

Underhill, E. 1923 *Mysticism.*

Van Gennep, A. 1909 *Les Rites de Passage.*

Wagner, G. 1949 *The Bantu of North Kavirondo,* vol. 1.

Walpole, H.R. 1941 *Semantics.*

Webster, H. 1948 *Magic, a sociological study.*

Whitehead, A.N. 1927 *Religion in the Making.*

—— 1928 *Symbolism.*

Wilson, Monica 1951 *Good company, studyof Nyakyusa age-villages.*

Young, K. 1946 *Handbook of Social Psychology.*

Young, T.C. 1931 *Notes on the Customs and Foklore of the Tumbuka-Kamanga peoples.*

Articles on *Symbolism* (Christian, Greek and Roman, Hindu, Jewish, Muslim Semitic) In Hastings *Encycloapedia of Relion and Ethics,* Vol. 12, 1921.

NOTES

1. This is the distinction drawn by C.G. Jung 91923, p. 601). Raymond Fifth 91951, p. 176) says that in a sign the relation between one entity and another is intrinsic or integral. "A symbol, on the other hand, is an object or action that represents another entity in virtue of some arbitrarily assigned conceptual relation between them." Heavy dark clouds are a *snig* of rain. In Australian mythgology the Rainbow Serpent is a *Sybmol* of rain and its concomitant, fertility.
2. Jacobi, 1951,p. 114, "The content of a symbol can never be full expressed rationally...We can make it rational component comprehensible to consciousness; its irrational component we can grasp only with our feelings."
3. Bailey, 1951, i. 367. It is one of the axioms of philology, we aretold, that vow lel sounds are equal to one another; the of of *sol* must therefore be equal to *el*, meaning God and power; and the French *soleil* may be equated with *sole il ro el.* the sole and solitary God, the Monocle or Lone Great Eye, i. 290.
4. Malinowski, 1930,p. 307. "Exactly as in the reality of spoken or written languages, a word without linguistic context is a mere figment and stands for nothing by itself, so in the reality of a spoken living tongue, the utterance has no meaning except in the *context of situation.*"
5. Riddles sometimes play an important part in the instruction given in initiation schools; see Lyndon Harries, "Makua song-riddies from the mitiation rities", *African Studies,* 1, No. 1, pp. 27 sqq.
6. Other examples are given by Rattray, 1932,pp. 140, pp. 140 sqq.
7. Field, 1937, p. 125 "Dramatic metaphor comes very easily to an African. It is probably in this region of struggle for expression, where he fails to convey by metaphor what he is not himself deceived about, that we must look for the birthplace of many invisible things. One has only to think of such modern jargon as the censor of consciousness.' `the sub-conscious *region'* to realise how difficult it is to escape metaphor the figures of which could easily begin to masquerade as something real."
8. Smith & Dale, 1920, i., 226 sq. The word *Chibumba* belongs to the personal class of nouns; it is to be referred to as "she" not " it". It means "the moulder"; cf. the Ila praise name of Leza, the

Supreme Being. *Lubumba* (also personal) formed from the same root. viz. *bumba*" mould, shape."

9. J. Davidson in *African Ideasy of God*. 1950, p. 167. See the index of God-names in this book.

10. Meyerowitz, 1951, pp. 94 sqq. Rattray collected gold weights and wrote (*Ashanti*, p. 302) of those in which the designs appear geometrical and were perhaps once symbolical: "I have not yet met a single Ashanti who can give any interpretation or assign any meaning to their symbols."

11. The word *amanga,* which Mrs. Wilson translates "mystical powers," is a plural abstract form of *bwanga* derived from the same root as *nganga,* "doctor, medicine-man." In various forms it occurs in Bantu languages from Southern Rhodesia to Lake Victoria, from the Atlantic to the great lakes. Dr. Malcolm, Guthrie has given me the names of 20 languages in which it is found. In Ila *bwanga* denotes the essential active principle in "medicines." It has the same meaning in Lamba (Doke, *The Lambas of Northern Rhodesia,* 1931, pp. 290 sqq., "the power for healing or for destroying, for protecting or for hurting") and in Bemba (R.J.B. Moore in *Africa,* xiii, pp. 211 sqq.). It appears to be mcu the same among the Kaonde (F.H. Melland, *In Witch-bound Africa,* 1923, pp., 231 sqq.). It is believed that *bwanga* may be strengthened by the infusion of divine power. A Luba doctor *(mpaka-manga.* "manipulator of *bwanga")* prays thus to God while preparing his medicine: "ubwele mu bwanga bwetu, come thyself into our bwanga" " (Van Caeneghem, "Gebeden der Baluba" in *Aequatoria,* no. i, 1947). But ht eoccult power is not confined to medicines; it is inherent in the secret rites of the Luba Budye society (Roy & Henroteaux in *Bulletin des Jurisdictions,* no. 4. 1945). Dr. Hastings in his (unpublished) work on the Ovimbundu defines *wanga* as "psychic power" and treats it as the equivalent of *mana.* Baumann *(Lunda,* 195) brings out the paramount importance of *wanga* which he interprets as *zauberkraft.* C.M. White *Africa,* xviii, p. 84) also reports that among the Lunda, Chokwe and Luchazi, *wanga* is "essentially the unseen power behind the concept of sorcery...the magical element of potency located in some material, the otherwise inexplicable"; it is not used for healing Writing of the Kwanyama, P.C. Estermann *(Africa,* vii, p. 440n.)described *ouanga* as "un pouvoir secret et imaginaire" attributed to

witches. Tribes of the Gabun are said to speak of *endjanga* as "witch-power: (Abbe Walker quoted by Webster, 1948, p. 411). Other observers report that the word is applied to specific medicaments. Thc Sukuma give the name *lwanga* to a mixture of flour and water used in purification rites. (H. Cory, *The temi,* 1951, p. 6). The *ovwanga* of the Kavironda Bantu is a paste of eleusine flour and wate rthat is "blown" upon warriors to give them *ovukali* (fierceneess, courage) and is used also in the rite which places an infant under the protection of its ancestors (Wagner, 1950, p.328). The Negroes of Haiti have preserved the word *wanga* for the active rpinciple of medicine; *wangataire,* in the Morcellins' novel *The Pencil of God* (1951) is "A sorceress who makes charms." Dr. Lorenzo Turner has found the word *Banga* among the so-called Gulalbs of South Carolina and the Sea Islands" he renders it" witchcraft."

The Sotho equvalent is *bongaka,* as in *senifare sema le bongaka,"* the medicine has (contains) bwanga!"

12. In the initiation schools of some East African tribes, instruction is largely given through songs and the lesson of each song is symbolized by a figurine of clay or wood (H. Cory in *Africa,* XIV, pp. 459 sqq.).
13. Diffidently I may suggest that these Dogon designs and their purpose afford an alternative explanation of rock paintings elsewhere in Africa and of the paleolithic pictures of Europe. Not that" the dancer idenatifies himself with th edesired animal executivn its movements in order to a attract it and lure it into his power" (Leonhard Adam, *Primitive Art,* 1949, p. 91) .
14. Various forms of this Himmel-Erde mythus in Baumann (1936); distribution map, p. 175: two centres, one in western Sudan, the other in North-East Africa.
15. In his Frazer Lecture (1923) Dr. Seligman reviewed the evidence for divine kings in Africa, including the Shilluk *reth (Egypt and negrio Africa).* More material has become available since then. See Evans-Pritchard's Frazer lecture, 1948: he thinks the killing of the kings ficctitious.
16. Note in *Africa,* xvi (1946), pp. 45 sq. Poem and translation by be Alxis Kagame, *Africa,* xvii (1947), pp. 41 sqq.
17. Aeschylus, *The Suppliants,* ii, 2. "Words are things....They are deeds: the man who brings word of a lost battle can work no comparable effect with the muscles of his arm: Iago's breath is

as truly laden with poison and murder as the fangs of the cobra and the drugs of the assassin" Raleigh, 1918, p. 108.

18. *Kono* "there"; *vukona,* "the essence of being there". H.P. Junod, 1938, p. 38.

19. Webster (1948: not very satisfactorily) and Baumann (1950 collate African (and other) names for the occult Manalike power. Baumann treats *Nyama* primarily as rehemacht and defines it thus: "nyama ist eine ubertragbare, halb sprititueIl, halb stoffich gedachte Mact, die von Menschen. Tieren und Manchmal auch von Baumen auseht und nach demmehr oder weniger gewaltsamen Tod des Nyama-Tragers an den unmittelbar anm tode beteiligten Rache Nahman kan." (1950,p. 228). Not seldom, he says, *nyama* appears as a king of "soul" "oder als vitale Triebkraft." The French anthropologists (Griaule and his coadjustors) write of *nyama* as "force vitale" and define it thus: "Le nyama est une energie en instance,impersonelile, inconsciente, repartie dans tous les hommes, animaux, vegetaux, dans les etres susurnaturels, dans les choses, dans la nature et qui tend a faire perseverer dans son etre le support auquel elle est affectee temporairement (etre mortel ou eternellement (etre immortel)" (Griaule, *Masque Dogons,* chap. iv.). Father tempels employs the same term "force vitale" in describing Bantu philosophy.

The word *nyama* is probably related to *naamis,* the active principle in the seminal fluids (not the fluids themselves) on which the Tallensi believe, procreation depends (Fortes, 1949, p. 20).

20. Quoted by permission of Blackwell Scientific Publications, Ltd.

---

* *Journal of the Royal Anthropological Institute* vol. 82. 1951

Chapter-4

Decorative Symbolism of the Araphao[1]

By A. L. Kroeber

Chapter-4

The Arapaho, a tribe of Plains Indians belonging to the Algonquian stock, practise a form of art very similar in material, technique, and appearance to that of the other Plains tribes, of whom the Sioux are the best known. This art is in appearance almost altogether unrealistic, unpictorial, purely decorative. For the greater part it consists now of beadwork, which has nearly supplanted the older style of embroidery in porcupine quills, plant fibers, and perhaps beads of aboriginal manufacture. The other products of this art are objects of skin or hide which are painted with geometrical designs. On the whole the decorative, geometric character of Arapaho art is very marked. Almost all the lines are straight. The figures in embroidery are lines, bands, rectangles, rhombi, isosceles and rectangular triangles, figures composed of combinations of these, and circles. The designs painted on hide are composed of triangles and rectangles in different forms and combinations.

On questioning the Indians it is found that many of these decorative figures have a meaning. An equilateral triangle with the point downward may represented a heart; with its point upward, a mountain. A figure consisting of five squares or rectangles in quincunx, the four outer ones touching the central one at the corners, is a representation of a turtle. A long stripe crossed by two short ones is a dragon-fly. A row of small squares at intervals represents tracks. Crosses and diamonds often signify stars. All this is in bead work. In painted designs a flat isosceles triangle often represents a hill; an acute isosceles triangle, a tent. Many other objects are similarly represented.

An ornamental feature is the symmetrical duplication of most designs. Bags, pouches, skins,moccasins, cases, and other

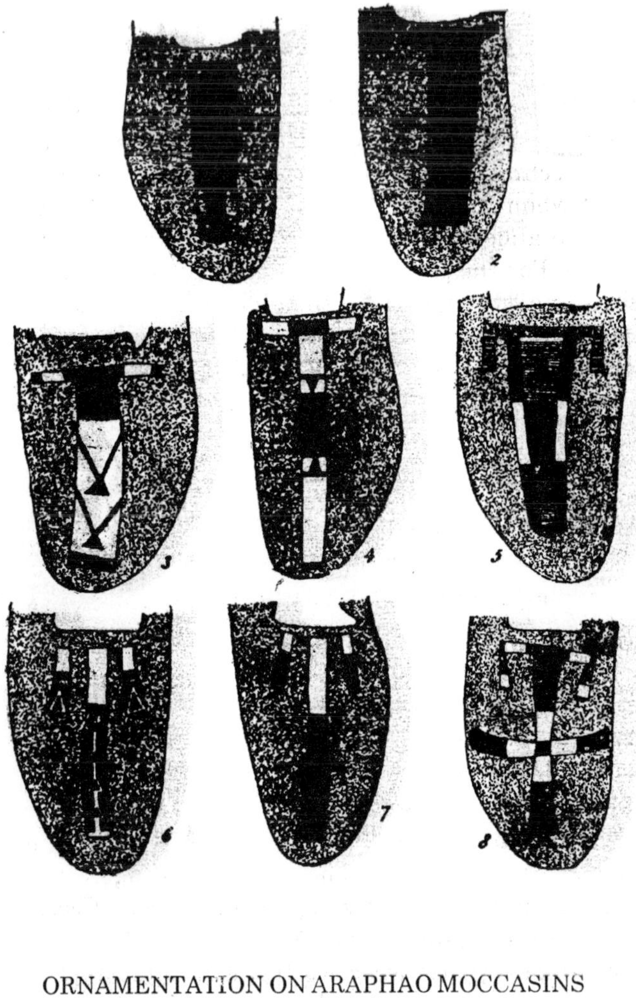

ORNAMENTATION ON ARAPHAO MOCCASINS

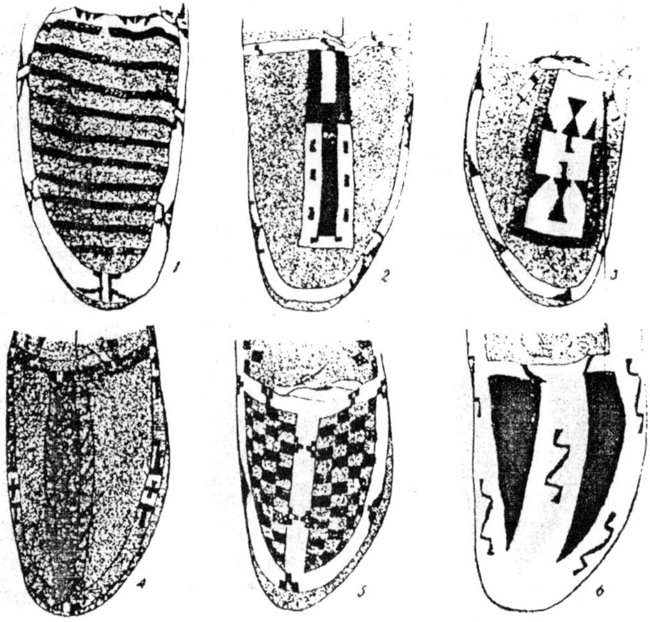

ORNAMENTATION ON ARAPAHO MOCCASINS

objects are ornamented by being treated as a decorative field within which the designs are symmetrically doubled, or even more numerously repeated. Thus a moccasin, if decorated with the symbol of a mountain on the outer side of the hell, has the same symbol also on the opposite inner side of the heel. Another purely ornamental feature of this art is repetition of a single figure to form a pattern. A stripe is often the representation of a path. This symbol is sometimes used singly, standing alone; sometimes it occurs double, owing to the tendency just mentioned, toward symmetry; and sometimes it is found in a pattern than my be described as a many-colored, drawn-out (i.e., rectangular,not square) checker-board, in which each rectangle or short stripe, whatever its color, still represents a path.

This strongly-marked decorative character of Arapaho art, however, is accompanied by a realistic tendency of such development as at first acquaintance would not be suspected by a civilized person. Several figures connected in meaning may be put upon one object and thus produce something approximating a picture containing composition. When as many as ten or a dozen symbols having reference to each other are combined, a star can almost be told by them. In this way the stiff embroideries on a moccasin or the geometric paintings on a bag may represent the hunting of buffalo, the acquisition of supernatural power by a shaman, a landscape or map, a dream, personal experiences, or a myth.

Arapaho art thus is at the same time imitative or significant, and decorative. Can the origin of this art be determined?

Since Arapaho art consists of the intimate fusion of symbolism an decoration, two theories as to its origin are possible. Either of its two elements may be the original. The Indians may have begun with realism, drawing or working life like forms in their art; then however,the obstacles inherent in the material asserted themselves, or the well-established tendency toward symmetry and repetition into a pattern came out, or perhaps other causes were influential, until the early imitative representations became abbreviated into the conventional decorations that have been described. Or it is possible that the Indians began with mere ornaments. Perhaps even these were not originally ornaments but peculiarities of construction of purely useful articles, which technical peculiarities were later considered beautifying and developed into pure ornaments. At any rate, whatever their own origin, decorations may in the past have existed *per se;* later, some conventional ornament may have accidentally suggested a natural object, where upon it was modified to resemble this object more closely; the same process occurred with other ornaments; until finally a whole system of symbolism was added to the older system of decoration. The first of these theories is that original pictures were conventionalized into decorative symbolism; the other theory is that original ornament was expanded into symbolic decoration. These are the logically possible explanations of the origin of Arapaho art because we recognize in it two factors, the realistic-symbolic and the decorative-technical.

Let us see if either of these theories can be rendered through the evidence of fact actually certain or at least probable.

One of the most frequent emobridered designs on Arapaho moccasins consists, in its simplest form, of a stripe or band which runs from the instep to the toe. This decorative motive takes varied forms,of more or less elaborateness. The following are a number of moccasins with this type of ornament.

One moccasin[1] (Pl. V, fig. I, catalogue number 1/5709) is embroidered merely with a stripe from the instep the toe. This stripe of breadwork consists of a number of bars or lengthened rectangles of different colors. No information was obtained as to the meaning of the design on this specimen.

Another specimen (Pl. v, fig. 2, cat. no.50/583) has similar stripe, about, an inch in width, running from instep to toe, and composed of bars or small stripes of six different colors. The distribution of these colors is not like that in the last described specimen, but the pattern and the idea of colour arrangement and identical.On this moccasin, however,there is one additional piece of embroidery, an narrow stripe across the instep, that is, transverse to the main stripe and touching it at its upper end. The large stripe as a whole, the smaller bars separately, and the transverse stripe all represent buffalo paths.

A third specimen (Pl. v, fig. 3, cat. no. 50/585) also has a stripe from instead to toe. This is white, except for a rectangular green portion in the middle. At the two ends of this green part of the stripe are two dark-blue (=black) marks, which are approximately triangular. Across the instep we again find a narrow transverse stripe. This represents a bow. The main longitudenal stripe represents a buffalo path. Its green rectangular portion is a buffalo. The black marks are arrow points shot into it. Small projections on these marks, which render them not really quite triangular, represent the barbs of the arrowheads.

Another moccasin (Pl. v, fig. 4, cat. no. 50/1021) again has the longitudinal strike. This represents path, probably with implication of the path traveled by the wearer of the moccasin. The major part of this stripe is white, but portions are beaded in darkblue(=black), red, and grayish-blue. These colors denote respectively night, day, and hazy atmosphere. On the white stripe are also two curious symbols, which are said to signify sunrise or going over a mountain. A narrow transverse stripe is found in this specimen also; but instead of being contiguous to the end of the main stripe, as on the last two moccasins, it is cut in two by it, so that it exists only in two fragments, one on each side of the large stripe. These two small bars represent insects that are desired to be out of the path,beside it, instead of being where the moccasin will travel in the path.

Another specimên (Pl. v, fig. 5, cat. no. 50/410) has the main stripe down the foot slightly modified in that it tapers a little toward the toe. In arrangement of colors, this moccasin resembles closely the second one described. In all the specimens just discussed, except the last, the bars of which the main stripe consists are arranged in three groups. In this moccasin this triple division of the stripe also exists. Moreover, in the middle section of this stripe there is a green rectangle, and in contact with this a small dark-blue mark approximately triangular in shape. These two symbols are very like the representations of the buffalo and arrowpoints on the moccasin above described as symbolic of the buffalo hunt. Unfortunately it is not known whether the design on the present specimen had meaning. So far, accordingly, this moccasin agress closely with those previously examined. It is further alike them in possessing a narrow, transverse stripe of beadwork at the instep. But a totally new feature is found in two smallest that start from the end of the transverse stripe. They are parallel to the main central longitudinal stripe, but very much smaller.

In all the preceding specimens but one (fig.4), the large stripe consists of three sections. In the exceptional specimen the upper third or fourth of the stripe is of one ground colour, the remainder all of another ground color. Such an arrangement is also found in another specimen (Pl.v, fig, 6, cat. no. 7/5707). The smaller portion of the stripe is white, the long part is blue with a pattern imposed upon it. Nothing is known of the significance of any part of this design. The two small bars are present, as in the lasts pecimen, and repeat the markings of the large stripe in simplified form. But the transverse stripe at the instep is missing.

Still another moccasin has its stripe divided into a short upper and a long lower portion of different colors (Pl. v, fig. 7, cat.no. 50/582). As in the last specimen, there are two small bars parallel to the central stripe and the transverse stripe is again absent. The stripes and bars all represent buffalo paths. In certain parts of the stripes are small squares colored light blue; these represent buffalo tracks.

The last specimen of this series (Pl. v. fig. 8 cat. no. 50/584) has the main central stripe, the transverse stripe at the instep, and the small bars repeating the markings of the large stripe. In addition to these three decorative devices that are found in previous specimens, it possesses a fourth one that is new. The central longitudinal stripe (slightly constricted toward its middle) is bisected by a duplicate of itself running transversely. These two stripes thus firm a cross. This cross represents the morning start, the variety of colors upon it denoting the variety of colors the star appears to assume. The transverse stripe at the instep represent the sky or horizon. The two small bars are said to be the twinkling of the start as it rises, in other words its rays.[2]

The symbolism of some of these designs is elaborate. The representation of the buffalo in his path shot by arrows from the hunger's bow is coherent and neatly compact. We do not low whether it is a commemoration of a particular event or the expression of a wish for plenty of food, but in either case it has pictographic function. In fact, it is a pictorial, except for the fact that its geometric form renders it illegible for anyone but its writer. The star-moccasin is also a pictograph in an ornamental dress.[3]

The conventionality of the decoration seems to have reached an equally strong development.It is apparent that the large stripe from instep totoe is the fundamental motive of this style of ornamentation. All the other motives are also stripes, and even of these there are only two (the transverse stripe and the two short bars), except in the one morning-star moccasin where the basal element is introduced in a new position as a fourth decorative motive.

In short, in these moccasins the tendency to realistic

symbolism and the tendency to decorative conventionalism are clearly about in equilibrium. Hence we cannot fairly say that either of these tendencies is the older and original. If one concentrates his attention on the symbolism, or happens to be temperamentally more interested in it, he is very likely to see it more abundantly than the decoration, to be more impressed by it, to consider the entire present art as merely corrupted or abbreviated symbolism. and to advance as a explanation of the origin oand development of these designs the theory of conventionalized realism. But if one thinks more of the decoration as such, or if one's mind runs naturally towards the ornamental and technical, he will probably notice mostly this side, regard the significantons of markings as triviall and irrelevant additions that may be ignored, and finally champion the theory of expanded decoration. With the one bias we are so overwhelmingly aware of the almost pictographic coherence in the buffalo-hunt moccasin, that we believer that pictures of such topics must have given rise to the present form. With the other bias the conventionality of the pattern that possesses this bufalo-bunt significance is no impressive that we come to think that decorative motives of just such persistence as this must have been the origin of the present form. A first investigator is so struck with the enormous difference of meaning between the ordinary path-stripe moccasins and the morning-star-cross moccasin that he cannot believe they had a common source; each must have sprung from a picture, which was as different from t he other as the objects represented are different. A second observer is so impressed by the fact that the morning-star moccasin with four decorative elements differs less from some of the buffalo-bath moccasins than many of these with from one to three decorative elements differ from each other, that he thinks that all these designs, however variable their superficial meanings, must have originated in one typical ornamental form.

Both these explanations are thus, in the case of these

moccasin designs, not only logically possible,but they are very naturally believed and advanced as the result of certain mental predispositions. But if we try to remain free from any such inclinations of mind, and if we remember how strongly developed and intimately fused are both the tendencies, we must come to the conclusion that, because symbolism and decoration balance each other, the two therories of conventionalized realism and expanded ornament, though logically admissible, are actually untenable. Rather it seems likely, since the two tendencies are vigorous, and combined, heat they are both well established, old, and long in close union; so that formetly designs on Arapaho moccasins, though perhaps ruder than now, were of the same general character, both symbolically and decoratively, as those we know.

Let us consider a second style of moccasin. Whereas in those just discussed the fundamental element of the embroidery was the longitudinal stripe, it now is a border running all around the foot just above the sole. In one particular specimen illustrated (Pl. vi. fig, I, cat. no. 1/5708) there is besides this border of bead-work a series of lines of quilwork filling the large space on the front of them moccasin, but as this is embroidery of a different material and appearance, we can disregard it in the present consideration and confine our attention to the ornamentation consisting of the border. It should be added that in addition to the border there is the narrow stripe across the instep.

In a second specimen (Pl. vi, fig. 2, cat. no. 50/953) their is besides the border and the transverse stripe, the large longitudinal stripe with which we have become familliar. As previsouly, this signifies paths.

A third specimen (pl. vi, fig. 3, cat. no. 1/5720) has the border,the large longitudinal stripe, and the two small lbars at its upper end, but lacks the transverse instep-stripe. On the central stripe are two representations of birds, but there is no information as to the meaning of the design.

It is evident that in these last two moccasins there is a combination of the stripe motive with the border motive.

In another specimen (Pl. vi, fig. 4, cat. no. 50/658), of whose symbolism we are ignorant, the longitudinal stripe is continued farther than previously, so that it meets the border. The stripe is not solidly embroidered: its edges are beads, but its interior is left open and merely painted red.

In any moccasins of this design there is left a blank space on each side of the foot. This is the area enclosed by the stripe, the border,and the transverse in step-stripe. It has the shape of a pointed right-angle triangle whose hypotenuse instead of being straight is convex. These two triangular or horn-shaped areas occur in another moccasin (Pl. vi,fig, 5, cat. no. 50/327). The border, stripe, and transverse stripe are all white. The two enclosed areas are half covered with a checker-board design in several colors, which is said to represent buffalo-gut. This checker-board embroidery also extends around the heel.

If, now, this half-open checker-board work were replaced by solid beading, we should have a moccasin completely covered with beadwork. Such specimens occur in abundane. In one (Pl. vi, fig. 6, cat. no. 50/1028), whose groundwork is white, the two triangular areas taken together represent buffalo horns. The buffalo trample the ground; this is represented by the coloring of the two areas. One is red, which denotes the soil, or bare earth; the other is green, which denotes vegetation or grass-covered earth.

A child's moccasin, also solidly beaded (cat. no. 50/1032), has as usual a groundwork of white. The two triangular areas are green, and represent horse ears—a symbol of good fortune and future wealth. Between them, the central stripe, slightly modified, represents a lizard.

A last moccasin (cat no. 50/1075) is solidly beaded in white. The two triangular marks are banded dark blue and white, and represent fish.

In these last cases, in fact in most fully beaded moccasins, the decorative elements of border, stripe, transverse stripe, and triangular area ar still visible in the embroidery; even though they often become identical in color and are not distinguished in the design, they are used technically.

If we follow the transition from the merely bordered moccasin to the solidly beaded one, and see the same technical or decorative features persisting in all parts of the series from the simplest to the most highly developed form, the ornamental nature of these productions is striking and their decorative origin seems probable. If we consider the realistic representation of, for instance, the buffalo horn, and the pretty symbolism of its coloring, the realistic origin of these decorations seems very hard to disbelieve. Of course there is no reason for leaping at either of these conclusions. Neither pahse of this art must be ignored, but both recognized. It is necessary to be aware both of the strong ornamental tendency influenced by symbolism and the symbolic tendency modified by ornamental system.

So far as these moccasins are concerned, it accordingly seems impossible to determine with certainty how the symbolic decoration originated.

Parfleches and bags of rawhide made by the Arapaho are painted on the front with designs that cover most of the surface. The back or bottom is sometimes left blank, or may have from six to ten straight lines (or narrow stripes) painted transversely across (fig. 3). These lines on the bottom usually represent roads or rivers. All parfleches are perforated in front to allow of being fastened with thongs. Occasionally, however, a cautious person winds a rope a number of times around his bag, in order to tie it up more securely.On one parfleche seen by the writer such transverse lines were painted across the bottom. The owner and maker declared that they represented a rope passing over the surface of the back several times for fastening the bag. She showed another parfleche in her possisession which was actually thus tied.

In this case the markings may appear to be an instance of the survival, as a decoration, of a anatrophied useful feature: first then these were left off but were represented by painting. This technical-ornamental theory seems at first glance to offer the true explanation of the origin of these lines on the back of all raw hide bags. But a moment's consideration shows that it is also within reason to believe the opposite: we candent that the line originated from attempts at representing rivers or roads, but that in this case the maker of the bag was struck by the resemblance of the line to a rope as it was occasionally used, and then gave the new signification of rope to what really were conventionalized representations of rivers or roads.

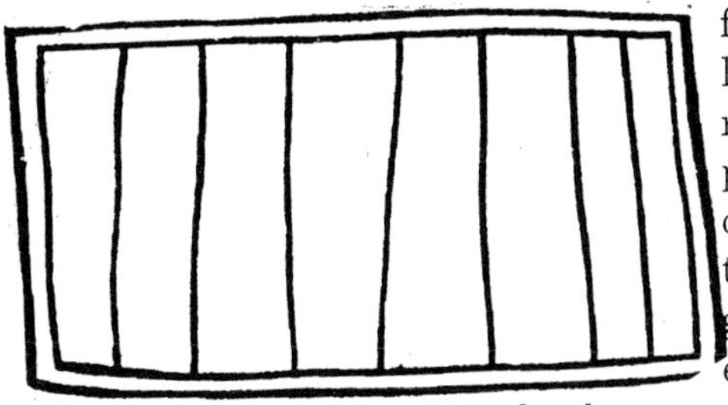

FIG. 3 — Marketing on Araphao bag.

So here again we have two explanations (there may be still more) that are plausible, while neither can be proved conclusively. As soon as we go beyond the description of existing circumstances into the inquiry of origin, we enter the realm of uncertainty, of irrefutable doubts.

A peculiar Arapaho medine-case shown unusual symbolism. The design painted on this is shows, spread out flat, in fig. 4 (cat. no.50/659). The ornamentation,which is less geometric than in most specimens of painting, represents the acquisition of super-natural power. Below, on the right side, is the sweat-house into which the owner and maker of the case went before beginning his fast to acquire supernatural power. This ornament also represents a small mound in front of the sweat-house, on which a buffalo skull is lying. The fish-tail ornament just above this is the mountain on which the man fasted, and hence also represents himself. To the right of this, the crescent topped design is "the overseer (the sun), also called "the one that lights." The pedestal or stalk of this figure represents "information" (supernatural power) flowing down from this being to the earth (the horizontal line). At the extreme left, the same design is a representation of himself after he had acquired information and power; and to the right of this, the fish-tail ornament now represents this very medicine-case. But the case is made of buffalohide, and his supernatural power consisted largely in control of the buffalo; therefore this same symbol also denotes buffalo. Below, on the left, is the sweat-house into which he went after his fast.

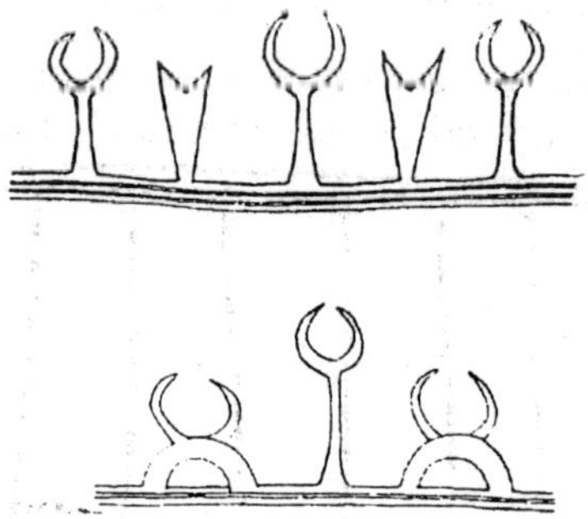

FIG. 4— Arapaho Medicine-Cases.

We have here an example of highly-developed symbolism. It might seem that when so long a story is told and so much abstract in formation is conveyed, the ideographic design must have arisen directly from the attempt of the artist to express his meaning, i.e., that the design is quasi-realistic in origin. But there is another medicine-case (fig. 5 a, cat. no. 50/401) with similar ornamentation (about whose signification we unfortunately have no information). The resemblance of the two designs is great. One consists of an alternating arrangement of two symbols, both forked, the other of an alternating arrangement of these two symbols with a third, the semicircle, added. some Arapaho say that this style of case was used by a powerful medicine-man and his followers or scholars; but it is uncertain whether this man invented the design or used an already existing one. It is doubtful whether even the symbolism was originated by this man or was similar to an earlier current of symbolism. The most usual ornamentation on Arapaho medicine-cases is a pattern of tents (fig. 5 b, cat. no. 50/688) or a combination of triangles and diamonds similar to that painted on parfleches. So her again there is pictograriic symbolism fused with a more or less conventional decoration, and it is impossible to say whether the symbolism or the decoration is the older and original.

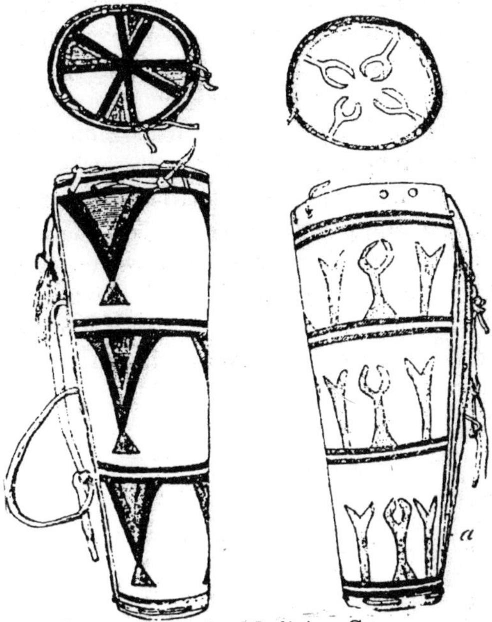

FIG. 5—Arapaho Medicine-Cases.

Small paint-bags—black skin pouches to hold body-paint—are in general use among the Arapaho. Some of these represent half of a double-ended fringed saddle-bag. The rest all represent small animals, such as the beaver, lizard, rat, fish, mussel, horned toad, and frog. The opening represents the animal's mouth, two strings that serve to tie up the opening are its forelegs, a loose flap at the end may be the tail, the pouch it self is the body, and other parts are indicated, as there is need, by beadwork, string, or attached ornaments. The resemblance to the animal represented is often detailed, but never accurate, being ideographic rather than visual, in keeping with all the symbolism of this art. It is generally impossible to recognize what species of animal is meant, and only the maker knows this. One pouch represents both a beaver and a fish (fig. 6 a. cat. no. 50/361), according to information given by its owner. When it is regarded as beaver, both pairs of strings are legs, and the scallops or notches at the opening are the prominent teeth. A design in beadwork on the pouch, which represents a steam with a dam and beaver-huts, also refers to this signification. When a fish is meant to be represented, the upper pair of strings are the barbles, the lower pair the pectoral fins. The fish-signification is

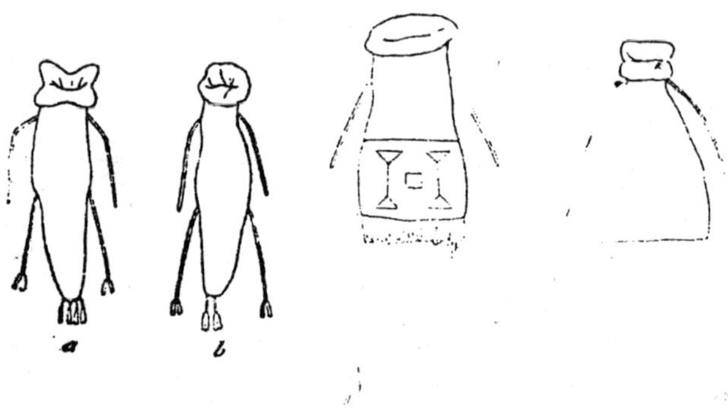

FIG. 6 —Arapaho paint pouches

strengthened by a rough line of beads at the edge of the pouch, which are interpreted as fish-scales.

A very similar pouch represents a lizard (fig. 6 b, cat. no. 50/362). Mouth, body , legs, and tail are represented in the conventional manner by opening, pouch, strings, and attached flap.

A pouch that lacks the long flap represents a frog (fig. 6 c, cat. no. 50/344). Two long strings indicate the frog's hind legs. A fringe at the bottom represents the grass in which it is sitting. A design in beadwork on this pouch denotes the shoulder and hip joints of the frog, and the food in its stomach.

Another pouch (fig. 6 d, cat. no. 50/601) differs in shape from this one only in lacking the two longer strings. It represents half a saddle-bag.

The realistic tendency Kanifested in the animal symbolism of these pouches is undeniable. A conventional,formal, decorative tendency is evident in the close similarity between the frog-pouch and the saddle-bag pouch, and between the beaver-pouch and the lizard-pouch. Both the tendencies come to light in the pouch with the curious double signification.

Some of the Arapaho say that at the beginning of the world, when the first men, their ancestors, obtained paint, they had only the skins of small animals to use for paint-bags, and that this is the origin of the animal symbolism of the present-day paint-pouches.

It is necessary not to be misled in to a belief of this origin and development on the authority of the Indians. Their authority on such a point is absolutely valueless. They believe that the time when the first men obtained paint-bags was four hundred years ago, just after the formation of the world by a solitary mythic begin floating on the water, and after a female whirlwind enlarged the minute earth by circling about it. Like all American savages they are almost completely without historical sense or knowledge. Occasionally a striking even may be remembered in a distorted form for a century or two, but on the whole, whatever of actual occurrence is retained in their tales in inextricably blended with mythic and supernatural elements. We have no right to reject the greatest part of their creation myth as so absurdly impossible that it would enter no one's mind to accept it as true, and at the same time to select here and there a point that is within the limits of possibility and proclaim it as historical and reliable. The mythic and historical elements in primitive legends are not simply mixed together so that they can be distinguished and separated, but they ar both equally wonderful and equally true for the savage. No myth can be intreprted into into history by mee elimination of its supernatural portions; it must be rejected in toto. Even thought it may be founded on a basis of actuality—and this must often be the case—it is altogether myth. In law, and exact science, and wherever evidence is judged, and account that is in great part manifestly absurd or palpably impossible is not accepted as true after the impossibilities have been subtracted, but is disregarded as a whole. So, too, it is necessary to attach no importance to the statement of the Arapaho as to the origin of these paint-bags.

We have considered several forms of Arapaho art—various objects, various styles, and various materials and techniques. In all cases we have found a well-developed symbolism and a conventional decoration. The symbolism and the decoration exist not side by side but in each other. It has been easy to manufacture explanations of the origin of this art that are plausible theories. But as soon as we are open to recognize all possibilities, such theories are seen to arise from our opinions and methods of interpretation, and to be unsubstantiable by fact. Therefore we can describe Arapaho art, we can characterize it, and distinguish its various coexisting tendencies. We can even, to a certain extent, enter into the spirit of the people who practise it, and understand (i.e., feel) their mental workings. We cannot in fairness lay claim to knowing the cause or origin of this art, nor can we hope to ascertain its cause and origin by studying its products.

In the art of other primitive races conditions very much resemble those just discussed. Everywhere art is conventionalized, under the influence of a definite style. Practically everywhere also it is decorative. This is obviously true of such high arts as those of the Japanese and Chinese. It is true also of Greek sculpture and of Renaissance paintings: though in our modern civilization we are in the habit of regarding the products of these arts detachedly, and enjoy them as if they were complete in themselves, yet every one is aware that the intent to decorate always accompanied the conception and execution of the clàssic and Italian masterpieces. Even so strenuously realistic an art as modern impressionism is unable to free itself totally form the reproach of begin ornamental; for whatever the purpose of the artist, the owner of such a picture has almost certainly secured it for the purpose, ostensible at least, of decorating a vacant wall. In primitive civilizations, the combination of the imitative and decorative tendencies is of course much greater. With very few exceptions, such as in some Eskimo tribes, the realistic, representative impulse is thoroughly impressed and influenced by the highly conventional style; and in all cases this conventional style is decorative. Correspondingly, most primitive decoration, no matter how metric or simple, has significance and thus is, visually or ideographically, realistic. This is a fact that has not become known until lately, because until tlatel savings were rarely questioned thoroughly.[4] Accordingly the main characteristic of Arapaho art, its fusion (which is more truly an undifferentiation) or the realistic and decorative tendencies, is also the characteristic of all primitive art.

In Bazil we know of tribes whose painted and incised designs, which are exceedingly simple and geometrical and usually in patterns, are all significant. Diamonds whose corners are slightly filled in are rhomboidally shaped fishes; a pattern of flat isosceles triangles stood up on end is hanging bats, and so on. There are also other representations of the same animals that are slightly more realistic. The same tribes use pots of oval shapes with half a dozen variously shaped projections at the rim. The whole vessel represents an animal, the projections being roughly modeled into head, tail and limbs. Birds, bats, mammals, reptiles, and invertebrates are indicated by very slight modifications. A civilized person unacquainted with the mode of sight and thought of the Brazilian aborigines might very readily mistake a bird-pot for a mammal-pot, and so on.

In Central Australia bullroarers and other objects are decorated with incised lines. These consist of concentric circles, bands of parallel lines, concentric arcs or curves, and rows of dots or small marks. The ornamentation is not symmetrical, nor even regular; it appears random and rude. Yet in general character these decorated bullroarers resemble each other closely. It has been found that the designs are all ideographic, though the total range of significance is apparently not very wide. Similar marks may on different objects mean things as different as trees frogs, edges, or intestines. It is interesting to note that while this art is remarkably crude and unformed both as regular ornamentation and as an attempt to represent objects accurately, it contains a system of realist expression as well as a system of decoration, both of which are conventionalized—or rather, the union of which is a convention.

The remarkable art of the North Pacific coast of America is certainly one of the most stylistic and conventionaized in the world, while its realistic character is sufficiently marked to give no one room to doubt its presence. Its decorative tendency is so strong that, in obedience to its demands, an animal that is being presented may be cut into parts which are then arranged as suits the requirements of the decoration and not as they are in nature. The chest of an animal may be put over its head, and the tail below; two opposite sides of an animal, which are of course invisible at the same time, will be represented,in order to meet the strong demand for symmetry. The chief decorative motive of all this art is an oblong figure whose corners are rounded an whose sides are very slightly convex the upper long edge generally curving the most. Almost everything that is represented is brought into this shape or some modification of it. Heads, eyes, mouths, ears, joints, tails, fins, are usually of this shape; the shole decorative field itself often it the same;

and in such cases the remaining portions occupied y unemumerated parts, such as back, belly, and wings, are almost necessarily of the same shape. Eyes an faces appear everywhere—on representations of joints, of the chest, of dorsal fins, of hands, in vacant spaces—and their shape is regularly the ornamental one described. Yet with this remarkably strong decorative tendency pervading and deeply influencing every representation, all examples of decorative art from this region are recognizably realistic in intent and often in execution. There is no geometrical ornament that one might take to be meaningless. In short, on the North Pacific coast of America all decoration is realistic and all realism is decorate.

It is of course impossible to prove by selected examples such as these that all primitive art consists of the combination of representative realism and ornamental conventionalism. But that such is the fact, that this undifferentiation continues often into a higher civilization, must be obvious to any one familiar with primitive art. This fusion of two differing tendencies is not merely a frequent or widely distributed occurrence, as are a great many special ethnic phenomena, such as circumcision or doctoring by sucking or angularity of ornament, but this fusion is a rule practically without exceptions. It is universal because it is necessary. Both the representative tendency and the decorative tendency are deep rooted in the human mind, so that it must be virtually impossible to suppress them for any length of time or among any considerable number of men. At times, indeed, as in European civilization, the two tendencies become more separated: our wall-papers are chiefly ornamental,our oil paintings chiefly realistic. But a glance at the past and present races of the world shows that this condition is exceptional, just as a civilization of the extremity of ours is exceptional. The more primitive a people is, we may say, the more intimately fused in its art will these two tendencies be, though, as there is no absolute or fixable scale of primitiveness and civilization, this rule cannot be applied to special cases but merely tends to be true. Other tendencies also are still combined with these two in a sufficiently early and rude condition of society. The symbolism of the Arapaho is as ideographic as it is realistic, and is as much a primitive method of writing as it is of a artistic representation. The Australian bull-roarers referred to are, in addition to other things, very primitive maps or charts; so that they are the products of diagrammatic, graphic, visually artistic, and decorative tendencies or activities still undifferentiated—all this in addition to their still more marked religious functions. Of course it is possible for a race to over-develop one of several related tendencies at the expense of others. To a certain degree this does happening all faces, and is what makes the difference between them. But every culture must contain among its motive forces more or less of every tendency, because the tendencies are in the human mind and hence ineradicable. These many tendencies are on the whole less differentiated in more primitive conditions of society. Hence all art, and especially primitive art, contains the combination at least of representative and decorative tendencies, perhaps of others.[5]

The invariable method of expert origin of an art his been to select that one of its tendency which was the most marked or appeared so to the investigator, to imagine the products of this tendency in its most isolated and pure form, and to pronounce these the original state of the art. An observer is struck by the fact that in a certain primitive art many ornamental features co-incide with technical ones that are present for practical reasons. He concludes that the technical pratical tendency which he has discovered among the decoration, is the original unmixed impulse that caused the art. Or he may become aware through inquiry or study of the fact that geometric ornament in an art has realistic significance. The realism impresses him; true, it is now modified an corrupt, but that only proves to him that originally it was pure. Ergo, this art began with representative pictures. Such has been the only method of explanation, however much the actual results in different cases different. No other method of ascertaining or explaining the origin of a primitive art whose history we lack, is even possible.

This method has the fundamental fault that it presupposes tendencies to have existed more unmixedly and separately at some former time than at present. In reality they must in all cases have been in the near past very much as now and in the very remote past more mixed or mutually undifferentiated. Thus we have seen that Arapaho art must some time ago have been very much as now. What is was still earlier we know even less definitely, but we cannot doubt, that its spirit must have been similar. Different objects may then have been represented, other ornamental motives employed in other materials,but even then there certainly was the combination of ideographic symbolism with crude, heavy decoration. As we go farther backward in time, we can be sure that the details of the art were more and more different from those of its present condition. Now perhaps one of its component tendencies was relatively stronger, then another. But whatever these temporary slight fluctuations, it is certain that if we only go back far enough we must arrive at a stage where the tendencies were even more numerously and more intimately combined than now. But if one should believe that Arapaho art can be explained, for instance, by the conventionalized realism theory, the realism being original and the conventionalization subsequent, he holds the view that at some time past this Arapaho art consisted of pictorial prepresntatons. This view is logically possible, but in reality it is absurd. This art could not have had so idealy simple a development that we could still trace its original condition, if it were very old. But if it, therefore, were comparatively recent in origin, there must until a certain time have been no art among the Arapaho, while at that moment it sprang up full-blown, not as a crude undifferentiated thing, but a highly-specialized pictorial art. Such an even would be extremely remarkable, not to say marvelous, and more in need of an explanation than the phenomenon it explained. By isolating any tendency that we find in any art, we are led to imagine a purely ideal condition which not only could not have been the original state of the art, but is probably even more different from its original state than from its present known state.

In short, it is impossible to determine the origin of any art whose history we do not know.

Let us briefly consider the field of mythology. There have been numerous explanations of myths and several theories of the origin of all mythology. The principal of these theories are the following.

What may be called the physical or science theory accounts for myths by making them the outcome of a desire to plain natural phenomena. The shapes or colors of animals, the motion of sun and moon, the existence of the stars, strange geologic formations, such phenomena are supposed to have stimulated the wonder of primitive man so much that he made myths to explain them.

The personification theory supposes that deities and other mythic characters, together with their actions,—in a word, mythology—are personifications of natural phenomena. Phoebus, India, Agni, are said to have originated in personifications of the sun, heaven, and fire. The solar myth theories, and others of an analogous kind, belong here.

The animal theory says that there was originally a belief in soul, out of which arose the various systems, of spirits and deities. it believes that myths originated from a state of the human mind to which all objects seemed equally endowed with human personality.

These three theories are at bottom the same.

What has been called the allegorical or ethical theory supposes myths to be allegorical inventions with a moral import. Miraculous stories of gods, men, and animals are thought to have been composed in order to teach, by illustration, ethical precepts. This views not so much in favor now as formerly.

The historical their makes myths the distortion of actual events. A power bulking of Crete gave rise to the mythic character of Zeus.

The etymological theory calls mythology a disease of language. Misinterpreted metaphors or false etymologies gave rise to myths. To use a familiar example, Zeus is thought to have been originally called Kronion, with the meaning "existing through all time." Later this epithet was misunderstood to mean son of Kronos, and thus gave rise to the conception of a god Kronos.[6]

As explanations, all these theories are untrue. But the tendencies which they recognize exist.

There is undoubtedly a tendency to explain natural phenomena in myths. The Indians of British Columbia have this story: The bear and the chipmunk disputed whether there was to be darkness or light. The chipmunk triumphed, and for the first time it became light. The angry bear attacked the chipmunk and pursued it. The chipmunk escaped by tearing itself from under the claws of the bear. From this it is striped down its back. This little story, whatever its origin, clearly reflects the tendency to mythologize about such natural phenomena as day and night and the color-markings of animals. Hundreds of similar myths concerned with the spots on the moon, or the blackness of the crow, or a certain peculiar stone, or a similar fact, are known from all parts of the world.

There is also a tendency to identify mythic personages with parts of nature; thor its thunder, for instance. And the tendency towards animism is so widespread and so deep-seated that it will be recognized without an example.

It must also be admitted that there is something of an ethical tendency in mythologies. Among primitive races ceremonial and ritual partly take the place of our later morality. And very frequently myths deal with ceremonial. The American Indian, the Jews, the Australians, and the Greeks have such myths.

The existence of a historical tendency in myths is demonstrated by the introduction of Attila into the Sigurd saga.

The etymological tendency, finally, is revealed in the following extract from a Dakota myth:[7] An old couple have adopted a foundling. When he grows up he is so successful in killing buffalo that he makes his parents very rich in dried meat. "Then the old man said: 'Old woman, I am glad we are well off. I will proclaim it abroad.' And so when the morning came he went up to the top of the house and sat, and said, 'I, I have abundance laid up. The fat of the big guts *(tashiyaka)* I chew.' And they say that was the origin of the meadow-lark *(tashiyakapopo)*. It has a yellow breast, and black in the middle, which is the yellow of the morning, and they say the black stripe is made by a smooth buffalo horn worn for a necklace."—From this point the myth deals with the adventures of the boy.

It is thus clear that for every one of these theories there really exists a tendency in primitive man which influences his myths.

This multiplicity of tendencies or causative forces necessarily refutes any explanation that uses and allows only one of them. Such have been all explanations of myths. Such they must be, for when more than one tendency or cause is admitted, we can have several tentative suggestions but no longer one positive explanation. The case is logues to that in art, and does not require detailed restatement. It may be said, in short, that all explanations of mythos consists of the ignoring of all the eternal and indestructible tendencies in man with the exception of one which is isolated and elevated as the sole cause of the myth. That such explanations, however clear and impressive they are, cannot be true, is obvious.

Thus we come to the conclusion that all search for origins in anthropology can lead to nothing but false results. The tendencies of which we have spoken are at the root of all anthropological phenomena. There fore it is these general tendencies more properly than the supposed causes of detached phenomena that should be the aim of investigation.

These tendencies, being inherent in mind,[8] are everlasting. On the other hand they are constantly changing and developing, and varying in heir differentiations and combinations. The phenomena of activity have changed as these tendencies and their relations to one another have become modified. Therefore the products of mind (the phenomena studied by anthropologists) arem like mind itself, beginning less (for us) They have no origin. All arts and all institutions are as old as man. Every word is as old as speech. They history of every myth is at least as long as the history of mankind. of course no myth was ever alike from one generation to the next; no decorative style has every remained unaltered. But no myth, no artistic convention, nor any other thing human, ever sprang up from nothing. it always grew from something previous that was similar. These principles are obvious, but they are ignored and implicitly denied in every search for an origin.

Every explanation of an origin in anthropology is based on three processes of thought which are unobjectionable logically but are contrary to blutionary principles and the countless body of facts that support these principles. First is the Assumption, implied in the word *origin,* that before etha beginning the phenomenon explained itself and its cause were absent; second is the belief that a suddenly arising cause singly produced the phenomenon; and the third is the idea that this cause as suddenly and completely ceased as it had before sprung up, and that its product has remained, unaffected by other causes, unaltered but for wear and tear, to the present day. These three thought processes are present in every explanation of the cause or origin of a human phenomenon,whether the explainer himself be conscious or unconscious of them. Generally, indeed, the origin is not state unhesitatingly and clearly enough for these three steps of thought to be visible in all their baldness. Often, perhaps, the investigator advancing a theory of origin would himself deny these processes to exist in his reasoning. Nevertheless, every determination of a origin, whether origin means the beginning of a phenomenon or its cause,must imply the existence of, first, a previous different state, secondly, a change produced by an external (non-inherent) cause, and, thirdly, the state that is begin investigated.

This three-step process of reasoning is not in itself wrong. When it is declared either that steam in a particular case was, or in general can be, produced from water by omheat, this method of thought is employed. The early state is the water, the altering cause the heat, and the present state the steam. In all the physical sciences thinking in this manner is not only permissible but necessary and is constantly done. It is when these thought-processes are used in anthropology[9] that their results become absurd. When we say that the origin of decoration is technique, or that the origin of marriage is promiscuity, or that the origin of the Polynesian Maui is personification of the sun, or that the origin of an alphabet is pictorial art, or that the beginning or cause of anything in human culture is a certain other thing—we assert or imply a distinct and separate antecedent condition and an isolated, definitely limited efficient cause. That such a condition and such a cause really existed we have shown in the consideration of primitive art to be so highly improbable as to make the belief in their reality absurd; and it must be obvious that in all other cases within the scope of anthropology the three suppositions made in every explanation of origin where direct historical knowledge is lacking, possess the same degree of improbability.[10]

If then, the specific causes or beginnings of specific phenomena are a delusion in anthropology and may not be sought, what can be the subject of investigation? The tendencies that have been referred to so much? Like words and styles and myths and ideas and industrial processes and institutions, all of which are their products, tendencies are both eternally living and everlastingly changing. They flow into one another; they transform themselves; they are indistinguishably combined where they coexist. So, if our view is wide enough, we cannot properly determine and separate and name and classify tendencies. They really exist only in the whole unity of living activity as parts in the endless . This great unity is the true study for the students of man. In it, as parts of it, cultures and civilization-movemens, tendencies and individual phenomena, are comprehensible. In it we know their interrelations. Only by understanding its totality can we really understand its smaller parts, those productions that have always a predecessor but never a beginning.

The fundamental error of the common anthropogical method of investigating origins is that it isolates phenomena and seeks isolated specific causes for them. In reality, ethnic phenomena do not exist separately: they have their being only in a culture. Much less can becauisative forces of the human mind, the activities or tendencies, be truly isolated. Every distinction of them is not only arbitrary but untrue. Both phenomena and causes can be properly apperceived only in the degree that we know their relations to the rest of the great unit that is called life. The more this is known and understood as a whole,the more do we comprehend its parts. This, the whole of life, is the only profitable subject of study for anthropology.

References

1. The Arapaho objects described in the course of this article are in

the American Museum of Natural History. Their catalogue numbers are given in parentheses.

2. Some of these moccasins,it will have been noticed, are with out known symbolism. This is due merely to their having been collected without inquiry being made as to the significance of their designs. Consequently, to judge from analogy, it is more probable that they do have meaning than that they really lack it.

3. Even in true pictographas free from decorative limitations and therefore drawn with the greatest realistic fidelity of with the Indian is capable, the symbols for the monging-star, the horizon,and rays of light are the same as those on this moccasin—a cross, a horizontal line, and vertical or sloping lines.

4. The scarcely suspected inherence of realistic significance in primitive ornament has been independently demonstrated from California, British Columbia, Central America, Brazil, Mississippi valley, Silberia, Indo China, Borneo, New Guinea, Australia,and Polynesia, in arts as diverse as pottery, weaving carving, basketry, drawing, and painting.

5. The differential here and previously spoken of a accompanying gor constituting evolution in vivilizationis at once too important and universal a matter to be proved here in a few incidental words, and too obvious to require it. A striking example of this differentiation is found in the mythology of our more primitive forefathers, in place of which, and more or less developed from which, we have products as different as romantic novels, fundamental scientific theories, and the doctrinary beliefs of our religions. There is no intention, however, of implying here by differentiation oa continuing separation. Where in a savage tribe every man, though in somewhat vary ingdegree, is hunter, warrior, participan tin government, sha man, artist, and myth-maker, a higher nation has its separate politicians, soldiers, food-producers, physicians, poets, and so on; but though the tendencies have in this transition differentiated, and have far more than formerly become specialized in individuals,yet they exist only in the culture as a whole: in this the only true unit, i.e., the only organic entity, they are all combined. For instance, our present-day science could not have arisen nor could it exist without modern industrialism, and this is equally dependent on science. Our literature is absolutely and intimately interwoven with our social conditions, not so much in that poets

and novelists actually describe these, but in that the memotions and ideas which form the content of their writing are the typical emotions and ideas accompanying our social circumstances. In proportion with the differentiation of tendencies in evolution proceed their combination and recombination. Very analogously, a mammal is far more highly diffentiated than a jellyfish, but none the less are its various organs interdependent and itself a distinct organic unity.

6. This does not necessarily exhaust the number of theories.

7. Riggs, *Dakota Grammar, Texts and Ethnography,* 1893.

8. The tendencies spoken of thought this essay must be understood to be the tendencies of social man. They are those tendencies which exist in individuals being parts of a culture, not in isolated individuals as such. there are psychological causes or mental conditions—generally considered physiological—which might also be called tendencies. Such are the tendency to fatigue, the tendency to form habits, the tendency toward imitation by suggestion, and others. These exist nearly identically in all men, whatever their degree of civilization; they seem even to occur with little modification in animals. It is evident that these physiological tendencies are totally independent of cultures. Our knowledge concerning them in due to a psychological study of individual men. On the other hand those tendencies which along are referred to above are determinable only from historical study of social groups. The manifestations of these tendencies are activities such as mythology, writing, ceremonials decorative art, castes, commerce, and language.

9. By the term anthropology there are meant here not those portions of the science which are clearly anatomical and physiological (i.e., resting upon mechanical science and included in it), but those domains generally covered by the titles ethnology, archeology, and history.

10. If it is true that origins cannot be determined, the supposed origins of words namely roots, must be imaginary. Whoever gives adherence to the currently accepted theory that language began with roots, deliberately or unconsciously commits himself to these beliefs: that previous to the making of roots language in the proper sense, as something articulate and definite, was

wanting. That with the roots, language began to be, essentially as it is now. That after the formation of the roots no new ones ever arose, but language remained unchanged except for modifications of its roots or their combinations into new words and inflectional forms. The improbability of such a process having ever taken place must be clear to any one who believes that never-dying, ever-changing, interrelated tendencies have unceasingly and unitedly been operative in man. The belief in roots as these sources of languages is totally unevolutionary: it is contrary to the axiom that nothing living ever comes but from what is similar and that all change is gradual development and not a process of finished creation. The weakness of the theory of roots is most palpable in the absurdity of the various explanations that are frequently given of the origin of the primary roots. It is true that there is something that may be called roots. In every language there are groups of words similar in sound and related in meaning. The ideal, non-existent centers of these groups of words can well be named roots, and they must be recognized and used in philogy. But roots that once existed as such, and gave rise to languages of words in which they can still be seen,—such there never were.

* *American Anthropoligist* vol. 3 1901

Chapter-5

Nyakyusa Ritual and Symbolism

By Monica Wilson

Chapter-5

The traditional religion of the Nyakyusa people has three elements: first, there is a lively belief in the survival of the dead and in the power of senior relatives, both living and dead, over their descendants; second, there is a belief in medicines, that is, in mystical power residing in certain material substances which are used by those who have the knowledge to do so; and third, there is a belief in witchcraft, an innate power to harm others exercised by certain individuals, and in a similar power, "the breath of men," exercised by villagers to punish wrongdoers in their midst.

There are two fundamental principles of social grouping in Nyakyusa society, kinship and age (Wilson 1951), and the distinction between the ancestor cult on the one hand, and witchcraft and the breath of men on the other, coincides with these. The ancestor cult, in its domestic aspect, concerns families and lineages; and in its public aspect it concerns chiefdoms for the chieftainship is hereditary, and dead chiefs are thought to have power over the countries and people they once ruled. In the villages, however, the hereditary principle does not enter; they are formed of groups of age-mates led by one of themselves, who *must* be a commoner, and may not be the son of a village headman of the previous generation. In the villages the power of dead kinsmen does not operate; but in its place there is the "breath of men" and the power of witchcraft. Power derived from medicines, on the other hand, is thought to be exercised in all types of relationship in Nyakyusa society; it is not confined either to kinship or to age relationship in Nyakyusa society; it is not confined either to kinship or to age relationships.

The belief in the survival of the dead and the power of senior relatives is expressed in a series of elaborate rituals, one set of which is directed toward the immediate ancestors of the participants, and another set of which is directed toward the immediate ancestors of ruling chiefs, and certain distant ancestors of the chief's line, heroes in Nyakyusa history. The name of one of these heroes, Kyala, has been used by the missionaries to translate the word "God," but all the evidence available goes to show that Kyala was, traditionally, but one of several distant ancestors to whom regular sacrifices were made on behalf of a group of chiefdoms.

In Nyakyusa society there is little development of arts and crafts except in relation to building—they build substantial and beautiful huts and long houses—and the main form of artistic expression is in ritual. Rituals are frequent and elaborate; great numbers of people attend them and the excitement is often intense. At death, at puberty and marriage, at birth-particularly at twin birth, and in misfortune, family rituals are celebrated; and annually, before the break of the rains, as well as in times of drought, flood, pestilence, famine, or other public misfortune, sacrifices are made on behalf of chiefdoms and groups of chiefdoms to immediate royal ancestors and the more distant heroes. The greatest ritual of all is that performed at the handling over of power from one generation to another, but it occurs only once in thirty years.

This paper is concerned with the family rituals. It would have been better had it covered all the rituals of Nyakyusa society, or at least all the rituals of the ancestor cult, but that would have been impossible in one paper. It must be realized, however, that no one ritual among the Nyakyusa is fully intelligible without reference to the whole series of rituals. The principle, propounded long ago by Radcliffe-Brown, that a symbol recurring in a cycle of rituals is likely to have the same significance in each, holds good for the Nyakyusa: certain symbols of shaving, washing, eating, spreading banana leaves, scattering grain, and so forth were similarly interpreted by our informants in the different rituals of the cycle, and their full significance is apparent only when a comparison of their various uses is made. Therefore we must focus attention on the ritual cycle, rather than on particular events in it.

The analysis offered here is based on the Nyakyusa interpretation of symbols.[1] We were lucky, among the Nyakyusa, in finding people who could, and would, interpret most of the symbols occurring in the rituals, and their interpretations were in substantial agreement. It seemed, from the evidence collected, that certain symbols were understood by everyone, e.g., a variety of plantain, *itoki,* stands for a man, and the *isèlya,* a sweet banana eaten ripe, stands for a woman, and this symbolism is as plain to the Nyakyusa as "breeches" and "petticoats" are to us; other symbols were understood only by some people. The most conscious of them were priests and doctors: Kasitile, a hereditary rainmaker and an elderly man, was our best informant on these matters, but there were a dozen others nearly as good. Here the interpretations must be taken on trust for there is not space to quote texts, but the texts are there and will be published.

Among the quarter million of people who are Nyakyusa-or-Ngonde-speaking, or dominated by them, there are marked variations in dialect and local custom, and corresponding variations in ritual; but we found in the two groups studied in detail, the Nyakyusa proper and the Kukwe, that differing symbols expressed common ideas and sentiments, and such knowledge as we gathered of the other groups showed that, among them also, there were differences in the symbols used but a very close agreement in the ideas expressed. Local differences in the ritual idiom are taken for granted by the Nyakyusa themselves, and are related both to differences in descent and to differences in the economy of local groups. "We do this because we are Kukwe, but the Penja do it differently," and so on, and they draw direct parallels between what they do and what their neighbors do. Contrary to the commonly accepted idea that ritual is more stable than the interpretation of it, we found the same conceptions expressed in varying ritual forms. The foods used in the ritual, the symbols of separation from the dead, of the union of husband and wife-these vary from group to group; but each time there is the ritual use of the staple food, the symbolic burial and casting away of the corpse, the elaborate purification, the symbolic marriage, and so on.

The ritual performed at death is the most elaborate of the family rituals and in it themes which recur in the others are expressed most clearly, so let us begin with it. It consists of two parts: first there is the burial, to which all relatives, and all members of the deceased's village, as well as special friends from other villages, should come; then, some days later, there is the "farewell to the dead" and ritual purification, which concern only immediate agnates and the widow or widows, if the deceased is a man, and siblings, children, grandchildren and the widower, if the deceased is a married woman (cf. Wilson 1939).

As soon as someone dies the women begin wailing, and messages are sent to agnatic kinsmen, affines, and the mother's father or brother. An autopsy is performed to discover the cause of death, and later the agent is sought by divination. The grave is dug in the swept courtyard of the homestead, close to the huts, and some hours after death and corpse is buried, wrapped in cloths and facing in the direction from which his ancestors came. A few utensils are buried in the grave and these, together with the cloths, and the cattle which are sacrificed, are believed to go with the dead to the world of the shades. (Unlike the Ila, the Nyakyusa are quite explicit on this point.) At least one cow from a man's own herd is killed at his death, and his affines-the fathers (or brothers) of his wives, and the husbands of his sisters and daughters-each bring a cow or bull to kill also. For a woman, her father and her husband each provide a cow or bull. Other relatives and friends bring cloths, or barkcloth mourning belts with which to tie up the trembling bellies of the close kinsmen of the dead, and so help to assuage their grief. Crowds of relatives and neighbors gather to wail, to dance and to feast; the greater the feast, the larger the crowd, the longer the mourning, and the greater the prestige of the family concerned.

Everyone who comes goes to the hut where the corpse is lying, or has lain, and there greets the chief mourners and wails with them a little. The men soon move away to talk and dance, but most of the women remain tight-packed in and round and hut, wailing in unison, swaying as they sit, and weeping unrestrainedly. The men, for their part, express their passionate anger in the war dance, charging back and forth over the new-filled grave, brandishing spears, and ready to quarrel and fight at any moment. Funerals commonly did end in battles between contingents from different villages.

The dance is a form of mourning. "We dance because there is war in our hearts—a passion of grief and fear exasperates us." "A kinsman when he dances assuages his passionate grief; he goes into the house to weep and then comes out and dances the war dance; his passionate grief is made tolerable in the dance; it bound his heart and the dance assuages it." With their spears, the young men slash at the bananas surrounding the courtyard; they are added to the sacrificed cattle and the cloth to accompany the dead on his journey.

Women dance also, threading their way among the men and calling the war cry to urge them on. Gradually, on the second or third day after the death, the war dance merges into a dance of sexual display. To the Nyakyusa this is in no way incongruous; they hold that friends who come to mourn should not leave without encouraging the bereaved to turn their thoughts again to life and laughter. At Christian funerals, also, this is very noticeable; on the second or third day there is a switch from mourning hymns to joyful ones.

Death, to the pagan Nyakyusa, is something very fearful and later ritual is directed toward cleansing the close relatives from the contamination of death, separating them from the corpse, and pushing away the dead from their dreams and waking thoughts. At the same time it ensures the entry of the dead into the company of the shades of the lineage, and he is invited back to his homestead hearth.

If the deceased were a married man his heir is formally recognized, being put into a hut with the widows; then a plantain flower, representing the corpse, is buried. "We are saying to him, 'You corpse, we have finished with you, do not come here again, it is finished for ever, do not look toward us, go away'." The heir and widows, and certain other agnatic kin who are the principals in this ritual, wash in a running stream, wash again with medicine in the doorway of the deceased's hut, and then grovel to eat from the ground plantains set with pumpkin seeds. This symbolizes both the sexual act and the action of a madman, eating feces, and is the essential prophylactic against going mad. The deceased's hut has been strewn with dry banana leaves on which the mourners sleep and sit; until the actions of a madman have been mimed it is left unswept, but now the litter is cleared out and burned.

Relatives and neighbors bring gifts of millet "to greet the shade" (and he is notified of who has come), then there is a final cleansing, sweeping what dust remains in the mourning hut onto the legs of the principals, and passing a flat basket of millet, mixed with pumpkin seeds and lentils, between their legs. This is a symbol of sex intercourse, and of getting rid of the shade from their bodies, for the shade is within men as well as without, and is expelled in the sex fluids. They go again to a stream to bathe, and throw away a stem of plantains, a symbol of the corpse, into the water. Returning home, the participants run into the mourning hut and out again, one by one, as the officiant pours water mixed with powdered medicine on the thatch above the doorway and the water drips onto their bodies. This is interpreted as "bringing back the shade to the home again."

The actions of a madman are mimed a second time, then the participants are shaved, the heir kills another cow and is presented to the children of the deceased as their "father." They reply, "Thanks be, father has risen from the dead."

From some of the millet brought by friends and relatives a paste is made and offered to the shade as the food he ate. With the rest beer is brewed, and the participants drink it with *ikipiki* medicine representing the blood of the lineage. Then they shave their sprouting hair with the lees of the beer, and anoint themselves for the first time since the death. If the deceased were a married man, the formal handing over of the inheritance follows, and the widows are admonished on their duties to their new husband. The heir sits in the doorway of the mourning hut, the senior wife of the deceased hands him a billhook (such as is used for pruning bananas) and he is adjured by the relatives and neighbors present to care for the children of the deceased as if they were his own. Then he enters the hut with the women he has inherited, and must have intercourse with all of them that night. One of them knocks on the wall when he has succeeded and the officiant raises the trill of triumph and shakes a basket of seeds by the door shouting, "Ours, ours, we marvel at the thing." Until this ritual connection the heir and widows must remain continent.

Next morning the heir is formally summoned out of the hut by a man crying, "War has come," i.e., sex intercourse has begun. He sits on a stool in the doorway and there is greeted by the children of the deceased with, "Good morning, father."

Each of the inherited women goes off to her own father's homestead with the filth of intercourse on her and takes with herd cooked plantains which she has smeared with her husband's semen and her own emission. These she buries in the banana grove in her father's homestead in which he prays to his shades. The heir similarly goes to his father's homestead, or that of his father's heir if he be of a junior branch of the family, and buries the plantains and semen in his father's sacred grove. Each drinks beer, mixed with medicines, with his own kinsmen. If it is a woman who has died she is replaced by a younger sister or brother's daughter, or if the family has no girl to send they offer a cow to draw water with.

This is only a very sketchy account of a complex ritual, and many of the details, which confirm the interpretation, have necessarily been omitted. There are in it nine main themes:

First, the driving away of the dead from the dreams of his close kinsmen, and measures to prevent his "brooding over them"-the word is that used of a hen brooding over chickens. A widow, in particular, must be separated from the shade of her husband before the heir, or any other man, dare have intercourse with her.

Second, the identification of the mourners with the corpse, and the separation of the shade from both. "What they do to the participants they do to the deceased....If they are not cleansed he is still muddy-his fellow drive him back and say, 'You cannot come yet, you have not bathed in the river.' We throw away the corpse, the contamination of death, into the river...we drive the shade away off our bodies to join his fellows...we separate the corpse and the shade."

Third, bringing back the shade as a beneficent spirit in the home. "In the ritual we tell the shade to go away and join his fellows and then to come back with them and warm himself by the fire in our house...At first the shade is in our bodies, we cast him out...at first it is as if we were still holding the corpse in our arms, but we throw the corpse away into the river...the spirit we bring back into our house."

Fourth, a miming of the actions of a madman as a prophylactic against behavior of the sort. The dead, if not separated from the living, brings madness upon them, and simulating madness is a protection against it.

Fifth, the corpse and faces are identified: "The corpse is

filth, it is excrement. And so when a madman for whom they have not performed the ritual eats filth, that is the corpse; he is still holding it, they have not done the ritual for him."

Sixth, the shades are identified with semen and seeds, and their control over potency and fertility is recognized. The Nyakyusa think that they are always present in sexual intercourse, and symbols of sex intercourse are interpreted as a means of driving out the shade from the participants' bodies.

Seventh, the "food which he fold" is symbolically given to the shade, the man who has just died, and he is urged to be satisfied: "You shade, do not think that there was little food at your ritual....The food which we have eaten you have eaten...do not create hunger."

Eighth, the shade is acknowledged as a kinsmen by eating with him food and beer mixed with *ikipiki* medicine, the symbol of kinship, before he is driven away.

Last, a dead man is formally replaced by his heir, a woman by her sister, or brother's daughter.

There is not space to describe the other rituals of the cycle even in the sketchy way in which the funeral rites have been described. It must suffice to show that the general form of the ritual is the same at death, at puberty and marriage, and at birth.

At puberty a girl is secluded in her mother's hut. Her mothers-in-law (for traditionally she was always betrothed before puberty) come formally to lay the litter on which she sits with her maids, girls a little younger than herself. There are latter spend the greater part of the day weaving mats, dancing and singing; there they entertain young men; and there they sleep. The girl washes ritually with her husband, using *ikipiki* medicine provided by his lineage as a symbol of their marriage, and eats plantains as in the death ritual. "The medicine is to create relationship. Using it means that the bride is now of my lineage." Feasts are exchanged between the two families, hers and her husband's, and after about three months she is elaborately purified and shaved, the litter is taken out and burned, she is admonished on her duties as a married woman and cries, "Put me down, mother." When her virginity has been proved, her husband brings a bull which is killed for a feast. The sacred cut (*ijammapa*) from it is buried by her father in his banana grove, and there he prays, saying: "Here is the meat. I have eaten the food of others, *come out a little,* may she bear a child at her husband's." After she has gone to her husband, she returns with plantains mixed with the sex fluids to bury in her father's grove, just as a widow does after her union with the heir.

The birth ritual is fairly elaborate at the birth of a first child, short and simple for other children, but prolonged and complex in cases of abnormal birth, that is, twin birth or breach delivery. (The same word, *ilipasa,* is used for both and the ritual is the same.) Abnormal birth is felt to be even more dangerous and terrifying than death, and a larger circle of relatives is held to be in danger than are in danger from a corpse. Affines, and mothers' relatives as well as agnates, gather for the purification. Isolation huts are built for the parents of twins, and they are formally inducted, a ritual litter being laid for them. A very large group of relatives gathers to wash that is brewed the temporary huts are burned, the parents and wins and relatives are shaved and anointed, splashed with scalding medicine, and given sausages of medicated porridge which they must eat from the ground. The parents have ritual intercourse and a mess of plantains is taken by the mother of twins of her father's grove, as by a bride or widow.

There are appreciable differences between the various rituals of the cycle: at death there is the wailing and burial; at puberty and marriage and rejoicing, the celebration of virginity; at birth an elaboration of taboos for the mother before her confinement; but here, in the space-available, attention is directed to the *common content* of the rituals, the common symbolic pattern.

The framework of all the rituals is the "induction" (*ukwingesia*) with a formal laying of the litter of banana leaves in a hut into which the participant is brought to live apart from other people; the retreat or "seclusion" during which he or she lives and eats apart and is regarded as filthy, for she is "brooded over" by the shades; and the "bringing out" (*ukusosya*) when the shades are driven away and she is purified.[2] During the seclusion the participant is not only filthy but *may not* wash or shave or use cosmetics; in the death ritual she embraces the corpse, smears herself with mud and ash, and mimes the actions of a madman. The madman is filthy like a corpse and so is the mourner. In the other rituals also the participant is filthy, brooded over by the shades, in danger of madness.

The symbols of purification are many: clearing and burying the litter; burning the clothes or leaves worn during the seclusion; elaborate and repeated washing and shaving; anointing the body with oil and rouge; and casting away some representation of the shade.

An element of the death ritual is the separation of the corpse and spirit, the final disposal of the corpse, and the bringing of the new shade back "to warm himself with the other shades" at the family hearth; but the distinction between the corpse which is got rid of, and the shade which is welcomed, is not maintained systematically. Repeatedly our informants spoke of the shade (*unsyuka*) being driven away from dreams and waking thought, and from men's bodies, as well as being separated from the corpse. The aim of Nyakyusa ritual is not that union with God, constantly sought in Christian ritual, but a separation, for close association with the pagan gods spells madness but death, not fullness of life. A measure of separation from the shades is a condition of fertility as well as of sanity.

Intercourse cannot be fruitful until the shades of her father's linease have "moved aside a little" from the nubile girl, the shade of a deceased husband from his widow.

All through the rituals the connection of the shades with potency and fertility is emphasized. The shades cause menstruation and sexual desire; they are present in intercourse and ejected as semen; they control conception; they control fertility in the fields. "The shade and the semen are brothers." "When they shake the millet and pumpkin seeds (after ritual connection) the seed is the semen...and it is the shade." The symbols of male and female, plantain and sweet banana (*itoki* and *iselya*), recur repeatedly, and the wearing of leaves of these plants is explicitly interpreted as a symbol of fertility. Intercourse between husband and wife is the culmination of the rituals of death, puberty, marriage, and abnormal birth, and is held to be essential to the health of the wife or the widow (even though she be old) as well as proof of the support of the shades for the husband or heir. A symbol of the ritual connection is offered to the shades of both lineages. Indeed the rituals of death and abnormal birth, as well as ritual of puberty and marriage, may be interpreted as a celebration of the union of husband and wife. For the parents of twins the end of the ritual marks the resumption of married life after a break during which contact between them was felt to be dangerous; for a widow and the heir of a dead man the end of the death ritual marks the beginning of their union. The manner in which a widow or the mother of twins, is admonished on her proper behavior as a wife, like a girl at her first marriage, underlines the fact that the death and birth rituals are, in a sense, also marriage rituals.

The virility of a lineage is symbolized by the *ikipiki* medicine interpreted as "our blood" or "semen." With it mourners, menstruating girls, bride and groom, the newborn babies and their mothers, and treated. To provide it or use it is to acknowledge kinship; husband and wife wash with it together in acknowledgement that the wife is now "one blood" with her husband; the grandmother washes her son's child with it in acknowledgement of its legitimacy; in the death rituals the mourners eat food with it acknowledging their kinship with the shade. To belong to a lineage is to be protected, and the *ikipiki* medicine is held to protect those who are empty from those who are heavy with real semen, or other medicines.

The shade, *unsyuka,* "he who is risen from the dead," may be interpreted as the principle of life, but at the same time he is "the one beneath" (*ugwa pasi*), filthy and fearful. What men worship is life; what they fear is death, corruption; and for the Nyakyusa, as for the Christian, the two are inextricably mingled. *I mindu* means dirt, dust, rubbish, the litter of the seclusion hut, and also the shade.

I have spoken of the Nyakyusa disgust of filth (*ubunyali*) which is associated with a corpse, menstruation, childbirth, intercourse, and feces, and all these are identified in some fashion with the shade. Feces "go below to the land of the shades." "The hair of a corpse is the shade's," the hair of a girl at puberty is "the filth of her menstrual blood." In all the rituals the "filth" is buried, shaved off, burned, washed away. At the death ritual "he who is risen" is brought to "warm himself" at the family hearth, but yet he dwells in the earth and is "dirty."

The conception of impurity, uncleanness, associated with the physiological functions of coition, excretion, menstruation, and with childbirth and death is, of course, a very widespread one. The Nyakyusa perhaps emphasize it more than their neighbors (though not more than the Jews or the Hindus) and their preoccupation with purification in the rituals is paralleled by the emphasis laid on cleanliness (*ubwifyusi*) in person, in house and courtyard, in cooking, and in disposal of excrement. Their extreme cleanliness, in contrast with their neighbors, was remarked by all the early travellers in the area and is still obvious. Houses and courtyards are swept and garnished, pots and dishes scoured, food housewife is *umwifyusi,* she who is clean. Men wash daily in running water, and children are trained to take a hoe with them when they go to defecate and to bury the feces.

The horror of filth is very closely associated with the fear of madness, which is, at the same time, a fear of too close association with the dead. It is when the dead have not been driven away, but return in dreams, when the necessary separation of living and dead has not been achieved, that men go mad. Madness is most often spoken of as the penalty for neglect of the death ritual, but it is not, in theory, confined to that. "All the rituals are the same if they are neglected men will become mad."

Besides madness, men fear sterility, debility, swollen limbs, and diarrhea "to get rid of the filth in the belly," if the rituals are neglected or taboos broken.

The Nature of Symbolism in Nyakyusa Ritual

Symbolism is always based on an association, a feeling of likeness between things. The intrinsic quality of an object or relationship, or event, is expressed in terms of another object or action which it is felt to resemble. The images men use, the things they feel to be alike, are determined in a general way by the form of the society: the poetry of Louis MacNeice, for example, could only be that of an industrialized society, and Nyakyusa images are in terms of bananas, staple grains, something on a primitive forge, lineage organization, and so on. There are "cultural idioms," accepted forms of expression, which frequently recur—we talk in terms of breeches and petticoats, whereas the Nyakyusa talk in terms of plantains and sweet bananas—and these one can learn. We can understand, when it is explained, that the *ikipiki* is a symbol for the blood of a lineage, that washing under a waterfall, or lying in a stream and letting pebbles flow between fingers and toes, are symbols of purification, and so on. But though one learns the symbolism of a culture as one learns the language, and is aware that certain forms of expression are common, one cannot predict with certainty what symbols will be used in a ritual, any more than one can predict what symbols a poet will use.

The symbolism of Nyakyusa ritual, and indeed all magical symbolism, differs in this way from the symbolism of poetry: in a magical ritual things felt to be like are taken as causally connected, whereas in poetry they are just a liked and that's all. In the rituals, the participants mime madness as a prophylactic against it; the pregnant woman does not linger in the doorway lest the child do likewise and delivery be protracted; the woman who is sleeping with her husband does not approach a smithy, for sex intercourse and smiting are alike and antagonistic.

This brings us to the next point: sometimes like produces like, as with the hesitation in the doorway or the "fierceness" or a pregnant woman which makes the game "fierce" if her husband goes hunting; and sometimes like things or actions are taken as antagonistic, as something and intercourse, seed in the belly and seed in the ground, war and "war of the mats," that is, sex intercourse. Within the field of anthropology I do not think that there are any rules, any general principles to be found, which would explain why some things are taken as sympathetic and others as antagonistic, or even why certain things are selected as like. It depends upon how the poet felt when he created his image, for the diviner or doctor who creates new ritual by modifying the old is, in this sense, a poet.

I have drawn the analogy with poetry. It is scarcely necessary to add that the same conception—purification, madness, what you will—is symbolized in many ways, and that the same symbol may present several things to the same person.

ANALYSIS

Now we come to the deeper analysis: what do the rituals really express? The recurring symbols of Nyakyusa society have been indicated and interpreted. What ideas and attitudes underlie them?

The funeral rites are an adjustment to death through a violent expression of grief, a passionate fighting of death itself, and an assertion of life expressed in dancing, flirting, feasting on meat, deliberately attempting to push away the dead from dreams and waking thoughts, replacing and dead through the levitate or sororate,[3] and finally, seeking a scapegoat.[4] The mourners are supported by all their relatives and neighbors who must gather to weep with them and also have the obligation of cheering them before they scatter.

All the rituals, including the death ritual itself, are an assertion of the supreme importance of procreation. Reproductive power is treated as sacred, hedged about with taboos, controlled by the shades; the climax of each ritual is the meeting of husband and wife, or wives; the overt purpose health and fertility.

One manifestation of the sacredness of the reproductive cycle is that it is polluting. All the physiological functions are felt to be polluting: the shade are associated with the corpse, and with procreation, and they are filthy, unclean. Those undergoing a ritual who are "brooded upon by the shades" are also unclean, and *may not* cleanse themselves until the ritual enjoins it. Madness comes from the failure to purify oneself in the ritual, to separate from the shades. This sense of pollution, and the horror of madness with which it is linked among the Nyakyusa,is an expression of fear, and comes very close to the sense of awe; what Otto called the "Idea of the Holy." Whether or not the sense of pollution is also linked with a sense of guilt I do not know. The Freudians would assuredly interpret it in that way, but I have no evidence that the Nyakyusa feel guilty. Of their terror at death and abnormal birth, and in a lesser degree of ordinary birth and menstruation, there is no doubt. All these are felt to be polluting.

The mutual dependence of kin, living and dead, is expressed again and again. Kinsmen are "members of one another" in the sense that the death of a kinsman, or the birth of twins to a kinsman or kinswoman, affects an individual directly. Health and sanity are thought to depend upon the performance of rituals with kin; procreation the fertility of fields are controlled by dead kinsmen. The separation and linking of lineages is also expressed in the conception of the *ikipiki* medicine, the "blood of the lineage," and the mess of plantains taken by a woman to bury in her father's banana grove. The differentiation of male and female, of lineages, and of local groups, is expressed in terms of crops and of cattle: what is *not* reflected in the family rituals is the age structure. It is the development of the individual rather than organized age groups which is symbolized.

All the rituals are a public and formal expression of change in status; a breaking off an old relationship which is incompatible with the new. The dead man joins his fathers as a shade; his widow pushes him away-to separate from him is a condition of her remarriage. The maid is acknowledged as a married woman, of one blood with her husband, and the shades of her father's lineage must "move aside a little." It is the end of childhood and dependence upon her parents. The newborn infant is accepted as a member of its father's lineage; until the birth ritual is performed it is not treated as a person or acknowledged as a kinsman, and at the end of the ritual the mother, who has been separated from her husband, returns to him.

Last, there is reflected in the rituals the value set on cattle, and the dependence upon bananas and on staple grains and relishes. The dead must take cattle with them if they are to be received by the shades; sacrifices offered them are primarily of beef and millet beer, and these are offered in the banana grove.

It has been clear, since the publications of the *Andaman Islanders,*[5] that rituals both arouse and canalize emotion; they teach men to feel and teach them what to feel. The family rituals of the Nyakyusa occur when emotions are aroused anyway, at the crises of life, and they enhance and direct these emotions.

Terror at the death of their kind is common enough in animals, and it is reasonable to assume that men have an instinctive fear of a corpse, but the society may play this up or minimize it. Nyakyusa society plays it up—men tremble at death—they are expected to do so—and in the ritual they receive comfort and reassurance. They turn from death to life. I suggest that there may also be an instinctive basis for terror at birth; that the cow or bitch in labor is a terrified animal. However that may be, in Nyakyusa society the re-productive process is felt to be fearful, and most of all an abnormal birth. Nyakyusa Christians are quick to point out that they do not fear death, or birth, or menstruation, as the pagans do—they disregard many if not all of the traditional taboos-and that the pagans themselves fear much less than formerly; in other words, that the fear is culturally determined, or at least *enhanced.*

In all the rituals the expression of certain sentiments is compulsory, whatever the individual may feel. Nyakyusa women commented freely on the fact that certain widows were not really grieved at their husbands' deaths: "Perhaps they are just thinking about whom they will marry next," they said, "but still they must wail and smear themselves with mud and ashes." And the expression itself tends to induce the appropriate feeling. Even to an outsider the pressure of the ritual is strong: the sense and grief when you are in the midst of a throng of women, close-packed, and weeping and wailing, is intense.

Radcliffe-Brown (1952:157) has argued not only that rituals develop certain sentiments in the minds of individuals, but that a society depends for its existence on the presence of these sentiments. It can, I think, be shown that the sentiments expressed in the Nyakyusa ritual are those necessary to the continuance of the society.

In every society men must overcome death, emotionally; they must turn to life. In the death ritual the mourners are distraught, terrified. They express their grief and put it behind them; their relatives and neighbors rally round them, share their sorrow, and help them to overcome it. It is true that the ritual enhance fear, but it also overcomes it (cf. Homans 1941). It is no accident that the Nyakyusa interpret all the rituals, and especially the death ritual, as a protection against going mad, against the disintegration of the personality.

And why should the death ritual enhance fear? Why not play it down? Because in their terror people are made to realize their dependence upon their kinsmen for cooperation in performing the ritual, and the necessity for following traditional custom. All the family rituals of the Nyakyusa enhance fear and make men turn to their kinsmen and to traditional observance to relieve it. The sense of awe (which is linked with the idea of pollution) expresses dependence upon the gods, the ancestors, and so upon kinsmen. In short, fear makes for the solidarity of the kinship group, and for cultural continuity. It is also apparent that fear of supernatural sanctions helps to maintain order in Nyakyusa society. The fear of the gods makes men "walk humbly and do justly." And in so far as the rituals nourish the sense of awe, they strengthen the force of supernatural sanctions.

The public acknowledgement of change in status, of new responsibilities expressed very pointedly in the adominition, impresses on individuals their changing obligations within the kinship group. The rituals are a symbolic weaning from childhood, from a former marriage, or from deceased parents, and compel acceptance of a new position.

Societies depend not only on sentiments of mutual dependence among their members, but also on their physical survival-on the will for reproduction among them. Certain groups seem to lose this, though we know little of the reasons why they do so. The Nyakyusa rituals express the supreme importance of procreation and regulate it. Procreation outside marriage is mystically dangerous, pregnancies are deliberately spaced, and the reproductive life of women limited by certain taboos. Thus conception is confined to the times when the chances for the child's survival are best, and the care of children in a family is ensured.

The word *ritual* has been used all through this paper and no reference has been made to ceremonial. I make a distinction between the two (Wilson 1939), using ritual to mean a primarily religious action, that is, an action directed to secure the blessing of some mystical power or powers. The action may be a negative, i.e., an avoidance or taboo, as well as a positive one. Symbols and concepts are employed in rituals, but are subordinated to practical ends. Ceremonial on the other hand, is an elaborate conventional form for the expression of feeling, not confined to religious occasions; any emotional situation, whether religious or secular, may be clothed in ceremony, and a ceremony is not enforced by mystical sanctions, only by conventional ones. In short, a ceremony is an appropriate and elaborate form for the expression of feeling, but a ritual is action believed to be efficacious. A ritual is often embedded in ceremonial which is not held to be necessary to the efficacy of the ritual but which is felt to be appropriate. Both ritual and ceremonial have a function in rousing and canalizing emotion, but ritual, by relating its symbols to some supposed transcendental reality, affects people more deeply than a ceremony, which some will describe as "mere play-acting."

Finally, I hold that rituals reveal values at the deepest level. There is much woolly talk of values and of how to study them, of how to achieve system and objectivity in the observation of them. Surely men express in ritual what moves them most, and since the form of expression is conventionalized and obligatory, it is the values of the group which are revealed. I see in the study of rituals the key to an understanding of the essential constitution of human societies.

FOOT NOTES

1. The field material on which this was based was collected by my late husband, Godfrey Wilson, and myself, between 1934 and 1938. We were indebted to the Rockefeller Foundation and the International African Institute for research fellowships.
2. Though the classic form of the *rite de passage* adumbrated by Van Gennep holds good, change in status is only one of several themes.
3. Sororate is used here to mean the replacement of a dead wife by her sister or other kins-woman, and distinguished from sororal polygany, the marriage of two sisters simultaneously.
4. The reactions to death postulated by Ruth Benedict as characteristic of different societies occur successively in Nyakyusa ritual. Cf. *Patterns of Culture, passim.*
5. My debt to Radcliffie-Brown in this analysis will be obvious to all students of anthropology.

REFERENCES CITED

HOMANS G.

1941, Anxiety and ritual: the theories of Malinowski and Radcliffie-Brown. American Anthropologist 43, No. 5:164-72. Menasha.

MACNEICE, LOUIS,

1949, Collected poems 1925-1948. London, Faber & Faber.

OTTO, R.

1926 The idea of the holy. London, Oxford University Press.

RADCLIFFE-BROWN, A.R.

1952 Structure and function in primitive society. London, Cohen & West.

VAN GENNEP. A.

1909 Les riets de passage. Paris, E. Nourry.

WILSON G.

1939 Nyakyusa conventions of burial. Bantu Studies 13:1-31. Johannesburg. South Africa.

WILSON, M.

1951 Good company: a study of Nyakyusa age-villages. London, Oxford University Press.

* *American Anthropoligist.* vol. 56. 1954

Chapter-6

Spatial Concepts of the Ainu of the Northwest Coast of Southern Sakhalin[1]

By Emiko Ohnuki-Tierney

Chapter-6

Presented here is the basic cognitive structure underlying the concepts of space among the Ainu of the northwest coast of southern Sakhalin, now resettled in Hokkaido. The spatial structure is examined by analyzing cultural meanings attached to the spatial categories and directions. The basic spatial structure may be best understood as a dyadic structure comprising a series of contrast sets in binary opposition, with the super-Ainu quality as the minimal distinctive feature.

I

This study represents an attempt to analyze the basic structure which underlies the spatial conception of the universe of the Ainu of the northwest coast of southern Sakhalin.

The study of space is a part of my work on the view of the universe, or, world view, which also includes the analyses of the temporal conception, the beings of the universe and communication among these beings. A preliminary analyses of the entirety of the world view is presented in Ohnuki-Tierney (1968), which is based on data obtained from fieldwork during 1965 and 1966 and a brief report on the temporal concept is published (Ohnuki-Tierney 1969a).

My discussion is based primarily on information gathered from Husko,[2] a gifted Sakhalin Ainu woman born around 1900, during fieldwork in 1965 and 1966, and three months in 1969. She is the only survivor who can coherently relate the life of the Sakhalin Ainu,[3] who occupied the northwest, coast of southern Sakhalin, where Japanese influence was not significant until the beginning of World War II.[4] The Sakhalin Ainu were relocated in Hokkaido at the end of World War II when southern Sakhalin was claimed by the USSR.

The following discussion thus represents the universe as seen by a single culture carrier. The positive side of using a single informant is that it allows the researcher to study in depth the whole cognitive structure of the culture carrier, rather than being forced to a common denominator, as in the case in most studies of world view which involve more than one individual since the cognitive structure of every culture carrier differ to some extent from those of his fellow man (Wallace 1964, ch. 1, esp. 31-41).

The assumption that man tends to classify his behavioral environment, as used in his study, often invites criticism that the researcher somehow distorts the data to fit into his classificatory system, rather than inductively arriving at the classificatory structure as consciously or unconsciously conceived by the people. For this reason, I have tried to distinguish carefully between what constitutes data and what comprises my interpretations.

My key informant Husko usually provided the best information when she volunteered it rather than responding to specific questions. During my fieldwork in 1965 and 1966, she provided so much information that I was usually on the receiving end. During my 1969 fieldwork, however, her voluntary information tended to be redundant, and thus I often structured my interview. Although my questions did not always stimulate satisfactory answers, the information I received in response to carefully constructed questions was exceedingly helpful. Her responses helped to explain more thoroughly what she had told me during my previous fieldwork, and at times they turned out to be a completely new set of data which otherwise might not have been uncovered.

Since this study of space represents a part of a study of

world view, its scope is necessarily limited to an analyses of spatial concepts as they are related to the structure of the universe. It is, therefore, not a study in proxemies which requires a more psychological approach.

My discussion of Ainu spatial concepts begins with a brief presentation of the framework of the Ainu universe. Next, I shall discuss the divisions of the horizontal plane of the universe in order to examine the cultural meanings of these divisions. Following is another attempt to examine the horizontal plane by analyzing the spatial arrangements of the Ainu house, which the Ainu consider to be a miniature universe. Then the directional terms of the horizontal plane are examined in order further to understand the cultural meanings assigned to these directions and the spatial categories which correspond to each direction. Then the vertical plane and its directional terms are examined in order to arrive at the categories and meanings of the vertical plane. Lastly, the possible locations of various enclaves of the universe are examined. These enclaves include the world of the dead Ainu, the worlds of the living and dead deities, the worlds of the demons, and worlds of the dead members of various beings of the universe. These worlds are believed to be invisible to ordinary living Ainu.

In the following, unless otherwise specified, the term "Ainu" means those Ainu who inhabited the northwest coasts of southern Sakhalin, north of *Rayviska* (Japanese call it Raichishika) to the former Russo-Japanese border, between 1900 and 1945.

II

The northwest coast Sakhalin Ainu term *mosiri* (universe) in its essential sense means the total sphere of physical and mental activities and phenomena.[5] It is the area inhabited by the Sakhalin Ainu, both living and dead, their deities, demons, and various other beings, all of which constitute the members of one society-the society of the universe; it is, from our point of view, southern Sakhalin, the adjacent sea and the atmosphere above. In fact, *mosiri* is the only term which the Ainu use as the designation for their country, or southern Sakhalin as we regard it.

The Ainu at present as well as in the past have had knowledge of other peoples on Sakhalin and, perhaps, elsewhere. The Ainu had long been in contact with other peoples engaged in the trade system, called the Santan trade, which had its northwestern end in Manchuria and its southern end on the Japanese mainland. The Ainu may have been involved in that trade since the seventh century or possibly earlier.[6] However, they are referring to an area where the Ainu are the only people. In this paper, I shall discuss the universe which is occupied exclusively by the Ainu.

The universe is characterized temporally by life cycles. Each cycle has the beginning, the middle, and the end, after which the universe is reborn (or *yayasirika*) and starts a new cycle. At the beginning and the end of each cycle, the state of some phenomenon was and would be the reversal of the one at the middle. Pertinent to the discussion of space is that sea and the mountains exchange their locations. In this paper, I shall discuss the spatial structure of the middle period of the universe; it is the state of the universe which the present day Ainu and their immediate ancestors have known.

III

Presented in this section are the major divisions of the horizontal plane. The focus of these analyses is on the the cultural meaning attached to the divisions. The essential features of the horizontal plane of the universe, are schemetically presented in Figure 1.

The general structure of the settlement and its location in reference to the surrounding nature, as presented in Figure 1, are shared by all the settlements, where my informant

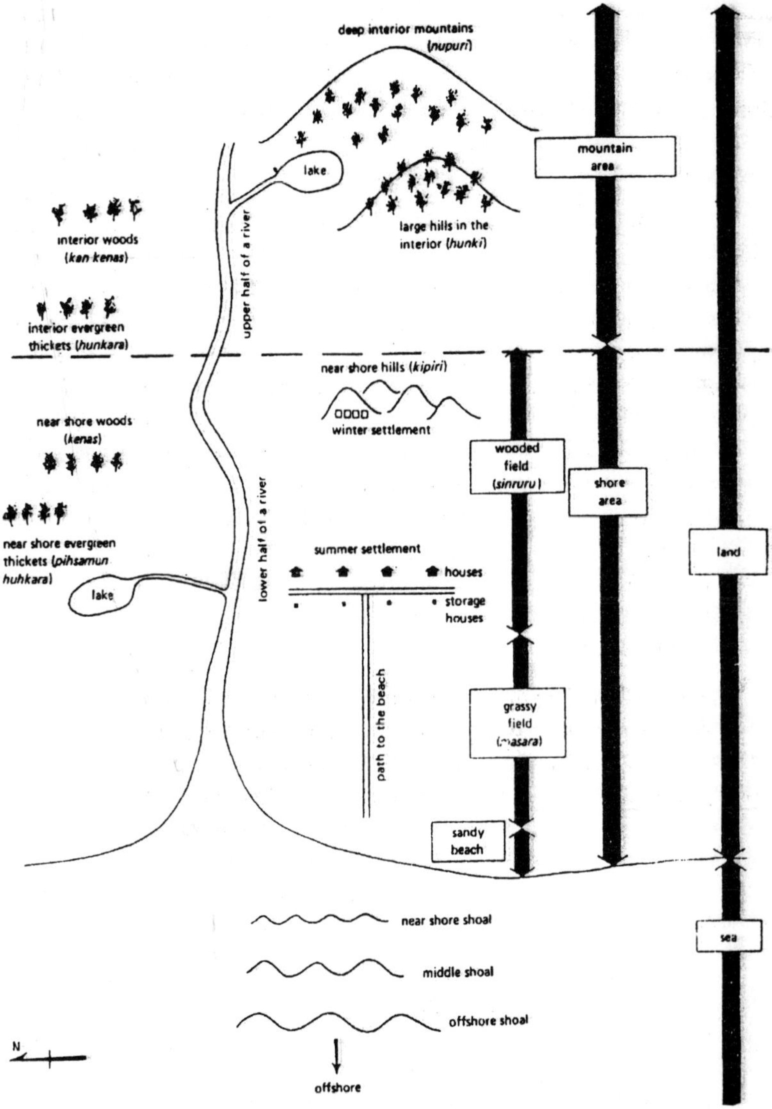

FIG. 1 The Horizontal plane of the universe.

Husko either lived or visited: several on the northwest coast, one on the southwest coast, and one in the east. According to Yamamoto's excellent sketches of the summer settlements at *Tarantomari* on the southwest coast and Shirahama on the east coast (Yamamoto 1943:55:56), these features are also shared by other Shakalin Ainu settlements.

The Ainu first divide the horizontal plane into land and sea. This division seems to be one of the familiar and unfamiliar. Thus terms which have ya (land) in their stem refer to the speaker's own people or place. For example, *yaun kotan* means "our settlement" or "our country." In contrast, terms with *rupan* (offshore or offshore area) refer to non-Ainu peoples or places. *Repun aynu,* as an example, means "foreigner." Of course, the Ainu live on the land, while the lands of other peoples are located beyond the offshore sea. Since the Ainu seem to consider that the offshore area represents the entire sea, this discussion indicates that the Ainu distinction between land and sea symbolizes their distinction between "we" and "you," or between the "Ainu" and "non-Ainu."

The major division of land is one into the shore area and the mountain area (see Figure 1). Husko clearly described this division, thus indicating that the division is a conscious one. She said that the shore area includes the shore and the relatively flat land with some trees and shrubberies, called *sinruru.* The mountain area, called *kimun,* on the other hand, includes the remaining flat land and the mountains themselves. There is no general term for the shore area.

Dividing land into the shore area and the mountain area is also seen in the way the Ainu classify some of their natural phenomena. The elevated area, i.e., hills and mountains, as well as wooded areas, receive different designations as well as different characterizations depending upon whether they are located in the shore area or in the mountain area.

The elevated land in the shore area is thus called *kipiri*, roughly translated as a hill, whereas the elevated land in the mountain area is called either *hunki* or *nupuri*. Although *kipiri* is usually the smallest, *hunk* next in size, and *nupuri* the largest, the primary distinction, according to the Ainu, is not the height of the elevated land but its distance from the sea. The farther from the shore, the more respect they receive.

Likewise, evergreen thickets on the shore are called *pihsamun hunkara* or *otaka un hunkara* (both *pihsamun* and *otaka un* mean "located on the shore"), whereas those in the mountain area are called simply *hunkara*. Thickets with various types of trees in the shore area are called *kenasi*, and those in the mountain area are called *kan kenasi* (*kan* means "upper" or "above). Of all the wooded areas, *kan kenasi* are most valuable to and respected by the Ainu.

The shore area is further divided into three parts: the sandy beach called *oya;* fields with shrubs and grasses, called *masara;* and fields with trees, called *sinruru*. I shall refer to *masara* as the grassy fields and *sinrur* as the wooded fields. Not everywhere on the northwest coast is there a gradual elevation of land from the sea toward the mountains, and thus there are often neither sandy beaches nor grassy fields. However, most of the Ainu settlements are located in areas which have all of these three divisions, since each provides important economic resources for the Ainu.

Both the summer and winter settlements are located in the wooded fields. In the summer settlements, the Ainu houses are built on a line parallel to the shorelinc on the part of the wooded field closest to the grassy field. The winter houses, called *riya cise*, are made by digging into the hills (*kipiri*) in the wooded area near the shore. Also located in the wooded field is the settlment's cemetery (*hamaskari usi*). It is situated some distance from the settlement in the wooded field. Lakes are often found in the shore area, as in the case of the *Rayviska* settlement where the lake is close to the sea.

Since the settlement is located on the shore, the shore area becomes the focus for daily activities of the Ainu. In their subsistence economy, however, most of the activities on the shore are women's work. The gathering of plants for food as well as for medicinal purposes is the responsibility of the women, although men are not forbidden to participate, if they so choose. The women gather plants in the grassy fields and the wooded fields plants in the wooded areas in the mountains.

Another economic activity of Ainu women is the gathering of dead fish, marine birds, sea mammals, and sea weeds washed ashore on the sandy beach. In the morning, the first work for Ainu women is to go down the path which connects the settlement with the beach to gather these dead though fresh animals, and plants from the sea. During the season, fish often come in abundance along the shoreline, so women simply scoop them up with their hands, or use small baskets. This part of the sandy beach, which is covered with water during high tide but is exposed during low tide, is the most important part of the beach. It is differentiated from the rest of the sandy beach and is called *pe:cara,* while the rest is called *ota noskekehe* (middle or center of the sandy beach).

Outside occasional kills of bears and other animals who wander onto the shore, the hunting and trapping in the shore area are confined to rabbits and birds. The rabbits, whose meat as well as fur are important to the Ainu, are often trapped by women. Birds are of little economic importance to Ainu life, and men only occasionally shoot them.

Along the man-made portion of the settlement the lakes are found. The Ainu engage extensively in net fishing when the lakes are not frozen. They ice-fish when the lakes are frozen but the ice is not too thick. A significant factor in lake fishing is that the women are allowed to fish as well as row the boats for the male fishermen. Both are strictly forbidden to women in sea fishing. It may be that the Ainu assign the shore area to women and thus allow women to fish on lakes which are often located on the shore. Women also gather plant food on the lake shore.

My discussion now turns to the deities who reside in the shore area. Just as female economic actitivities strongly characterize the shore area, a female deity, the Goddess of the Hearth, dominates other deities on the shore. Not only are all the shamanistic rituals dedicated to her, she is also addressed during all the Ainu rituals because she is the mediator between the Ainu and other deities. The ash renewal rites, which ensure the rebirth of the Goddess, are important Ainu religious rites.

The relationship between the Goddess of the Hearth and the shore needs further consideration. As we shall see in section IV, the Ainu house is conceived as a miniature universe. The Goddess of the Hearth is most directly associated with the hearth, which is believed to be the heart of the house. Therefore, the Goddess seems to represent the house, and hence the shore area, in one sense, but the universe in the other.

Other deities in the shore area include the deity of the ground, *Itarakoro Kamuy,* and the deity of the settlement, *Kotankoro Kamuy.* On the northwest coast, however, these deities receive little attention.

This information about the shore area seems to indicate that it is an Ainu area. With the settlement being located on the shore, much of Ainu life centers around this area. However, in viewing the subsistence economy, the female activities predominate. Moreover, the pre-eminence of the Goddess of Hearth over all other deities in the shore area seem to reinforce the interpretation that the Ainu assign the shore area to females. Besides, the Ainu house on the shore is considered as a miniature universe.

Now the other half of the land, namely the mountain area, must be examined. Of the two elevated sections of the mountain area, *hunki* (a large hill) is close to the shore, smaller in size, and has trees extending to its top. Because it has trees at its top, a *hunki* is also called *nius nupuri* (interior mountain with trees). However, Husko specifically mentioned that a *hunki* is not a true *nupuri,* or a deep mountain in the interior. The *nupuri,* on the other hand, is farthest from the shore, largest in size, and only has trees on its lower slope. I shall use approximate translations of these terms and refer to *hunki* as large hills and *nupuri* as deep mountains.

Although both the large hills and deep mountains offer good hunting game and useful trees, and deep mountains are especially respected by the Ainu. Hunters must perform a ritual of making and offering *inaw* (ritual sticks with wood shavings) to the mountain deities before they go to a deep mountain; otherwise mist will descend from its top, and the hunters will not be able to climb it. Women are strictly forbidden to approach the deep mountains. The large hills, on the other hand, do not require that men perform such rites before going hunting there. Although women ordinarily do not go to the large hills because they are forbidden to hunt, they can climb a large hill when it is necessary for them during their travel.

In these two types of interior mountains, the Ainu hunters seek important game such as bears, marten, reindeer, and musk deer.[7] Marten hunting is especially important due to the value of marten fur as a trade item. In the beginning of the cold season, the hunters build temporary huts for a prolonged stay in the mountains for marten hunting. This animal is caught primarily in the rivers in the mountains. They hibernate in dens which are dug in the slope of a large hill. In these dens, bear cubs are caught by Ainu hunters and then raised for the bear ceremony.

The thickets composed of miscellaneous trees in the mountain area are called *kan kanasi,* and form the most important type of wooded area for the Ainu, for in it are found such evergreens as Yesso spruce and Sakhalin fir, as well as white birch and elm;[8] all are considered precious by the Ainu. Moreover, it is in the *kan kenasi* where bears, the most important group of deities and also the most important food resource, are abundantly found. They are especially visible in the early spring when there are few fish to eat in the rivers. Also in these thickets are an abundant supply of edible plants such as corydalis, Kamchatka lily, peony, asparagus, and leek.[9] The Ainu use the roots of the first four plants. Thus Ainu women frequent the woods despite the danger of bears in order to gather these edible plants. These thickets, however, are unimportant in the gathering of useful grasses, which are far more abundant in the shore area.

Although they are not as important as the *kan kenasi,* the *huhkara* or evergreen thickets, in the mountain area, have some economic value. Important evergreens such as Yesso spruce and fir and found there. Various types of berries are also abundant in this type of thicket, and the women gather them not only for immediate use but to dry them for their winter supply. The men trap and hunt squirrels,[10] martens, reindeer, and some bears, although the bears are far less numerous in the *huhkara* than in the *kan kenasi.*

There are a few other areas of vegetation in the mountain area which the Ainu differentiate from the regular *kan kenasi* and *huhkara.* The grass land at the edge of the *kan kenasi* is called *nitah.* It is a good place for women to gather good leek and cow parsnips.[11] If the flat land between two large hills is a boggy area coveredwith mosses and lichens,[12] it is specified by the designation *nuh.* Women go there to gather cranberries and raspberries,[13] which are abundant in the area. Men hunt for reindeer which frequently roam in the area, grazing on mosses and lichens. There larch[14] predominates, although some white birch also grows in the thickets; both of these trees are frequently used for various purposes. Women gather raspberries and some vacciniaceous berries here.[15] Cotton grass[16] found in the larch thickets is of better quality than that found elsewhere, and women eagerly gather them for use in their shoes as insulation.

In addition to considering the mountain area as the home of abundant game, good trees, and some plants, the Ainu regard it as the home of all the mountain deities, i.e., the land animals which are considered to be deities. These deities, which are collectively called *kimun kamuy* (mountain deities), are considered to be male.[17]

The Ainu believe that all important things ultimately belong in the mountains. This idea is expressed by the term *makoraye* (ultimately return or belong to), and a part of this verb is *mak,* which means "interior."

The Ainu notion of *makoraye* is most vividly expressed is the bear ceremony. The Ainu repeatedly emphasize that the purpose of this ceremony is to return the bear to the mountains where it belongs (*makoraye*); this can only be achieved by killing the bear so that its soul is released to travel to the mountains where it somehow rejoins its body. In fact, all of the worlds of dead deities, including that for the bears, are considered to be located in the mountains. Therefore, all the bones of the important land mammals are brought to certain locations in evergreen thickets in the mountain area. Proper treatment of the bones assures the well-being of the souls of dead animals. Even the world after death for kitchen utensils is in a small lake high on a deep interior mountain.

The above description of the mountain area indicates that activities in the mountain area belong primarliy to men. This is in contrast to be shore area which is characterized by female economic activities. Thus, hunting and cutting trees, both done by males, are the most important activities in the mountain area. Although the women gather plants in the woods in the mountain areas, it is a minor economic activity in contrast to hunting and lumbering.

The foregoing discussion considered the two categories of land: the shore and the mountains. The division of land into these two areas is seen also in the division of rivers, which run through both areas, into an upper and lower part.

The Ainu use a pair of terms, *penram* and *panram,* in differentiating the two parts. The terms *penram* and *panram* originally referred to the upper and lower parts of the human body. The Ainu divide the human body into the *penram,* which includes all the body above the *uto otuy* (the lower-most rib), and the *panram,* which includes the parts below the *uto otuy.* Since the Ainu consider the head and heart as the most critical parts of the body, the upper half of the body, which includes these two parts, is considered more important than the lower part.

The Ainu believe that a river enters land and flows up toward the mountains, rather than flowing down from the mountains. The source of a river in the mountains, then, is the head of the body and is called *nay sapa.* Consequently, the upper half of the stream is called the upper part of the body or *nay penram.*

The lower part of the body of a river lies in the shore area. The part which lies just before the river mouth is sometimes specified as the shin of the river, or *nay kuhnisah.* It usually lies in the grassy field next to a sandy beach. Since the body of a river lies with its head in the mountains, the entrance part at the sandy beach is called the public region of the river (*nay opuh*). Here Chiri's information about the Ainu concept of rivers helps to explain the use of the term *nay opuh.* He states that the Ainu during the aboriginal times considered a river as a woman. Thus the Ainu considered what we call a river mouth as the vulva (Chiri 1954a:460). Another designation for this part of a river is *nay caruhu*, the river mouth. Chiri suggests that the concept of a river as a woman lying with her head toward the mountains is a traditional one, while later the Ainu started to refer to the part next to the sea as "river mouth" (Chiri 1954a:457-460). It may be that the Japanese use of the phrase the river mouth may have influenced the Ainu.

The qualitative dichotomy of the two parts of a river is well illustrated in the following tale in which the upper part of a river is associated with super-Ainu quality and old age.

The tale concerns three brothers and a demon rat. The oldest brother is called *Penke an kuh,* because he lives along the upper part of a river. The second brother lives along the middle reaches of a river and hence is called *Nuthom un kuh.* The youngest lives along the lower reaches of a river and is referred to as *Panke an kuh.* The settlements of the two younger brothers have been threatened by an invisible demon who has been stealing the food supplies of the settlements. The oldest brother, living along the upper reaches of the river, has the super-Ainu power which enables him to see the demon. He kills the large hairy demon rat, and thereby saves the people in the settlements from starvation. (The complete story with Ainu texts is presented in Ohnuki-Tierney 1969b, Tale 9.[18])

The story indicates that the Ainu assign superior quality, super-Ainu power in particular, to the upper part of the river, which lies in the mountains. The assignment of the oldest brother to the upper part of the river reinforces the Ainu association of that part of a river with super-Ainu quality. The Ainu consider that the aged are closer to the deities since they are closer to death. Some of the respected elders upon death acquire super-Ainu power; these deified elders, just like other deities, can punish the living with misfortune if they do not receive proper respect from the latter, or they can protect the living and bring them good fortune if they are pleased with their behavior.

In addition to the Ainu assigning super-Ainu quality to the upper part of a river because it is located in the mountains where the deities reside, they appreciate the upper part of a river because of its better fishing. Riverine fishing to the Ainu is as important, if not more so, than fishing in the sea. An important part of a river for fishing is the shallows (*uhka*) situated next to deep water along the upper reaches of a river (*hahtara*). It is found at the curves of meandering rivers dug deep by the current. The Ainu fish in the shallows by wading up to their waists with fish spears called *ma:reh*. It is also in these shallows where many salmon end their lives spawning. The Ainu association of the upper stream with the old age may well come from their observation of salmon dying in the shallows along the upper stream. Ice-fishing is also done in this type of shallows.

The last area in this discussion of the horizontal plane of the Ainu universe is the sea. The Ainu distinguish between two areas of the sea: the near shore, *ehanke atuy;* and offshore, called either *t̊uyma atuy* or *repun atuy*. As the English translation of these terms clearly indicate, the distinction between these two areas of the sea is the distance from the shore line, and naturally the offshore tends to be deeper. Thus, we see here the same principle operating in the divisions of horizontal space as in distinguishing different types of mountains.

Ainu fishing is primarily nearshore. Sea mammals, however, are hunted both nearshore and offshore. During early spring, seals are hunted with a gun while they are on the ice giving birth to their young. Both fishing and hunting are conducted exclusively by the males; these activities are strictly forbidden for women.

The coastal area is divided into two to three zones according to shoals. From the coastal line to the offing, they are: *yanke sahma* (i.e. *ya un sahma,* the shoal close to the land); *inoski un sahma* (i.e. *inoski oma sahma,* the shoal in the middle); and *repun sahma* (shoal in the offshore). Of the three, the middle shoal seems to be of less importance as a marker. It is important for fishermen to recognize the three waves, called *rekoy ukam* ("the three waves on top of one another"), which are created by these three shoals, and to be able to go over them without overturning their boats.

The offshore area (*repun atuy*) is the area between the offshore shoal and the horizon. The major Ainu activity in that area is the hunting of sea mammals. We have seen that the Ainu consider the offshore area as being unfamiliar or foreign. The most dominant picture in their mind about the offshore area, however, is that it is the homed of the sea deities. The sea deities compose the two most important groups of deities, those whom the Ainu do not identify in terms of actual species of sea mammals, and all the sea mammals. These deities of the sea are considered to be males.

Just as in the case of land, the sea is then divided into two areas: nearshore and offshore. The nearshore area is characterized primarily by Ainu activities of fishing and some sea mammal hunting, whereas the offshore area is an unfamiliar area, characterized as the residence of the sea deities, and used for hunting sea mammals.

In the previous discussion, I did not present information regarding the demons and their residence because the Ainu characterization of the demons has little to do with their spatial orientation; the demons seem to reside almost everywhere in the universe. The most powerful demons, who have the power to exterminate a whole settlement, still reside in the mountains or offshore (see Ohnuki-Tierney 1969b, Tales 1 and 3).

In summary, it appears that the Ainu recognize two major areas on the horizontal plane of their universe: land and sea. Each area is further divided into: the mountain area and shore area; and the nearshore area and offshore area. In Table I, I have used the subsistence economic activities and the residents of the area as criteria,and then presented the dominant characterizations of each area.

IV

In the previous section, different parts of the universe were examined with particular emphasis on the cultural significance assigned to these parts. For the same purpose it is now essential to examine the orientation of Ainu houses, because the Ainubelieve that the house represents the unvierse in miniature scale, and hence it should reflect Ainu concern for spatial orientations.

During aboriginal times, the Ainulived near the shore during the warm season and further interior in a semi-subterranean house during the cold season.This discussion starts with the summer house *saha cise).*[19]

The essential spatial orientations of an Ainu summer house in relation to its surroundings are presented in Figure 2. The diagram is based on information provided by Husko.

This discussion starts with the cultural meaning attached to the four areas of the Ainu house, which constitute the space between the hearth and each wall.They are placed in a definite hierarchical order. The *rounso:* (the main side) is the most important andis the sacred side.The other three follow inthis order: *si: monso:*(rihgt hand side), *harikiso:* (left hadn side), and *a: kes* (rear side). I shall use the apprcpriate English tralsation of these terms.

The main side, which is located on the side of the house nearest the mountain area, is first of all the seat for the bear deities. When a bear is killed, either during a bear ceremony or otherwise, it is brought into the house through a sacred window, *(kamuy puyara)*, which is in the wall of the main side. Because this is the sacred side ofthe house, all of the important family treasures are also kept against the part of this wall closest to the right hand side of the house. Another use of the main side of the house is to seat male elders, as the Ainu believe that the male elders are closest in status to the deities; hence they are the most revered of humans.

The right hand side, which is next in importance, is for the man and wife of the house. It is located on the side corresponding to our north. The head of the house (*cisekoro*

TABLE 1.

CATEGORIES OF THE HORIZONTAL PLANE

		Subsistence Economic Activities	Participants in the Activities	Objects of the Activities	Residents inthe Area
LAND					
	mountain area	hunting and lumbering	male Ainu	male deities (land mammals)	male deities (land mammals)
	shere area	plant gatherign	female Ainu	plants (notdeified)	Ainu
SEA	near shore	fishing & sea mammal	male Ainu	fish (notdeified) & male deities (sealmammals)	fish
	off-shore	sea mammal hunting	male Ainu	male deities (sea mammals)	male deities (sea mammlas and others)

nispa) is seated on this side ner the main side; whereas his wife (*cisekoro (kahkemah)* is seated next to her husband near the rear side. Behind them and next to the wall is an elevated platform which the couple use for sleeping. Their charms and ritual sticks hand on this wall when not in use.

The third important is the left hand side, which faces the south side of the house. On this side young males, both family members and guests, are seated. Charms and ritual sticks of the family members hang on this wall.

The rear side has the least status, as the term *a:kes* (a:, to sit; *kes,* end) indicates. It is on the side of the house nearest the sea. This side is for females, family members as well as guests, since in Ainu society the females occupy the lowest position. Older females are seated on this side toward the right, and younger females are seated toward the left. The entrance is on the rear side, which is adjacent to storage.

The storage structure (*mosem*) is rectangluar and attached to the house. The Ainu store such items as grass to spread on their beds, grass for insulation in their shoes, spare shoes, and tools. Usually there are two entrances to the storage structure, one on the side facing the sea and the other in the direction corresponding to our north.[20] To the Ainu, the entrance to a house is the back entrance, rather than the traditional front entrance in the United States.

Beside having a hierarchical order of significance, the four sides of the house constitute two directional sets, having opposite sides, constituting a pair.

As in the case of the Ainu universe, the Ainu house is considered as the "body." Thus, in the language of the elders, the main side and the rear side are paired and respectively called the "upper side" (*pe:na un pa"*) and the "lower side" (*pa:na un pa:*). Likewise, the right and left sides of the house are considered to be the right and left sides of the body or trunk. The Ainu consider the hearth, which is situated at the center of the house, represents the heart. Thus, the body of the house is pictured as lying on its back with its head facing the mountain, its right side facing our north, and its heart at the hearth.[21]

The foregoing discussion of the hierarchical order of the four sides of the house indicates that the right hand side is more important than the left. Etymologically, the term *si: monso:* means "true," whereas *har* in *harisiso:* comes from *ar*, meaning "one side" when there are two sides. The preference of the right hand over the left is, however, an implicit cultural assumption of the Ainu. On the conscious level, the Ainu do not stress their preference for the right hand. In addition to the higher status given to the right hand side of the house over the left, there is other behavior which also supports the preference for the right. For example, a man sleeps to the right of his wife. In the Ainu culture, the males are considered superior to the females and closer to the deities.

Not only do the Ainu consider the main side as greatest in importance and the right hand side next, they also consider the direction between these two sides, namely, our northeast, as the holiest. Thus, the sacred window on the main side wall is located on the right hand side. As mentioned earlier, the window is used to bring the bear deity, who sits on the main side as the sacred guests, into the house. The corner between the main and right hand sides, called *so:pa,* is the residence of the deity of the house. Among the deities who reside in the house, this male deity is second in importance to the Goddess of the Hearth. A pair of male and female ritual sticks for the deity are placed in the corner.

Another indication suggesting the importance of the direction coresponding to our northeast is the location of the ritual sticks for the Goddess of the Hearth, the most important household deity. They are placed in the square hearth in the corner corresponding to our northeast.

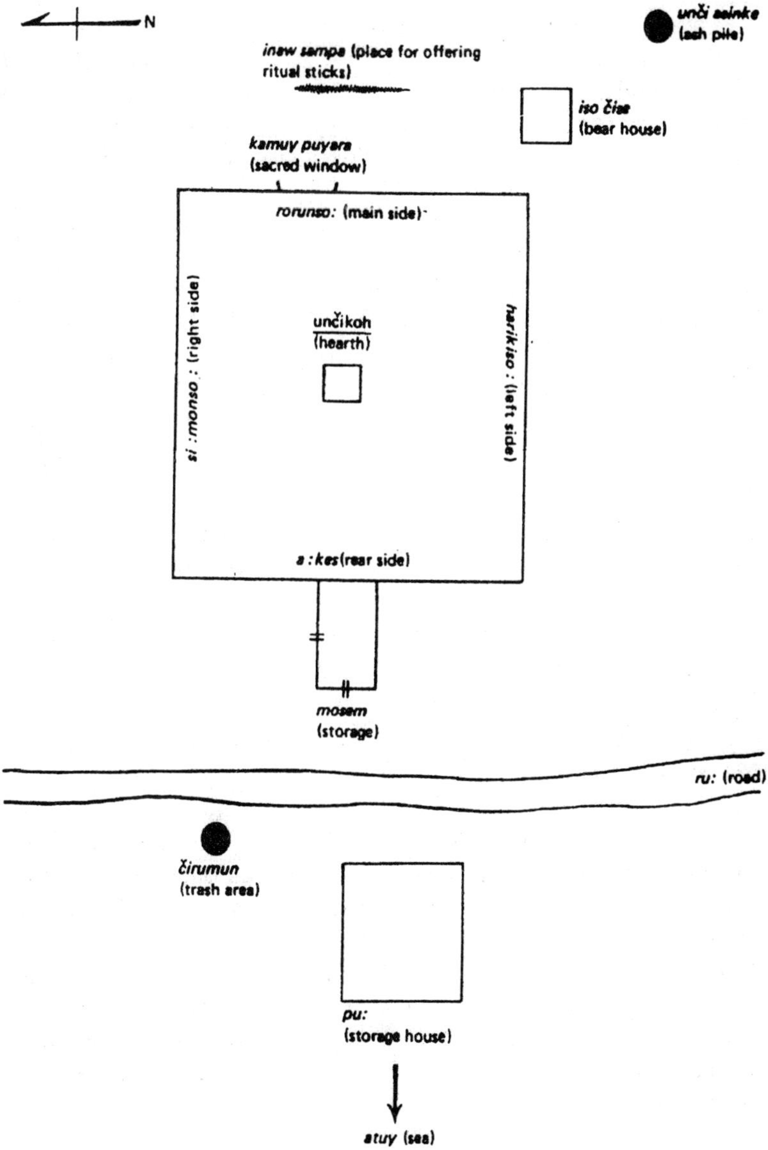

FIG 2. The Ainu summer house

Not only do the Ainu place relative values on the four sides of the house and the highest on the "northeast" direction, they also extend these values to the shore area outside the house. Thus, all three structures connected with the deities are found on the side of the mountains. The altar, used for rituals, is located outside the house on the side of the mountains. Both the house used for the captured bear deity, called *iso cise*, and the ash pile, called *unci asinke*, are situated on this side of the house. The Ainu periodically perform the ash renewal ceremony, which is considered to renew the life of the Goddess of the Hearth. During the ceremony they remove the ashes and sand from the hearth and replace them with fresh sand from the beach. They then carry the old ashes and sand to the ash pile to deposit there.

In contrast, the trash area, or *Cirumun,* is located on the rear side. The Ainu relieve themselves in this general area as it is strictly forbidden to do so in the area adjacent to the main side and the right hand side of the house. The storage house (*pu:*) is also located here. The Ainu consider the storage areas, both *mosem* and *pu;* as belonging strictly to human beings and hence place them on this side.

In this discussion, I have referred to the side corresponding to our east as the side of the mountains or as the main side of the mountains or as the main side of the house. Now it is necessary to examine whether this side is considered first of all the side of the mountains or side of sunrise. I tried to solicit an Ainu answer or explanation by asking direct questions on several occasions. The attempt failed. On the conscious level, the mountains and the sun are equally important, though in different ways. Other cultural data suggest, however, that the sacred value attached to this direction comes from associating this direction with the location of the mountains where the mountain deities reside.

The utmost importance which the Ainu place on the deities of the mountains is demonstrated by bear ceremonialism. This ceremony is not only the most elaborate celebration, but is the only Ainu ceremony of supra-community scale; even the east coast Ainu will join the celebration on the west coast. It involves the capturing of a bear cub, which requires much courage. The cub is then raised by the members of the entire community for a year to a year and a half. Although the bear ceremony in a limited sense includes only an evening and the next day, the Ainu consider the celebration to last throughout the winter, starting with month-long preparations, and ending with the after-celebration marking the end of the cold season.

A more decisive evidence for the pre-eminence of the mountain area over the sun results from an examination of the spatial orientations of the Ainu of the east coast of southern Sakhalin, where the location of the mountains and the sunrise do not coincide. There, the mountains lie to the west of the Ainu settlements opposite to the sunrise in the east. As elsewhere, the Ainu settlements are located along the shore.

According to studies by Yamamoto (1943:58-62) and Chiri (1956:19), the main side of the house and the sacred window are placed in the direction of the mountains, namely, our west. Outside structures, such as the altar of ritual sticks, the bear house, and the sacred ash pile, are placed on the side of the mountains. Thus, it apears that the mountains determine which side is the most sacred.

This discussion of the spatial orientations of the summer house is based on information about summer houses on the north-west coast. The essential spatial orientations in relation to their surrounding natural settings do not show major discrepancies from dscriptions by Yamamoto of east and west coast Sakhalin Ainu houses (Yamamoto 1943:79-100), Chiri's description of the Ainu houses on the east coast of Sakhalin (Chiri 1944:43-48, 1956:19, 50-51) and Sentoku's information about east coast Sakhalin Ainu houses (Sentoku 1929:21-22).

Interpretations by some of the scholars, however, differ from mine. For example, Chiri presents a convincing argument that the Ainu designations for the parts of the house indicate that they conceive of a house as an erect body. Chiri further argues that the Ainu consider the house as a woman facing the east, with a child on her back. He supports this conclusion with various descriptions of houses in folktales and prayers. Although Chiri does not specify the sources of his information, it appears that he is talking about an Ainu house in Hokkaido. He wrote the article when visiting an Ainu house being built by some Ainu from Niputani, Hokkaido for the museum at Hoya, Tokyo (Chiri 1950:76-77).

Munro, too, suggests a different interpretation of Ainu spatial orientation. He studied the Ainu of Niputani in Hokkaido. Munro stresses that solar worship used to be very prominent among the Niputani Ainu andthat the sacred window among these Hokkaido Ainu is oriented toward the rising sun (Munro 1963:13-14). In the Niputani area, the direction of the mountains and the sunrise coincides. Since Munro did not investigate the importance of the mountains among his people. I have no way of evaluating his conclusions.

I have based my discussion of the directional arrangement of the Ainu house on the summer hoses an summer settlements. Information about Ainu winter houses is ver searce. The Ainu discontinued using semi-subterranean winter houses around the turn of the century and adopted the Rusian-style log-cabin for their winter residence.

Since Husko only spent part of her first year of life in a semi-subterranean house (toy Cise), she remembers little about it. She has seen, however, some deserted winter houses and said that they were built against a near shore hill; the entrance, which was built on the slope of the roof, faced the direction opposite the hill. She did not know anything about its internal structure. In response to my question about the spatial orientations of winter houses in relationship to the surrounding nature, she said that accordign to her elders it was the same as that for the summer house.Obviously, this reply supplied little information.

Reliable as well as detailed information on Ainu winter houses in Sakhalin comes from the study by Yamamoto (1943:23-43). Yamamoto combed through available descriptions of winter houses by early explorers and such scholars as Torii and Pilsudski. In various parts of Sakhalin he also personally asked the older Ainu for the information. Although his information relates more to winter houses on the east and southern coast, he did check essential points on the northwest coast houses. According to his investigation, spatial orientations in relation to surrounding nature are the same as for summer houses (Yamamoto 1943:42).

As a miniature universe, the Ainu house reveals some of the essential features of Ainu spatial orientations. The four sides surrounding the square hearth in an Ainu house are placed in a hierarchical order, and this order as well as their division into the four sides are extended to the shore area. Thus, with the hearth in the center, the entire shore area is divided and placed in the following hierarchical order: the side between the hearth and mountain area; the right side of the house which lies to the north, in our sense; the left side which lies to the south, in our sense; and the side between the hearth and the sea. The supreme importance of the mountain side is based on the presence of mountains where the mountain deities, including bears, are believed to reside.

Since the universe is considered analogous to a human body, so is the miniature universe, namely the Ainu house. Thus, the "body" of the Ainu house lies on its back with its head toward the mountains, and the right side of the body toward our north; its heart is represented by the hearth which is situated in the center of the house.

V

In order to understand fully the Ainu arrangement of the horizntal plane, an examination of the directions is necessary. I shall do this by examining the directional terms.

All Ainu directional terms are paired, each designation being 180° opposite to its mate. An examination of these terms indicates, however, that the Ainu recognize four cardinal directions. The correspond roughly to the four directions of Western directinal schema: north, south east, and west. The Ainu directional orientation resembles the Western orientation only superficially. Their directions are not mechanically determined absolute points on compass, as Hallowell points out in his study of Saulteaux directional orientation (Hallowell 1955:189-192). The Ainu directions refer to objects, or more precisely, the natural phenomena and beings of significance in the Ainu culture.

My discussion starts with a pair of terms: *penram and panram*. In the earlier discussions of the division of a river and the Ainu house, we have seen that the terms *penram* and *panram* originally meant the upper and the lower parts of a human body respectively. The Ainu conceive of the unvierse as analogous to a human body. Thus, what we call the horizontal plane is considered by them as a body lying on its back, while the vertical plane is an erect body.

Considering the unvierse as a human body, the Ainu picture the body lying with its head pointed toward the Russo-Japanese border, or our north. That directon is referred to as the upper part *(penram)*. As discussed earlier, the upper *Penram*. The application of these terms to the body of the universe thus indicates that the Ainu considered the direction corresponding to our north as more important than the opposite direction.

This pair of terms, *penram* and *panram*, are used in various ways. The northern end of a settlement is referred to as the head (*kotan sapa*) or the upper part of the body of a settlement (*kotan penramuhu*) or simply the end of a settlement (*kotan kes*).

Not only is the set of terms *pen* and *pan* used denoting opposite ends of a contiguous area, but they are also applied to similar natural pheonomena in a certain area. Thus, if there are two rivers in an area, the one to the north (lying in the direction of the head of the universe), is referred to as the upper river (*penun nay*), whereas the one to the south (lying in the direction of the lower part of the body of the universe) is called the lower river (*panun nay*). Similarly, two small hills inthe same area are referred to as the upper hill (*pe:na un ori*) and the lower hill (*pa:na un ori*). If there are two paths (*ruesan*) which connect an Ainu settlement with the shore, they are the upper path (*pe:na un reusan*) and the lower path (*pa:na* un ruesan*). (Those examples were all found at the* Rayciska *settlement.)*

The foregoing information indicates that the term pen (upper) is applied either to our east or north, whereas lower (pan) is applied to our west or south. Since the term pan (upper) designates a quality superior to pan (lower), it follows that the directions corresponding to our east and north are considered to be superior to the directions corresponding to our west and south.

Although it is not a directional term, the designation for the horizon suggest that the Ainu perceive of the sea as a body. Thus horizon is called atuy ousike, which means the posterior or lower part of the sea. The sea thus has its head at the shore, i.e., our east, and its posterior at the horizon, i.e., our west.

The perception of the universe as a human body seems to be widespread among various Ainu groups. Pilsudski reports that on the east coast of Sakhalin the Ainu believe that the head of the universe lies in the east or north whereas the opposite part (mosiri kes) lies toward the west and sometimes to the south (Pilsudski 1912:34). Chiri, however, found at Tonnai on the east coast of Sakhalin, where Pilsudski had worked, that the head was to the direction of our south and the end was to the direction of our north (Chiri 1944:29, 1956:51-52). Among the Hokkaido Ainu, at places where the coast line stretches east and west, the head is in the east, and the end is in the west. At places where the coast line runs north and south, the head is the north, and the end is the south (Chiri 1944:29).

Chiri states that the set of terms referring to the head and posterior of the land are extremely significant in suggesting the "route of migration" as well as direction (Chiri 1944:29). I am not sure what he means by "migration," and unfortunately, neither Chiri nor Pilsudski provides information as to how the Ainu whom they investigated use body terms in relation to the sea, rivers, mountains, and hills.

Another set of directional terms which correspond to our north and south are *reputoro* and *yautoro*. *Ruputoro* refer to the direction corresponding to the upper part of the body of the universe, namely, our north; whereas *yautoro* refers to the opposite direction, i.e., our south.

The application of these terms of the directions corresponding to our north and south is somewhat puzzling. Etymologically the term *reputoro* cómes from *repun* (offshore) and *yautoro* from ya (land). Thus in the original sense of these terms, *reputoro* should mean the west as the sea lies to the west on the west coast of Sakhalin; *yautoro* should mean the east.

However, these terms may have been applied to these directions because of other meanings of the terms. Thus *repun* (off-shore) also means " foreign," whereas *ya* (land) may mean "belonging to one's own country." Since northern Sakhalin is a "foreign land" occupied by non-Ainu, north might have received the designation *repun*. On the other hand, the land was continuous to the south from the point of view of the Ainu on the northwest coast, and it was occupied by their own Ainu people; therefore, the south might have been referred to as *yautoro*. A less likely speculation is that it indeed the Sakhalin Ainu had migrated to Sakhalin from elsewhere, some of their directional terms may have been shifted in thc course of their migration.

Without knowing why these terms are applied to the directions north and south, it is impossible to infer values which may be attached to these directions.

The Ainu also orient themselves in relation to the direction of sunrise and sunset. On the west coast, the direction of sunrise coincides with the direction of the mountains, and the direction of sunset is the direction of the sea. The direction of sunrise is considered sacred because it is where the Goddess of Sun rises in the morning, where as the direction of sunset is a tabooed direction. The direction of sunrise is called *cuh ka utoro* (where the sun is), *cuh rikin* (the sun rises), or *cuh ekanray* (cah, sun + *eken*, to meet, to welcome, to receive+*raye*, push away). The direction of the sunset is called cupehoose (sun sets), *cuh ahun usiikehe* (where the sun goes in), or *cuh pokutoro* (*pok*, below).

Ainu behavior regarding the direction of sunset relates to death and sickness. Thus, clothes of a deceased person have to be disposed of outside the side of the house facing the direction of sunset. Likewise, the ritual sticks with wood shavings (*inaw*) which were used by the deceased have to be placed in the same direction. While the corpse is in the house until after the funeral, the head has to be facing the sunset. Only during the time when it is carried out of the house to the cemetery, is the head facing the direction of sunrise. This is done so that the legs are carried out first; this procedure ensures that the deceased will not look into the house. If this happens, the soul back into the house. If this happens, the soul may hesitate leaving the house. At the time of burial, however, the deceased again is placed so the head faces the sunset.

Similarly, the ritual stick (*inaw*) used during the shamanistic ritual to purify a sick or what we call insane, person is placed outside in the direction of the sunset. When a sick person visits a distant horse, he has to purify himself upon arrival at the entrance by gently striking himself with a branch of fir (*yayuh*). Then he has to place the branch on a bifuracted crotch of a tree standing in the direction of the sunset.[23] Fir branches are also used by older women during the exorcism rite against demons. The exorcism rite a part of the funeral for the drowned and the curing rite for the insane. These branches also must be placed on bifurcated crotches of trees in the direction of the sunset.

The Ainu thus connect the direction of the sunset with death because the head of the dead person is placed toward that direction, and thus it is toboo. (The Ainu of the north-west coast believe that the world of the dead is located somewhere on the shore, and they have no directional specification for its location.)

An intersting comparison of the association of west and death is found in Fujimoto's descriptin of the Shizunai Ainu of Hokkaido.the Shizunai Ainu believe that the world of the dead is located in the west. They, however, place their dead in the ground withthe head facing the east, so that when the corpse stands up, it can face the dead which is in the west (Fujimoto 1964:215-216). Fuimoto does not explain why the Ainu believe that the world of the dead is located in the west. He gueses that the basis of the belief is the fact that the sun sets in the west. Whatever the Ainu explanation may be, the Shizunai Ainu associate the direction which corresponds to our west with death because of the location of their world of the dead in the west.

Arutoro and *teutoro* are another pair of directional terms which corespond to our east and west. Etymologically, the terms seems to have originally meant "that way" as opposed to "this way." However, in their current usage, they are directional termsb referring to our east and west. Husko explained that the term *aurtoro* means "to insert mountains between." I could not get a further explanation of this term during either field session. On the west coast, however, it designates the direction of the Ainu settlements lyign on the east coast beyond the mountains when viewed from the west coast. Conversely, when the term is used by Ainu on the east coast, *arutoro* would be the direction of the Ainu settlements on the west coast. However, the opposite term, *teutoro,* refers to the location of the speaker. Thus on the west coast it means the west coast. However, the opposites term, *teutoro*, refers to the location of the speaker. Thus, on the west coast it means the west coast. However, it is most commonly synonymous with "*tan atuy kopahka*" (the direction of the sea). These terms alone do not indicate a value differentiation between the directions.

In the beginning of this section I stated that the Ainu directional terms only superficially resemble those in the Western schema. The fundamental difference between the two must now be emphasized. Although in the foregoing discussion I have used the English terms of north, east, south, and west, the Ainu directional terms differ from these in that their directions do not extend beyond the Ainu land. Ainu terms refer to specific objects in the Ainu universe and do not refer to abstract points on the globe.

The Ainu term referring to the direction of the sea typifies their notion of directions. Although this direction is referred to as the direction of sunset or the direction of the sea, the reference points are confined to the land area and thus do not extend to the sea. My interpretation rests on the assumption that when the Ainu place the objects related to death in the direction of the sea, they place them on the shore. Also, as mentioned earlier, the Ainu do not postulate the world of the dead as being either on, under, or beyond the sea; it is located on the shore.

The foregoing survey also indicates that the Ainu directional terms are paired, each term in the pair referring to the direction which is 180° from the direction of its mate. Furthermore, except in the pair arutoro and teutoro, or positive-negative opposition in the values attached to the directions. Thus, the direction of the Russo-Japanese border is believed to be superior to the direction of Hokkaido. Likewise, the direction of the mountains, which is also the direction of the sunrie, is a good and basically sacred direction, whereas the direction of the sunset is associated with death and hence taboo. Thus the values revealed by these directional terms reinforce findings in the preceding sections.

VI

The discussion in this section starts with an illustration of the Ainu conception of the vertical plane of their universe, which might be pictured as layers of a cake. Next is a description of the Ainu view of life on the upper layers. Lastly is a discussion of the directional terms for the vertical plane and their cultural meanings.

The vertical sphere of the Ainu universe consists of several layers. The exact number is unclear. Husko often explained the Ainu views of these layers with an Ainu expression, *wan kanto wenka* us. Literally translated it reads: six skies piled on top of one another. The expression *iwan kanto* (six skies) and their perception of the sky as expressed in this phrase are found among various Ainu groups. Ainu scholars have translated the phrase as "six" skies. However, the number six in many Ainu dialects also means "many." Especially in folktales, the number six is almost always used to express "many." therefore, I am inclined to interpret the number "six" in the Ainu description of the sky as "many."

At any rate, the "six" layers of the sky are symbolized in

the decoration on the tall ritual stick for the Goddess of Sun, called *soyuncikara*. She is the most important inhabitant of the sky. On this ritual stick, which is mảde of Yesso spruce, three horizontal strips of bark are peeled off. This produces three bands, which are white (*tetara*) in color. These white bands are considered to represent the there layers of sky, whereas the three unpeeled bands represent the layers of earth. the unpeeled bands are black (*kurasno*) in color. Two of these black bands are located between the three white bands, and the third black layer is between the shavings at the top of the ritual stick and the upper white layer. Althugh there are only three white layers representing the skies, the Ainu explain that the black and white layers, "six" in all, represent the "six" skies.

Each of these six layers seems to comprise a structure which is schematically drawn as follows (see Figure 3). Each larger layer consists of a layer of ground, a layer of sky, and the space between. The layer of ground (*toy*) is considered narrow, as only the surface of the ground, called itara, is significant to the Ainu. The space between the ground and sky is literally called "between" *uturukehe*). No special meaning is attached to the area. In the upper part of this between space, there are clouds, although they receive little emphasis. The Ainu term for sky (*kanto*) refers to the bluish part of the sky, *siwnin niskuru* (*siwnin*, blue; *niskuru*, clouds or sky). When the Ainu talk about these layers in the sky, they do not refer to the sea.

C sky (kanto)

B space between
(uturukehe)

A layer of ground
(toy)

Fig 3. Structure of a layer of sky

The foregoing description of the vertical plane of the universe pictures the Ainu as living on the ground belonging to the bottom larger layer, with six larger layers, identical in structure, on top. This picture emerges in the Ainu mind, however, only when an outsider, like myself, asks them to describe the structure of their vertical plane.

A more realistic picture, however, is that the Ainu collectively consider whatever is above to be "the above," in contrast to the ground where they reside. "The above" is called *kanna* (above) *pohna* (below). When "the above" and "the below" are contrasted, the former is primarily characterized by the presence of various deities and "the below" by the Ainu themselves.

To the Ainu, the most dominant beings of "the above" are the Goddess of the Sun and Moon, and the Dragon Deities.

The Ainu consider the sun and moon to represent one entity. Her womanhood is symbolized by a pair of earrings, which are made of branches and attached to the ritual stick. Her movements regulate the performance of all Ainu ceremonies except shamanistic rituals. The Ainu believe that only during the period between a new moon and full moon can they perform ceremonies, because only during this period is the Goddess in good spirits and thus their prayers will reach her. She is the mediator between the Ainu and other deities, and hence they believe that her mood is crucial in their efforts to reach the deities.

While the Ainu believe that the Goddess of Sun and Moon resides in the sky which is visible to the Ainu, they believe that the Dragon Deities, *Kanna Kamuy* ("deities of the above"), reside on the ground which is above the sky occupied by the Goddess. The Dragon Deities are next in importance to the Goddess of Sun and Moon. The Dragon Deities are numerous, and occasionally they fight among themselves. Lighting is considered a reflection of their swords used in fighting.

Although their residence is the ground above the sky, periodically a Dragon Deity will come to the Ainu world to drink water from a stream.

At one time, the war among the Dragon Deities was very violent. During a noisy thunder storm, a dragon fell from the sky and landed at Horokes on the northwest coast. Only after a sagacious old woman waved her underwear and prayed to the diety did he return to the sky. Simultaneously, many musk deer, rabbits, vipers, and worms, all halved, fell from the sky. They also lived on the ground above the sky and were victims of the war among the Dragon Deities; the swinng of swords of the deities had accidentally hit these animals. This incident occurred before Husko's time, although she could still clearly see traces of the claws of the Dragon Deity on the cliff where he had climbed going back to the sky.

The sex of the Dragon Deities is unclear. When I inquired of Husko, she replied that there are male and female dragons. however, this would be a standard answer for her, as she believes every "species" of beings has both sexes in order to reproduce and thus continue their line. Unsolicited information on the Dragon Deities suggests, however, that to the Ainu the dragons usually fight with swords. This suggests that the dragons are considered males, as fighting is considered a male occupation among the Ainu; when Ainu women fight in emergencies, they use small daggers and spears,but not long swords.

There are many deities residing in the "above," or more precisely on the ground above the sky. The Ainu conception of these deities, however, is very vague. My only definite information is a folktale about the Ainu culture hero (Ohnuki-tierney 1969b, Tale 1). In this tale the culture hero is raised by a deity of the sky, but there is no information in this tale about the life of the deity.

The Ainu postulate about the lives of many deities since

they occasionally see things descending in the sky. These objects are believed to have been dropped by the deities. They say that when these objects land o the ground were the Ainu live, they roll rapidly, and one has to chase after them in order to catch them. They can identify these objects very easily as the workmanship on these objects is too fine to be made by humans. A small sword which a deity dropped and which was later found by an elder has been one of the family treasures of the leading family of the *Rayciska* settlement.

There also are demons in "the above." Somewhere near the sun, the Ainu believe that there is a country occupied by cannibals, or *cuhkampe* ("the people of the sun who eat their own people"). The Ainu classify them as demons. The chief of these demons owns manybowls made from human skulls. Whenever an important guest visits the house, the host will even offer his only daughter to the guest; this act indicates that the host is a great man. She will be dressed in her best clothing and later strangled with the crotch of a bifurcated branch.

Among the humans, the drowned are believed togo to "the above." In the mortuary custom pertaining to the drowned, the Ainu strictly for bid the use of any color on the shroud; the shroud for the drowned has to be white (tetara). Not only is the material without colors, but even the use of colored thread for embroidery on the shroud is forbidden. They use as the shroud a garment woven with natural elm thread. The white shroud, *Tetara imi* (white garment), symbolizes the sky, which is the destiny for the drowned. As we saw in the he symbolism of the six layers of the sky on the ritual stick for the Goddess of Sun, the color called *tetara* (white) is associated with the sky.

All dead Ainu, except for those who were drowned, go to the world of the dead Ainu. It is located somewhere on the shore which is on the same plane as the world of the living Ainu. When I asked Husko why the drowned go to the sky, she said that she knew of no exlanation for it. She assumed, however, that there were some deities who would receive the drowned.

As mentioned, musk deer, rabbits, vipers, and worms are also believed to reside in "the above." These animals, however, are thought to be somewhat different than their equivalent in the Ainu world; details of these differences are not articulated in the Ainu mind. For example, an elder at Horokes, who once saw a musk deer which had fallen from the sky, thought that the color of the musk deer was some what different.

All of the deities and animals who occasionally descend to the world of the living Ainu reinforce the belief that there is ground above the sky where they live.

So far discussion has been focused on the Ainu notion of "the above." It is necessary now to discuss Ainu thinking about the space below the ground where they reide. This grounds perceived as a thin layer. I attempted in various ways to understand the Ainu perception of the space under the ground. Since they perceive the ground as a thin layer, the Ainu do not postulate any activities or inhabited space under the ground. I specifically attempted to clarify this point since many Ainu scholars report that "hell" is located below ground. The northwest coast Ainu believe that the wicked are punished after death in the world of the dead Ainu. This world is located on the same horizontal plane as the world of the living Ainu.

The lack of any conception about "under the ground" may also be seen in their notion of caves. The Ainu attach particular significance to caves since they are considered as either entrances to the world of the dead Ainu or the residence of a deity or a demon. these caves, however, are always described without vertical dimensions. Thus, when a living person visits the world of the dead during what the Ainu call temporary death, he crawls through a horizontal cave which connects the two worlds. Similarly, demons are found in Horizontal caves (see Ohnuki-Tierney 1969b, Tale 1).

The last topic of discussion here is the directional terms for the vertical plane. In contrast to the rich assortment of directional terms for the horizontal plane, there is only one terms for the vertical plane. They are *kanna* (upper) and *pohna* (lower). In the language of the young, they correspond to *riswaan* (upper) and *rawwaan* (lower).. When applied to the universe, *kanna* refers to the sky or the direction toward the sky, and *pohna* refers to the ground were the Ainu reside. This set of the terms is also used in referring to a set of body parts separated horizontally. Thus, they are used in referring to the upper and lower edges of the eyes, teeth, lips, and jaws.

Various larger objects of the universe too, are conceived essentially ass analogous to an erect human body. Thus, the mountains (*nupuri*) are perceived as standing on their legs (*kema*). A storage house is more clearly perceived in this manner. Not only are the four stilts called legs (*kema*), the ground underneath the structure is called the armpits, *pu: ciyarapoh* (*pu:*, shed + *cise*, house + *yarapoh*, armpits). The idea of the storage house as a body with four legs is well illustrated in a riddle, a favorite a gavorite game of the Ainu. The question is: *ekemasahkuh iwan kotan ka: ama kemakorokuh ohacirun ta hemata*? (What is it that travels around six (many) villages without legs setting traps, when the storage house with four legs is left at home?). The answer is *cis* (boat). The term *kemakorokuh* in the question literally means "a person with legs," and refers to a storage house. I have no data, however, to assume that this analogy extends to the entire vertical space.

In sum, the Ainu first of all postulate "six" layers in what we call the upper atmosphere, each consisting of ground, sky, and the space between. The upper layers, however, are collectively perceived as "the above" and characterized by various deities, especially the Goddess of the Sun and Moon, and the Dragon Deities. "The above" contrasts with "the below," which is the ground occupied by the Ainu.

The second most salient feature is the Ainu conceptualization of larger objects as analogous to an erect human body.

VII

The last topic of discussion is the world of the dead Ainu. The primary focus will be on its location in relation to the world of the living Ainu, since the particular way in which the Ainu place this world in their universe reveals an important characteristic of their spatial orientations.

The most commonly used term for the world of the dead Ainu is *auru un kotan*, which means "the next settlement" or "the world next to ours." The implication of geographical proximity will later be discussed in more detail. The world of the dead is also called *aynu oiwakusi* (place where the souls go), or *ramah oiwakusi* (place where the souls go). The latter designation reveals the Ainu concept of death: death occurs when the soul leaves the body and goes to the world of the dead.

Life in the world of the dead Ainu is depicted as basically identical to that in the world of the living Ainu—the dead live as they did when they were alive. Thus the Ainu visualize the world of the dead Ainu as being entirely different from that of "hell", either in Christianity or in Japanese Buddhism. As Chiri states, Japanese scholars have often misinterpreted the Ainu notion of the world of the dead because of their own notion of hell (Chiri 1956: 4-5).

All that the Ainu know about the world of the dead comes from those who have experienced "temporary death." The Ainu often talk about their temporary deaths, during which their soul visits the world of the dead Ainu. Upon its return,the individual regains consciousness, and then describes what his soul has seen in the world of the dead Ainu. Somehow these descriptions by various Ainu, including those now deceased, coincide. Since everyone cannot die a temporary death, Ainu who can are called *uhsuye aynu* (men who are born again), and they are esteemed by others. The Ainu often experience "Temparary deaths" during sickness, and the phenomenon seems to correspond to their loss of consciousness or what we call deep sleep.

The location of the world of the dead Ainu in relation to the world of the living is not consciously defined by the Ainu. An analysis of the tunnel, however, which is believed to lead to the world of the dead Ainu and of the spatial orientations of the world of the dead Ainu as perceived by living Ainu, provides clues to its location.

The tunnels *(tuhso)* are often situated in a large rock. Some are located on the beach, and others somewhat away from the shore in the wooded area; they are, however, never in the mountain area.

Although not every settlement has a tunnel connecting with the world of the dead, there are often one or two in an adjacent settlement. For example, there was a tunnel entrance in a large rock on the beach at the *Hurooci* settlement, and it was believed to be the tunnel leading to the world of the dead Ainu. One of the most famous on the northwest coast was at the *Ustomonaypo* settlement. It was wellknown because there was definite "proof" that this tunnel was connected with the world of the dead. The "proof" was based on the statement by an Ainu who claimed that his soul used this tunnel traveling to the world of the dead during his temporary death.

Just as the world of the dead is called "the world next to ours," these tunnels are also called "the tunnels next to ours," *(oyasirun tuhso*).

Husko claimed that she experienced "temporary deaths" twice in her lifetime. Her description of traveling to the world of the dead offers some clues as to its location in relation to that of the living Ainu. Although she is not certain, she thinks that both times the tunnel entrance was in a large rock in a wooded are a with a vast grass field in front. The tunnel was long, narrow, and horizontal, and it was pitch dark inside. She came out of the opposite end of the tunnel which was in a large rock in a wooded area. There she saw an Ainu settlement—the settlement of the dead Ainu. A beautiful blue sea was beyond the settlement.

The dead continue to live in the world of the dead as they did in the world of the living. Even the wicked are sent there; they are punished in a special area in the world of the dead.

Thus, it appears that the world of the dead is located on the same horizontal plane, and on the shore, just as the world of the living, although possibly on the other side of a mountain. In other words, it composes a mirror image of the world of the living with the mountain area in between. Although the mirror image description is my interpretation based on information received from Husko, the location on the shore of the world f the dead is definite and is stressed by all Ainu who have been there.

The spatial orientations in the world of the dead are essentially identical to the world of the living Ainu. The temporal orientations, however, are partially reversed. The seasons are opposite in the two worlds. When Husko visited the world of the dead during her temporary death in the spring, the Ainu were drying fish which they ordinarily do in the fall. (Further details of the temporal orientations are discussed in Ohnuki-Tierney 1969a.).

It is worth noting here that the world of dead humans is an important and well-developed theme among many Ainu groups. Many of the Sakhalin Ainu ideas about the world of the dead are shared by the Hokkaido Ainu. the latter also believe that the Ainu settlement in the world of the dead is located on the shore, and that it is reached through a tunnel (Chiri and Yamada 1956:4-11, Storeis 1, and 2; Chiri 1956:4-5).

Chiri made an extensive study of the supposed location

of the tunnel among the Hokkaido Ainu and the Sakhalin Ainu on the east coast (Chiri and Yamada 1956). According to his informants, the tunnel is located either on the side of a cliff along the shore, or along the river bank near the deep mountains of the interior. In some cases, there actually are caves or tunnels which are considered to be the entrances to the world of the dead. In other cases, it is simply believed that somewhere there is a special cave which leads to the world after death (Chiri and Yamada 1956:1-33).

There are significant differences, however, in the spatio-temporal orientations of the world of the dead Ainu between the Ainu of the northwest coast of Sahalin and the Hokkaido Ainu. the Sakhalin Ainu place the world of the dead, both the good and the wicked, on the same horizontal plane as the world of the living Ainu. The Hokkaido Ainu, however, locate it on a different plane from the world of the living. According to Kindaichi's analysis, they consider the world of deities to be located in the sky and the equivalent settlements for the living are in the middle of these two worlds (Kindaichi 1925:296-298, 1961:4-5). Chiri also reports that the world of the deities is located in the sky (Chiri and Oda 1956:37-49); the souls of the dead Ainu which go to the eastern sky return to this world to be reborn, whereas those which go to the western sky never return (Chiri 1954a:244); and among the Saru and the Horobetsu Ainu the world of the dead Ainu is located underground (Chiri and Yamada 1956:4-11). Munro also reports that among the Ainu at Niputani the location of the world of the dead Ainu is underground (Munro 1963:121). Among the Shizunai Ainu, it is located more specifically underground and to the west of the world of the living (Fujimoto 1964:215-216). Kitagawa quotes a song sung during the bear ceremony at Piratori, Hokkaido, in which the world of the bear deity is described as being located in the eastern sky (Kitagawa 1961:143). Takakura also indicates taht during the bear ceremony the Hokkaido Ainu symbolically send the bear back to the sky by shooting a blunt arrow toward the sky (Takakura 1966:23). Generally the writers cited do not state from which group of Hokkaido Ainu they gathered infomation. According to these statements then, the Hokkaido Ainu conceptualization of the spatial relationship between the world of the living and that of the dead is vertically oriented, which contrasts sharply with the horizontal orientation of the Ainu of th enorthwest coast of Sakhalin.

VIII

As suggested in my preliminary interpretations in each section, the basic structure underlying the Ainu spatial concepts is dyadic. A domiain or culturally codified area is dichotomized and, in some cases, each sub-area is further

TABLE II.

DYADIC STRUCTURE OF THE AINU SPATIAL CONCEPTS

I. Domain	II. Super-Ainu areas +	III. Ainu areas 0
1. horizontal plane	sea sond mountains	shore
2. mountain area	interior mountains	nearshore mountains
3. sea	offshore	nearshore
4. shore area	eastern-northern half	western-southern half
5. right & left	right	left
6. body of the universe	upper half	lower half
7. river	upper half	lower half
8. vertical plane	the above	the below

dichotomized. The basic dyadic structure may be understood

in terms of a series of contrast sets in binary opposition with the super-Ainu quality as the minimal distinctive feature.

The term "super-Ainu quality" refers to the properties of the deities. I chose the term "super-Ainu" because the Ainu consider the eities as more powerful than of the Ainu either by providing sufficient food or by punishing them through famine and other disasters

In Table II, spatial categories in the same horizontal column I and III constitute a minimal pair in the domain defined in column I. Each spatial category in column II may be understood as the area which is characterized by the deities and their behavior, when it is contrasted with its partner defined in column III which is characterzied by the Ainu behavior. Since the Ainu believer that the deities possess power over them, the entire column II is marked "plus." By contrast, column III, which is marked zero, represents the absence of super-Ainu quality; the areas in column III belong to the Ainu, who do not have the power which the deities enjoy. Further elaboration of the super-Ainu/Ainu opposition will be presented later.

In Table II, the first line represents my analysis that the entire horizontal plane is divided into the non-shore area and the shore area: the former is considered as the the home of the mountain deities, and the sea is the home of the sea deities. The Ainu exclusively occupy the shore area where both their summer and winter settlements are located, and much of their activities, except hunting, lumbering, and fishing, is conducted.

When the mountain area is considred alone, the area is divided into the area away from the shore and the area close to the shore. Of these two sub-mountain areas, the one away from the shore is the location of the deep mountains, which are spatial symbols of the supreme deities of the mountains. The other area, on the other hand, is less sacred, or more profane.

Although the sea, in contrast to the shore, is a super-Ainu area, when considered the super-Ainu area because it is the residence of the sea deities. The nearshore is characterized primarily by fishing; fish are not deified by the Ainu.

The shore, an Ainu area when considered as a whole, is divided into the eastern-northern half and the western-southern half, thus cutting the shore area diagonally into two triangles. The eastern-northern half of the shore is the super-Ainu area; however, not because it is the permanent residence of the deities, but because the Ainu use this area to visit and communicate with the deities. The Ainu supreme deitty, the bear, is brought into the house through the sacred window, situated in the northern half of the eastern wall. The deity then is seated on the eastern side of the hearth during the ceremony. During the deity's absence, the male elders, believed the closest humans to the deities, are seated on this side. All offerings to various deities, through which the Ainu convey their respect, are also placed against the eastern wall. Outside the eastern side of their house, the Ainu construct the altar. They convey their respect and requests to the deities through prayer. The bear house, where the supreme deity is raised, is also situated in the eastern-northern half.

The Ainu half, on the other hand, is characterized by an ultra-Ainu or ultra-profane quality. Inside the house, the young, who are considered the most Ainu or human, are seated with males on the southern side and females on the western side of the hearth. The latter symbolizes the Ainu notion of the ultra-profane. The Ainu consider the females as most impure and hence offensive to the deities; the smell of the their menstrual blood and blood during birth, which supposedly continues to smell even after washing, is detested by the deities. Females are therefore forbidden to hunt and fish because deties are other the objects of the hunt, and fish is considered the product of a sea deity. The placing of the young females on the western side, considered the lowest of the four, epitomizes the

Ainu notion of the ultra-profane.

The same ultra-Ainu quality characterizes the exterior area adjacent to the western and southern sides of the house. The trash area is situated on this side. The Ainu, who do not have toilet facilities, relieve themselves in this area; it is a strong taboo to use the other half of the ashore. Likewise, grass soiled by women blood has to be buried under the grass in this area. Furthermore, the Ainu associated this side of the shore with sickness and death—the symbols of mortals. Thus, the ritual stick used to purify the sick either during the shamanistic curing rite or before their entry in to a house has to be disposed on this side of the house. The fir branches used during the exorcism rite have to be placed on bifurcated crotches of trees standing on this half of the shore. The personal belongings of the deceased, such as clothes or ritual sticks, are also disposed outside the western side of the house.

As indicated in column 5 of Table II, the right and left hands represent the Ainu/super-Ainu opposition. Inside the house, the northern side of the hearth is called the right hand side and southern side the left. The northern side belongs to the super-Ainu category whereas the southern side belongs to the Ainu category. Therefore, the Ainu are one of those peoples who choose the right hand to be preeminent or sacred (cf. Hertz 1960).

What results from dividing the shore into the eastern-northern half and the western-southern half are indicated in columns 6 and 7 of Table II. The Ainu consider the unvierse or a river to have "body." They postulate that the head or the sacred half of these bodies is either on the north in the case of the universe or on the east in the case of the river. Conversely, the lower half, i.e., the profane half of the universe or a river, lies to the south and west respectively.

The super-Ainu/Ainu opposition is also seen in the categorization of the vertical plane. "The above" is collectively opposed to "the below." The six layers above are collectively the area for the Goddess of the Sun and the Dragon Deities, whereas the "below" is the ground occupied exclusively by the Ainu.

My interpretation of such symbols as trash, menstrual blood, sickness, and death as being ultra-profane requires further clarification, since much has been discussed on the relationship between pollution, taboo, and the sacred. This is not the appropriate place to start a discussion of the history of this subject, which is well presented in Douglas (1966, especially 7-28, 159-179). The opinion of more recent scholars, however, provide a point of departure for my discussion.

Developing van Gennep's thesis on symbolic classification, Leach has explored the source of the negative power. In his 1958 article (Leach 1967a), he claims that abnormal, special, other-worldly, royal, taboo, and sick compose the sacred category, and that it is the ritual situation which endows these sacred objects and phenomena with power or dangerous potency. An example of a sacred symbol is the Hindu attitude toward hair clipping; as soon as hair is cut from the head, it is regarded as "dirty," and having power to pollute. In his 1961 article (Leach 1967b), however, Leach places such objects and phenomena with negative power into the category of "mediation.: This he describes as a third category—a category outside of the dual categories created by binary opposition.

The entire book by Douglas (1966) is primarily dedicated to the question of relation of pollution and taboo to magico-religious behavior, namely, the sacred. She contends that although there are many objects in a particular culture which are considered to be polluting, only few of them are chosen to be placed in ritual context, thus becoming the source of dangerous power. Thus uncleanliness and the sacred are not synonymous. Sh also argues that the source of the dangerous power of these sacred polluting objects is their marginal status. This includes those lacking identity, such as dirt.

In view of these opinions, my interpretation of the Ainu classification of such symbols as trash, blood, human excreta, sickness, and death into the Ainu or profane category, rather than either the sacred or the marginal category, requires further clarification. This I shall attempt by discussing such related problems as: the demons, which constitute the other source of power in the Ainu universe, the Ainu attitude about these tabooed objects in relation to other objects and beings in the universe; and finally the boundaries between different spatial categories and their symbols.

A brief discussion of Ainu demons is necessarysince, in my analyses, the demons constitute the marginal in the Ainu classificatory schema. In my previous analysis (Ohnuki-Tierney 1968, 1969a), I interpreted the demons as representing a super-Ainu power, as do the deities; only the demons have a negative power in that their power is destructive to the Ainu. I later realized, however, that the destructive power of the demons comes from their marginal status in the society of the Ainu universe.

Most of the demons have a unique existence. They do not constitute a class or a group, as do the deities. Often they appear in pairs: male and female, or silings; or as a stray member of an ordinary class of beings which has become a demon.

In the case of "famed demons," which constitute the central theme of most folktales, their marginal status is further emphasized. For example, the most dreadful demon couple, and husband and wife, constitute the central theme of a folktale which Husko repeatedly characterized as the most reversed Ainu folkatale (see Ohnuki-Tierney 1969b, Tale 1). The demon couple are not members of an actual species, as for example, the bear deities. Further more, the demons have only one eye, which is as large as a full moon; the upper jaw reaches to the sky, while the lower jaw digs into the ground; and their skin is so hard that nothing can penetrate it. Thus, the demons are marginal in that they have a unique existence, and their forms is anomalous.

Another story concerns two demon brothers. Two musical instruments, which are deserted by their owner, turn into demon brothers and are ready to exterminate a whole village. They disappear in the air, however, when the chief of the village, the Ainu culture hero, sagaciously answers questions about their identity. The musical instruments thus are demons only as long as they lack identity, i.e., they are of marginal stauts in the society of the Ainu universe.

Therefore, I consider that demons constitute the marginal category in the Ainu classification of the beings in the universe. The polluting objects and phenomena associated with the western-southern half of the shore, however, do not symbolize demons.

Now I will turn to Ainu beliefs and attitudes about these polluting objects and phenomena. One thing common to all of these is the Ainu belief that exposure of these objects and phenomena to the deities is most offensive. Thus, the Ainu cannot scatter trash anywhere but must bring it to a specified area to the west of the house. Likewise, they must relieve themselves in this general area.

Blood is the most potent. The Ainu, however, discriminate between "fresh" and "old" blood; only the latter, which is the blood at child birth and menstrual blood is offensive to the deities. The "old" blood is considred so potent that even its smell remains after washing. Thus, it is taboo *(ihomah)* to expose women's underwear to the Goddess of Sun and Moon or to Ainu males who are oin contact with the deities during hunting and fishing. The offensive nature of such blood to the deities may, however, beutilized by the Ainu in emergencies to ward off a deity or demon. Thus, when Ainu encounter a deity or a demon, they can wave a woman's underwear to chase away the deity or demon.

My interpretation of "old" blood as being profane is further supported by Ainu treatment of old women. Duirng old age, even women gain prestige because they are no longer impure with "old" blood. For example, in the legal area certain old women may express their opinions even though normally the judgment of criminals is a matter exclusively for male elders. Whenever female deities disguise themselves to visit the Ainu, they take the form of older women. Therefore, I hold that while the younger women represent the ultra-profane, old women approach the super-Ainu state.

It is the "old" blood which characterizes the western side of the shore. Young women are seated on the western side of the hearth, and grass which has been soiled by blood during mestructionor child birth has to be hidden among grass to the west of the house. Sickness and death are also offensive to the deities. Thus, in one folktale, women who had just returned from the county of the deities were instantly killed when they encountered a funeral service. This happened because they had not gone through the smoke from the shamasnistic ritual, which would have properly cleased them by removing their odor. Humans acquire such a smell when they visit the country of the deities. The breach of this regulation invoked the anger of the deities. The Ainuconsider sickness called *araka* as being similar to death, since *araka* is a serious disease, which might lead to death. They distinguish between araka and minor aches and pains. Only araka requires a shamanistic ritual for diagnosis and treatment.

Thus, the objects and phenomena associated with the western-southern half of the shore are characterized by the power to offend the deities. None are used in the Ainuritual context whereby they gain sacred power. Thus, I consider these objects and phenomena as symbols of ultra-profanity rather than marginal or sacred.

The last part of my discussion on this subject is the boundaries of the spatial categories. In the spatial domain of the Ainu, there is little conception of the marginal or in-between, although it is developed in other domains of the Ainu cosmology (cf.my discussion on time,Ohnuki-Tierney 1969b).

A space between two definite categories of space is often called uturu in Ainu. thus, the vertical space between the ground and sky is called uturu, The Ainu ascribe no meaning to this space between the ground and sky nor to any other areas called uturu. Although there is seldom an intermediary space between two categories of space, the boundary between these categories is very well marked. Free traffic between spatial categories without the properritual results in punishment, often lethal, of the transgressor.

The color white symbolizes the boundary between the world of the deities and the world of the Ainu. Thus, a human being going to the country of the deities must pass through white fog and observe the rule—that he shall not speak about that country. One returning from the country of the deities to the Ainu world must, of course, pass through the white smoke of the shamanistic ritual. Any thing which he brought from that cuntry must remain outside the house. Similarly, a white fog descends from the mountains and a man is unable to climb them unless he has observed the special purification ritual; inner mountains, of course, are the most sacred Ainu land. White smoke during the shamanistic rituals symbolizes the spatial boundary between the territory of the deities and that of the Ainu, as during that time deities come from their world to that of the Ainu.

The boundary between the worlds of the living and dead Ainu, however, is marked by a pitch-black tunnel connecting these two worlds. Things brought from the world of the dead Ainu must be left outside the house till the odor of the other world disappears.

Therefore, although the concept of the intermediary is little developed in Ainu spatial thinking, very strict rules against the mixing of spatial categories govern their concept of space.

It is precisely because of this rule against the mixing of spatial categories that the western-southern half of the shore have polluting power. That is, these objects and phenomena acquire polluting power only when they are exposed to the deities; the profane are mixed with the sacred. They become the source of dangerous power when they are out of place.

It is necessary to speculate as to why trash, old blood, human excreta, sickness and death, are chosen as symbols. A quality common to all these objects and phenomena is their state of being ambiguous. As Douglas suggests (1966-160-161), trash, which originally was food, wood, étc., is in the stage of losing its identity. Its nature is ambiguous; it is, for example, neither food nor dirt, the latter representing the stage of total disintegration. The “old blood” is also of ambiguous nature, since it is still blood and yet not the “fresh” or normal kind which the Ainu believe to be the essential substance for life. Human excreta has the same unidentifiable quality as trash. Death, and sickness which leads to death, represent ambiguous stages of life. For the Ainu who believe in the continuation of life after death, death is an ambiguous stage between life in this world and the world of the dead Ainu; as van Gennep pointed out a long time ago (1960: 146-165), funeral ceremonies are rites of passage.

It thus appears that the objects and phenomena associated with the western-southern half of the shore are singled out because of the ambiguous status. In the classification of the beings of the universe, however, they are symbols of the profane rather than the marginal.

The nature of my Ainu/super-Ainu opposition is further illustrated by distinguishing between my use of these terms and the widely used terms of “sacred” and “profane.” My Ainu/super-Ainu dualism corresponds only in a limited sense with the sacred and the profane as used by many scholars (e.g., anthropological use of these terms stating that "sacred" refers to the abnormal, special, other-wordly, royal, taboo, and sick; whereas "profane" refers to the normal, everyday, of this world, plebeian, permitted, and healthy (Leach 1967b:97). My super-Ainu category does not involve the abnormal. "Taboo" and "sick," classified by Leach inthe sacred category, are in my Ainu category. Moreover, Leach's list of the profane are too positive for my Ainu category.

<table>
<tr><td>(+) interior mountains</td><td>(0) near shore hills</td><td>(+) offshore</td><td>(0) near shore</td><td rowspan="2">(+) eastern-northern half</td><td rowspan="2">(0) western-southern half</td><td rowspan="3">(+) the avove</td><td rowspan="3">(0) the below</td></tr>
<tr><td colspan="2">(+) mountains</td><td colspan="2">(0) sea</td></tr>
<tr><td colspan="4">non-shore (+)</td><td colspan="2">shore area (0)</td></tr>
<tr><td colspan="6">horizontal plane</td><td colspan="2">vertical plane</td></tr>
<tr><td colspan="8">UNIVERSE</td></tr>
</table>

TABLE III
HIERARCHICAL LEVELS OF THE DYADIC STRUCTURE

I must also mention that my Ainu category is not as powerful as the profane category is not as powerful as the profane category defined by Hertz, a most influential scholar in the anthropology of symbolic classification, he saw affinity and even equivalence between the profane and the impure, arguing that the profane is an active and contagious nothingness in that it is "the antagonistic element which by its very contact degrades, diminishes, and changes the essence of things that are sacred" (hertz 1960-, 1909:94-95). The Ainu category, however, is characterized by lack of power; it is like a vacuum. As indicated earlier, the Ainu believe that their life is subject to the demands of the deities, whose mood controls the supply of food and disasters, including attacks by demons.

The basic difference between my Ainu/super-Ainu opposition and the classical Durkhe mian sacred and profane is the fact that the former is a classificatory principle. Thus, to use Needham's expression, it represents "a mode of classification which orders the scheme," and it does not signify the possession of specific property or properties (Needham 1960:26).

Unlike the Durkheimian sacred and profane, the Ainu/super-Ainu opposition is a complementary one. A system of complementary opposites is not a dualism of mutually antagonistic forces (see Freedman 1968:7). Because the Ainu/super-Ainu opposition is a classificatory principle and represents a complementary opposition, it can operate onmore than one plane or level. Consequently, the Ainu/super-Ainu dichotomy does not characterize any area in absolute terms, and thus on the next level a super-Ainu area may become an Ainu area.

Therefore, in Table II in horizontal columns 2 and 3, a super-Ainu area is dichotomized into a super-Ainu and an Ainu area. thus, both nearshore mountains in column 2 and nearshore sea in column 3 are Ainu areas when contrasted with interior mountains and offshore respective;y; however, they are super-Ainu areas when the horizontal plane of the universe at large is in consideration. Likewise, in column 4, the shore an Ainu area, is dichotomized into a super—Ainu area and an Ainuarea. Thus, the eastern-northen half is a super—Ainu area when contrasted with the western-southern half of the shore, although it is with the Ainu area of the shore (see Table III).

Since the super—Ainu quality represents a minimal distinctive feature in categorizing spatial domains which possess many other properties, other binary oppositions may also operate between certain spatial categories. These, however, are of more limited applicability. For example, male/female opposition divides the universe into a male area consisting of the mountains, sea, and ground above the sky, and a female area comprising the shore and sky.

The male area is characterized by Ainu male subsistence activities and as the residence of male deities. Hunting and fishing, done exclusively by Ainu males, are the primary activities of the Ainu in the mountains and the sea, and both the duties of the mountains and the deities of the sea are perceived as male figures. Dragon Deities, which are also male, reside on the ground above what we call "." The shore, on the other hand, is characterized by economic activities of Ainu females and as the residence of the Goddess of the Hearth. The other female deity, the Goddess of the Sun, resides in the sky.[24]

In summary, the basic structure of Ainu spatial concepts may be best understood as a dyadic structure comprising a series of contrast sets in binary opposition with the super-Ainu quality as the minimal distinctive feature. It is a complex structure because of: multiplicity of planes of classification, equivocality of each symbol and yet univvocality of each symbol on each plane in binary oppsotion (see Turner 1960: 1-43).

In this discussion, I have attempted to convey the basic structure of Ainu spatial concepts—how the Ainu classify the universe. Like most cultural behavior, the spatial concepts in the main are not consciously, constructed in the mind of the people (see the discussion on the world view in Hallo well 1964:50). Thus, the basic structure presented in this paper is my interpretation and abstraction based on ethnographic data. I hope my presentation clarly differentiates my inferences, interpretations, and abstraction from the data, since I believe that the foremost task of the anthropologist is, as Goodenough most appropriately put it, "to make available to his colleagues the detailed findings of his research" (Goodenough 1968:v.)[25]

Reference

1. The fieldwork was conducted under a grant from the National Science Foundation. I am very grateful to the Foundation, and to Dr. Chester S.Chard of the University of Wisconsin who was very instrumental in obtaining the grant. I am most grateful to Dr. Jamn Vansina in his generous allocation of his time for reviewing my study. His criticisms and suggestions of the initial version of this study, my dissertation (Ohnuki-Tierney 1968) and of the draft of this paper were most helpful.
2. All the italicized Ainu terms are in phonemic notation.For phonemic transcription, see Ohnuki-Tierney (1969b:5-8)
3. To my knowledge, all the Japanese scholars of the Ainu agree with this. Only two linguists, Dr. S. Hattori and Mrs. K. Furukawa, from the Language Institute of Tokyo, howevr, have been working extensively with Husko.
4. Husko spent most of her pre-married days in the Hurooci settlement, and all of her married life until 1943 at the Rayciska settlement. Althoug there were some Japanese near these settlements, the contact between the Japanese and the Ainu, although not hostile, was not intimate. She lived the Ainu way of life and Ainu was her only language until the beginning of World War II. With the opening of World War II, the japanese government in Sakhalin penetrated into the Ainu settlements in this area. Husko's husband, who was chief of the Rayciska settlement, caused her to have some contact with the Japanese officials. She learned Japanese during this time.
5. In a more limited sense the term may also mean simply a

locality as in So:ya Mosiri (place name at the northern tip of Hokkaido; Japanese call it Soya), or an island as in Ri:sir Mosiri (Japanese call it Rishiri-to) and repun Mosiri (japanese call it Rebun-to).

6. For a detailed discussion of Ainu contact with other peoples and the trade system, see Ohnuki-tierney (1968-20-79)
7. bears—is in Ainu; ursus arctos collaris (Chiri 1962:149)). Martens—hoynu in Ainu; Martes zibellina brachyura (Temminck) (Chri 1962:147). Reindeer-tunakay in Ainu; Rangifer tarandus sibiricus (Schreber) (Chiri 1962: 173). Musk deer—opokay in Ainu; Moschus moschiferus L. (Chiri 1962:173).
8. Yesso spruce—sunku in Ainu; Picea jezoensis Carr (Chiri 1953:236). Sakhalin fir—yayuh in Ainu; A bies sachalinenesis Fr. Schm. (Chiri 1953:234). White birch—tahni in Ainu; Ulmus laciniata Mayr Chiri 1953:165).
9. The root of corydalis is called toma in Ainu. Corydalis ambiqua cham. et Schl. (Chiri 1953:134). The root of the Kamchatka lily is called hah in Ainu. Fritillaria kamtschatcensis Ker-Gawl (Chiri 1953:203-204). The asparagus is called sewah in ainu. Aralia cordata Thunb. (Chiri 1953: 68). The root of peony is called home-su: in Ainu; *Paeonia Japonica* Miyabe et Takeda; Paeonia obovata Maxim (Chrii 1953:150). The leek is called kito in ainu; Allium victorialis L. var. *platyphyllum* Makino (Chiri 1953: 195).
10. Squirrels are called *rohse* in Ainu. Sciurus vulgalis rupestries (Chiri 1962: 170).
11. Cow parsnip is called in Ainu. *Heracleum* lanatum Michx (Chiri 1953:63).
12. The General term in Ainu for both moss and lichen is siprus.
13. Cranberry is *katam* in Ainu: *Vaccinium Oxycoccus* (Chiri 1953: 54). Raspberry is *etakay* in Ainu: Rubus Chamaemorus L. (Chiri 1953:124).
14. Larch in Ainu is kuy: *larix dahurica Turcz.* (Chiri 1953: 237).
15. One of the vacciniaceous berries is called sahtureh in Ainu. It is: *Vaccinium chamissonis* Bong, *Vaccinium ovalifolium* Sm. (Chiri 1953:55); *Vaccinium* Smallii A Gray (Miyabe and Miyake 1915:302). The other kind of vacciniaceous berries is called *Cuhtureh:* It is: *Vaccinium uliginosum* L. (Chiri 1953: 56).
16. cotton grass is called *Cius mun* in Ainu: *Eriophorum* Chiri 1953:219).

17. When asked directly about the sex of these animals, the Ainu say that there are both male and female deities and thus of spring is born. However, when the Ainu think of them as deities, they perceive them as males.
18. Chiri discusses the stories of *penkankux* [sic] and *pankankux* [six] in detail, giving examples of stories collected on the east coast of Sakhalin and a few from Hokkaido (Chiri 1955). The above story told by Husko is quite different from Chiri's examples. In all of Chiri's toreies from the east coast of Sakhalin, the penkankux is the fool and the pankankux the wise. Chiri, However, points out that in some areas such as Teshio on the northern tip of Hokkaido, the pankankux is the fool (Chiri 1955: 257-258)
19. The Ainu summer hoses are made of logs of either Yesso spruce of Sakhalin fir, and the roof is made of Yesso spruce bark which is held in place by wooden nails, or nivinkiw meciroh, with a few logs covering it. On the northwest coast, it is square in shape, although its shape range from square to rectangular depending upon the region (Yamamoto 1943:67).
20. There seem to be some regional differences in the location and the number of entrances built in the storage structure (Yamamoto 1943:67).
21. In view of the classical study of Hertz, Husko's analogy of a house as a body in lying position is interesting.Hertaz generalized that east and south are the sacred directions, whereas north and best are profane (Hertz 1960, 1909:96, 110). He explained that among peoples who practiced solar worship, a person facing the rising sun has his sacred right to the south. Of course, he assumed erroneously the universality of the sacred right. We now see cultures where there is a sacred let, e.g., many African cultures (cf. Needham 1960). Huski's statement indicates that the right hand may face the north, and hence north is sacred.
22. For example, on the northwest coast, the winter when Husko was born in 1900 was the last winter which her family of orientation spent in the winter settlement along the masaramamma river, a tributary of the Tomarikesnay he (Japanese call it Esutori-gawa). At Naibuchi on the east coast, the Russian style log cabin replaced both the summer and winter houses around 1901 (Sentoku 1929:20). there change is

also noted by Pilsudski (1912:56) and Yamamoto (1943:32).

23. During my 1965-66 fieldwork, I had mistakenly noted that the branch may be placed toward the direction of sunrise. In 1969, I checked on this point at several different occasions.

24. The female area is thus located in the center of the universe, while the male areas are located on the outer s[here. This spatial arrangement is particularly interesting as women, as noted earlier, have the lowest status in the Ainu society and therefore are furthest away from deity status. Also pertinent here is that the two female deities are mediators between the Ainu and the deities. In folktales, it is an Ainu female who marries a deity and thus becomes a medicator in a broad sense between the Ainu and the deities. I know of only one folktale in which an Ainu elder is married to a female diety; in that case it is the Goddess of Sun. A discussion of the full range of inferences on the Ainu concept of women would require separate treatment.

25. Ever since Durkheim and Mauss argued that symbolic classification is a reflection of the basic classification in social organization, most of the studies on symbolic classification include a discussion of categories in social organization. I did not include spatial analysis of the Ainu social organization, since most of the Ainu settlements, including those on the northwest coast, are very small. They trace descent bilaterally and the basic social unit is often an extended family consisting of cognatic kin. There is little in the Ainu social classification that may be meaningfully related to their symbolic classification. Other common approaches in spatial analyses of social organization,such as analysis of settlement pattern and generalogical distance, are not presented, since they too show little correspondence to the spatial classification of the universe. Therefore, the Ainu society supports Needham's insight that a striking correspondence between social organization and symbolic classification is actually uncommon in simple societies (Needham 1963:xxxvii) and that a correspondence of structure between the two orders is often seen in lineal systems with prescriptive affinities llianal (Needham 1960:22).

REFERENCES CITED

Chiri, Mashio,

1944, Karafuto Ainu no Setsuwa (Folktales of the Sakhalin Ainu). Karafutooho Hakubutsukan Iho 3((1):1-146.

1950 Ainu Jukyo no Kansuru Jakkan no Kosatsu (Some notes the Ain dwelling). Minzokugaku Kenkyu 14(4). 74-77 (336-339)

1953, 1954, 1962 Bunrui Ainugo Jiten (Classified dictionaries of teh Ain language), 3 vols. (Vol. I, Plants, 1953; Vol. II, Animals, 1962; Voo. III, Human, 1954). Tokyo: Nihon Jomin Bunka Kenkyujo.

1955 Ainu Sanbun Monogatari-- Kawashimo no mono no Mukashi Banashi (Panampe-uwepeker Ainu folk tales of the true and untrue type [sic]). Hoppo Bunka Kenkyu 10:251-319 (1-69).

1956 Chimei Ainugo Shojiten (Dictionary of Ainu place names). Sapporo: Nire Shobo.

Chiri, Mashio, and Kunio Oda

1956 Yukara Kansho (Evaluations of the Ainu epic). TokyoL Gengensha.

Chri, Mashio, and Shuzo Yamada

1956 Anoyo no Iriguchi (An entrance to the other world).. Hoppo Bumka Kenkyu 11:1-33.

Douglas, Mary

1966 Purity and Danger. London: Routledge and Kegan Paul.

Durkheim, Emile

1965 The Elementary Forms of the Religious Life. New York: Free Press. (First Published in 1915).

Eliade, Mircea

1961 The Sacred an dth eProfane, W.R. Trask, Trans.. New York: Harper and Row.

Freedman, maurice

1968 Geomancy. Proceedings of the Royal Anthropologicla Institute of Great Britain and Ireland. pp.5-1.

Fujimoto, Hideo

1964 Ainu no Haka—Kokogaku kara Mita Ainu Bunkashi (Ainu tombs—Ainu culture history as seen from arch aeology). Tokyo: NIhon Keizai Shinbunsha.

Goodenough, Ward H.

1968 Anthropological Studiės: A New Publication Series of the American Anthropological Association. American Anthropologist 70 v.

Hallowell, A. Irving

1955 Culture and Experience. Philadelphia: Unviersity of Pennsylvania Press.

1964 Ojibwa Ontology, Behaviour, and World View. Primitive views of the World. S. Diamond, Ed. New york: Columbia Unviersity Press. Pp. 49-82.

Hertz, Robertt

1960 Death and the Right Hand. Glenocoe: The Free Press. (First Published in 1907 and 1909.

Kindaichi, Kyosulke

1925 Ainu no Knkyu (Study of the Ainu). Tokyo: Naigai Shobo.

1961 Ainu Bunkashi (Culture History of th eAinu). Selected essays of Kyosuke Kindaichi, Vol. II. Tokyo: Sanseido.

Kitagawa, Joseph M.

1961 Ainu Bear Festival (*lyomante),* History of Religion 1 (1): 95:151.

Leach, Edmund

1967a Genesis as Myth. Myth and Cosmos. J. Middleton, Ed. New York: Natural History Press. pp. 77-108.

Miyabe, Kingo, and Tsutome Miyake

1915 Karafuto Sokubutsushi (Flora of Sakhalin). Toyokara Japanese Government in Sakhalin.

Munro, Neil Gordon

1963 Ainu creed and Cult. New York: Columbia University Press.

Needham, Rodney

1960 The let Hand of the Mugwe: An Analytical Note on the Structure of Meru Symbolism. Africa 30(1):20-33.

1963 Introduction. Primitive Classification. E. Durkheim and M. Mauss. Chicago: University of Chicago Press. pp.vii-xivii.

Ohnuki-Tierney, Emiko

1968 A Northwest Coast Sakhalin Ainu World View. Ph.D.

dissertation, University of Wisconsin.,
1969a Concepts of Time Among tho Ainu of the Northwest Coast of Sakhalin. American Anthropologist 71:4880492.
1969b Sakhalin Ainu Folklore. Anthropological Studies 2. Washington, D.C.: American Anthropological Association.

Pilsudski, Bronislov
1912 Materials for the Study of the Ainu Language and Folklore. Cracow: Spplka Wydawnicza Polska.

Sentoku, Taroji
1929 Karafuto Ainu Soa (Stories of the Sakhalin Ainu). Tokyo: Shikodo.

Takakura, Shinichiro
1966 Vanishing Ainu of Northern Japan. Natural History 75:16-25.

Turner, Victor. W.
1969 TheRitual Process. Chicago: Aldine.

Van gennep, Arnold
1960 The Rites of Passage. Chicago: University of Chicago Press. (First Published in 1909)

Wallace, Anthony F.C.
1964 Culture and Personality. New York: Random House.

Yamamoto, Yuko
1943 Karafuto ain no Kukyo (Ainu dwellings in Sakhalin). Tokyo: Aizawa Shobo.

* *American Anthropoligist*. vol. 74. 1972

Chapter-7

The Stranger as God: The Place of the Outsider in Japanese Folk Religion[1]

By Teigo Yosida

Chapter-7

The object of this paper is to examine the meaning of "stranger" in the traditional context in Japan. While the Japanese are reputably hospitable to foreigners, at the same time Japanese society is also said to be essentially closed to foreigners, strangers, or outsiders. The ambiguity in the Japanese attitude toward foreigners and strangers implied by these contradictory observations is related to symbolic aspects of the notion of "stranger" found in the past and in contemporary rural Japan.

Special attention is also given to the association of animal spirit possession and strangers in Japanese villages, the mystical powers and evil qualities attributed to newcomers in the villages, the belief that a stranger unexpectedly appearing in a village in fact may be a god in human guise, and the oppositional structures inherent in the symbol system pertaining to strangers in Japan.

THE AMBIGUITY AND POWER OF STRANGERS

First, let us consider animal spirit possession as it relates to the place of strangers in Japanese villages. In villages in Oita, Kochi, Shimane, and Gunma Prefectures, some family lines are believed to "hold" certain animal spirits that may possess other people, causing them to become mentally deranged or ill (cf. Yoshida 1967). A curious, underlying social pattern is commonly found in this custom. The founders of families holding animals spirits were generally not the earliest settlers in the villages, but were later arrivals. Villagers contend that the founding ancestors of the animal spirit holding families were initially strangers (*yoso-mono*) in their respective villages. Moreover, the fact that were strangers is often emphasized by the inhabitants. For example, the founder of the Murata family, known as a "fix-spirit family" (*kitsune-mochi*), moved into the village of Tagawa, Shimane Prefecture, from a neighboring village in the middle of the seventeenth century. The household head of either the third generation, who died in 1743, or of the fourth generation, who died in 1779, is said to have brought into his house as his mistress "a woman whose past is unknown." The woman has subsequently discovered to be a "fox-spirit holder," according to the villagers, and since then the Murata family has been a fox-spirit holding family (Yoshida & Ueda 1968).

Our next example shows a similar pattern. Two brothers, ancestors of the Nakao family, moved from another village to the village of Sato, Nogi-Gun, Shimane Prefecture, and settled there during the Genroku Period (1688-1704). According to the present household head of the "branch house" of his family, the Nakaos were not initially fox-spirit holders. The "main house" of the family became a fox-spirit holder in the second generation of the family, because the heir to the headship of the main house took a woman from her original husband, a man known as a *"kajiya-mono,"* and married her. The term *kajiya-mono* derives from the word *kajiya,* meaning blacksmith which usually denotes in this area a stranger and a fox-spirit holder, although many blacksmiths have entered villages to practice their craft. The heir of the Nakao main house was the village headman. Utilizing his political power, he forcefully married the blacksmith's beautiful wife. Since then the main house of the Nakao family has been regarded as one of the fox-spirit holding families. Members of the Nakao branch house have served their relations with the main house to prevent the spread of fox-spirit holding to themselves. Thus, the original branch house of the Nakao family has not been regarded as a fox-spirit holding family although all three later branches of the main house retained the fox-spirit holding character.[2]

To take a slightly different example, in a village of 38 households in Tano-Gun, Gunma Prefecture, there was one household considered by the villagers to be holding fox-spirits. In this area we find holders of both fox-spirits and *osaki* spirits. *Osaki* is the local term for a type of weasel believed to possess people. In this particular village there was no *osaki* holder and only one fox-spirit holding family (*kitsune-mochi*). According to some older informants of the village, the founder of the fox-spirit holding family was a *gyo-ja*, or magico-religious practitioner. He had come from the outside and settled there after marrying a woman in the village. Until the 1920s it is said that there were many *gyo-ja* in this area. They were believed to use fox-spirits in their magical curing techniques. Generally *gyo-ja* were strangers coming from outside. Even in villages of the area where the origins of family lines of animal spirit holders are not known, villagers emphasize that holders were initially strangers and later arrivals in the villages (Yoshida 1972:66-80).

The attribution of mystical evil qualities to newcomers may be a reflections of the Japanese villagers' traditional fears and suspicions of outsiders and strangers. In many northeastern villages strangers and outsiders are not permitted to settle without establishing fictive kinship relations with one of the prominent families of the village. The newcomers' status in the village is then defined in terms of the pre-existing village social structure. For instance, on the island of Tashiro-jima, Miyagi Prefecture, it is customary for outsiders to settle down by creating fictive kinship relations with one of the main houses or long established stem families of a village. This is accomplished by obtaining permission from the household head of a main house to become his branch house or family. It is worth noting that in the villages of this island there are no animal spirit holding families, just as there are practically none throughout the northeast region of Japan.

Inhabitants of traditional villages used to recognize many

kinds of strangers. Visitors from the outside world included smiths, carpenters, masons roofers, and other craftsmen, peddlers of medicines, fancy goods peddlers, traders, horse dealers, shamans, priests and other religious practitioners, travelling drama players, story tellers, and so on. Smiths and other craftsmen, as well as the religious practitioners, were attributed with mystical powers (Takeuchi 1960b).

The fact that newcomers and outsiders who become holders are typically prosperous, powerful, highly skilled, or possess valued and rare objects is matched by the fact that they are regarded as dangerous for some reason. In this we see the underlying pattern of ambiguity. Japanese attitudes toward foreigners who came to Japan from the West during the sixteenth and following centuries also contained much that was ambiguous. The foreigners were often attributed by Japanese as having mystical powers. On the one hand, they were seen as mystically dangerous; yet, on the other hand, they were often considered to have some supernatural ability, e.g., the power to find miraculous stones which could bestow longevity and even eternal life.

The Portuguese who came to Japan during the sixteenth century were considered to have come from *"tenjiku"* and were referred to as the *tenjiku-jin* (people of *tenjiku*). *Tenjiku* is an ancient name for India and denotes a remote place, a mountain peak, the sky, and a foreign country. It was believed then that Europeans came to Japan from such a distant place. Obviously, the people of *tenjiku* were associated with supernatural power in the minds of most Japanese of the day. For example, Francisco Xavier, a Spanish Jesuit missionary, was once walking in heavy snow in some moun-tainous region when he met a Japanese who requested that he, "a man from *tenjiku,"* reduce the amount of snowfall (Okada 1955: 159). According to historical documents, Japanese during that time often believed that Western missionaries ate children, disemboweled dying people to make poisons, and could make grass and trees wither just by touching them. It was also believed by the Japanese that human excrement and urine were effective in eliminating the magical powers of those foreigners. That Christianity, introduced to Japan by strangers from *tenjiku* during the middle of the sixteenth century, was first understood by Japanese to be a religion of black magic and witchcraft, is no surprise. Christianity, it was thought, had much evil power. It was called "the religion of the *tenjiku*" (Okada 1955: 159-174). Even later when Commodore Matthew C. Perry came to Uraga with his squadron of four "black" ships in 1852, the Japanese were frightened by the mystical powers of foreign visitors. According to some documents written in that period, they believed that by the use of magic Americans could find personal treasures hidden in houses (Okada 1955: 146).

There is an Edo Period folktale in Nagasaki about a Dutchman with mystical ability. The Dutchman asked a Japanese to sell him a stone from his garden. With the consent of the Japanese the Dutchman gave him five *ryo* and left Nagasaki or his home country, asking the Japanese to keep the stone for him until his return three years hence. Since the Dutchman had not returned to Nagasaki after six years, the Japanese man, not being able to wait any longe, broke the stone. To his surprise, a red living fish jumped out of the stone. The next year the Dutchman returned and to his regret found that the stone had been broken. He then told the Japanese about the stone; that it was of the most valuable kind and found only in Japan. Possession of such a stone would greatly lengthen life. With great polishing it would become so transparent that one could see a red "immortal" fish swimming inside. Looking at the fish inside the stone every morning and evening would enhance longevity. The Japanese then asked the Dutchman to reach him how to recognize such valuable stones, but he left for Holland without sharing his secrets (Okada, 1955: 155-156).

Although there exist different versions of this sort of tale of magically endowed strangers, the motif is essentially the same. In earlier folk tales written before the Edo Period the stranger who can recognize the mystical value of such stone or other materials is a Chinese. The Chinese are replaced by European visitors in later versions. Although this type of story originally may have been made it their own and in turn applied it to European stranger. It is worth noting here that in Chinese folktales mystical power is attributed to Japanese travellers and visitors, and that in European folk stories Orientals are often attributed with supernatural qualities (Okada 1955: 157).

As stated above, the Japanese notion of stranger is connected to both inauspicious and auspicious powers. Strangers, visitors, beggars, and even stones coming from distant places are often believed to bring good luck. This belief can be historically related to the notion of *marebito* in ancient Japan. The word *merebito* means a god who occasionally visits villagers from the other world (*tokoyo*), located far beyond the sea, for the purpose of bringing good luck to the inhabitants (Origuchi 1975a, 1975b, 1976). The visit of *marebito* is the basis for certain widespread village rituals. In one ritual, for example, a young man dressed as a god visited every house in his village to bless it with good fortune. In later periods the *hokai-bito,* or "people who offer felicitations," were attributed to being *marebito,* and treated as gods. *Hokai-bito* often came in the guise of beggars (Origuchi 1957b; Nagano 1973). The notion of *marebito* has not disappeared, but survives to this day. The well-known practice of *nama-hage* in northeastern Japan, in which young men wearing goblin masks and dressed as monsters visit every house of the village to bring about a good harvest and human fertility, is based upon a similar notion of "visiting gods" (*maroudo-gami*) (Takeuchi 1960a, 1960b; Okano 1960). The notion of visiting gods is also found today in various rituals in villages on the island of Tokunoshima, one of the Amami Islands, in extreme southwestern Japan. For instance, in the practice called *"muchi-tabore"* (give us rick cake) in the village of Tete on the north coast of the island, young men and boys, each wearing a white sheet (actually a bed sheet) over hid head, visit every house of the village to promote fertility, and are given *muchi* (rice-cake) at each house. The *muchi-tabore* is performed on July 15th of the lunar calendar, the last day of the *bon* (festival honoring the ancestors).

The notion of visiting gods is also the basis of the folktales in which a rich man who refuses to allow a beggar-priest to stay in his house becomes poor, whereas a poor man who lodges the priest becomes wealthy (Seki 1960). A similar motif can also be found in ancient myths. In a myth from the *Fudoki,* a god called Mioyano-Mikoto, after having visited various places, asks the god of Mount Fuji for a night's lodging, but is refused. Mioyano-Mikoto then curses the god of Mount Fuji, saying, "In your mountain it will be very cold with snowfall and frost in the summer as well as in the winter, and no one will offer you and food." He then went to Mount Tsukuba, and asked the god of Mount Tsukuba for lodging. Since he was warmly treated by the god of Mount Tsukuba, he said, "Many people will come to your mountain, and they will always offer you much food." This is why Mount Fuji is perennially snow-capped white Mount Tsukuba is visited by many people bearing offerings.

In another myth of the *Fudoki* a god called Muto, on his way to marry a girl of the South Seas, is refused lodging by a wealthy man named Shorai. However, Shorai's elder brother Somin, who is poor, welcomes the god Muto. Some time later this god conquers Shorai and his people, but saves Somin and his people. It is eventually discovered that the god Muto is none other than Susa-no-o-no-Mikoto, brother of the Sun Goddess.

The folk belief in visiting gods can be found today in legends told by contemporary villagers. In the village of Inokawa on the east coast of the island of Tokunoshima, Kagoshima Prefecture, there is a shrine called Ibiganashi dedicated to a flat rock. According to a legend told by the villagers, once upon a time an old man wearing worn-out clothes came to the village from far away, beyond the sea, riding on a flat rock. One villager threw stones at the old man, but another man offered him food, after removing lice from his hair. The family line of the man who had thrown stones has been childless. The women who became wives in his family line have been barren with wombs "like stones" due to the mystical power of the old man. However, the descendants of the man who had been kind to him have had many children, "like lice," and have become prosperous. The old man also assured the kind man that his descendants would suffer no shipwrecks, smallpox, or difficult childbirths. According to the present village headman, who claims to be a direct descendant of the kind man, what the old man promised has proven true. Ever since the old man suddenly disappeared from the village, villagers have worshipped the flat rock on which he had arrived. This sacred stone is also known as the god Ebisu among the villagers.

Ebisu

The belief in visiting gods obviously is related to the god called Ebisu who has been worshipped by Japanese fishermen as the god of fishing, and later by merchants as the god of commerce. The god's name seems to be related to the word *ebisu,* meaning a stranger, foreigner, or person from a remote place. Ebisu is thus originally a god coming from a remote land bringing good luck. This is reflected in the fishermen's practice of worshipping stones or items washed up on the beach as manifestations of the god Ebisu. A fisherman of a village in Oita Prefecture curiously found similar stones three times in his fishing net. Villagers decided to worship these stones as the god Ebisu in a shrine which they built near the beach (Fujiwara 1949). It is also the custom of some fishing villages that at the time of a large catch visitors casually passing by are created with special hospitality as the god Ebisu (Takeuchi 1960b). At another time a traveller visiting a fishing village was invited to join in the fishing. The crew he joined caught so many fish that they called the visitor "Ebisu-san." When other fishermen learned of this good luck, they asked the visitor to sail on their boats too, hoping to have similar large catches. The poor fellow was obliged to sail in one boat after another (Sakurada 1968:201). The association of the notion of stranger with benevolent and mystical power still persists strongly today. When I was visiting the Oki Islands, Shimane Prefecture, with a French anthropologist and his wife in the fall of 1977, we accidentally came across a fishing port in Urago where people were performing a launching ceremony. Noticing our unexpected visit, they repeatedly exclaimed, *"man ga ii* (we are lucky)," hoping that the strange visitors would bring good luck to the boat.[3]

The same notion of stranger can be recognized in novels, movies, and television dramas of contemporary Japan. In many traditional stories "master-less *samurai (ronin-mono)*," "migratory strangers (*watari-mono*)" or mysterious strangers passing by, rescue people in distress by eliminating the malicious bosses who are the source of the people's affliction. Famous those stories are the "Seven *Samurai*" and other films of Akira Kurusawa.

Also the series of movies with Zatoichi as the hero are among the most popular of the post-war era. Zatoichi is a blind, homeless, travelling priest skilled in fighting with a sword cane. Set in the pre-modern period, these movies show him accidently becoming involved in helping people oppressed by unjust authorities. Zatoichi's fighting skills help eliminate the oppressors, thereby rescuing the afflicted common people. After each episode he returns to his journey, becoming a stranger once more. Zatoichi movies have been repeatedly shown on television and a new series, especially made for television, is currently being shown once a week. A similar and equally popular television drama is "Kogarashi Monjiro," in which the hero, a wanderer (*watari-mono*) highly skilled in fencing, rescues people in distress by fighting the powerful oppressors. There are many other television dramas that follow this basic pattern. Can we not say that the appeal of this generalise in something more than the sword fighting alone, and is linked with the *ebisu* or *marebito* idea.?[4]

One of our findings in the fishing village of Katsumoto-ura, Iki Island off northern Kyushu, is that when a fisherman finds a corpse adrift in the sea, he usually takes it into his boat and buries it in his home graveyard. They believe that this practice will help them catch fish, for they regard a drifting corpse as the god Ebisu. A fisherman mentioned that he had picked up drifting corpses twice in two successive years, and that during those two years his catch was particularly good. This practice of retrieving corpses co-exists with the villagers' quite contradictory notions of impurity. Contact with death, childbirth, menstruation, and women are all considered unclean. Such pollution (*kegare*) will bring about poor catches and bad luck (Namihira 1978).

As described elsewhere (Yoshida *et al.* 1974) this village has achieved notable technological improvement in its fishing industry; yet, in spite of the improvements of the boat engines, the rapid increase of power-driven fishing boats, the introduction of transceivers and radar, and other innovations, the villagers still retain their traditional folk beliefs. Even today they generally avoid taking women along in their fishing boats, for it is believed that women pollute fishing boats. Likewise a fisherman does not go out fishing f or three days after his wife bears a child. Many other rules are still strictly observed in order to avoid pollution. When his wife becomes pregnant, a fisherman always goes to the Shomo shrine dedicated to a tutelary god of the village to have himself purified by the priest before going out fishing. When a fisherman attends a funeral ceremony, he takes a different road home. He is purified at a small shrine called *odo* by drinking *sake* with his relatives and friends, passing the *sake* cup counter-clockwise.

This way of passing a *sake* cup is a symbolic contrast to the way fishermen circle their boat clockwise in port before going out fishing. After purifying themselves at the *odo* they always go to the beach to purify themselves again by sprinkling salt water on themselves or by wetting their feet in the sea.

If a parent dies, his or her sons should not go out fishing for 49 days. A man should not go fishing for twenty days if his paternal uncle or aunt dies, while the period of the taboo is ten days if his maternal uncle or aunt dies. Villagers attributed the tragic shipwrecks of 1972 and 1973 to the fact that crew members of the wrecked boats broke the taboo period of 49 days after their parent's death. Also, poor catches in other years were attributed by villagers to someone's failure to observe those rules.

Despite all this concern with pollution, and especially with the pollution death brings, fishermen will pick up a drifting corpse because they regard it as bringing good luck. Special procedures, however, must be followed to keep pollution from the boat. The part of the boat where the corpse was placed must be carefully purified by salt after the body is taken from the boat. The fishermen also purify themselves by drinking *sake,* and a Shinto priest of the village shrine performs a purification ceremony for the boat and for the *funa-dama* (guardian spirit of the boat) enshrined within it. The word *funa* means boat and *dama* means a spirit or soul. In Katsumotoura the belief in *funa-dama* strongly persists today. A *funadama* is enshrined in every fishing boat without exception, even though all fishing boats are equipped with powerful engines. A small wooden box containing *funadama* is placed at the foot of the main mast or in the central part of each fishing boat. However, some fishermen contend that the guardian spirit actually resides in the bow of the boat. The fishermen of this village always pray to the *funa-dama* before embarking on a fishing trip and offer some fish and rice to it after returning to port.

The belief that a drifting corpse in the sea can bring good luck if it is picked up and properly buried is widely distributed among Japanese fishing communities. Reports of the belief are known for the Goto Islands, Nagasaki Prefecture, villages on the northern coast of Fukuoka Prefecture, Koshiki Islands, Kagoshima Prefecture, and for villages in Tokushima, Shimane, Wakayama, Fukushima, Miyagi, and Iwate Prefectures (Makita 1966:85-7). It is also reported from the Miyake Islands, and I found the same belief in Tsudo, a fishing village, Dogo, in the Oki Islands, Shimane Prefecture in 1977.

In fishing villages of the Koshiki Islands, and in Uchino-ura, Kagoshima Prefecture, a young man, blindfolding himself, dives into the sea to pick up stones to dedicate to Ebisu Shrines. In those villages stones thus taken from the bottom of the sea are worshipped as Ebisu. In villages in Fukushima-cho, Miyazaki Prefecture, stones worshipped as Ebisu are replaced with new stones if fishermen suffer continuous poor catches. In the fishing village of Tamano-ura, Goto Islands, a new stone is taken from the sea every year to replace the old ones at the times of the annual festival of the Ebisu Shrine (Sakurada 1968:208-9). The stone worshipped as Ebisu in a village in Wakamatsu, Fukuoka Prefecture was caught in a fishing net. In Gokamura, Oki Islands, Shimane Prefecture, stones found in fishing nets customarily have been brought home and worshipped as the god Ebisu in the *kamidana* (small shrine) of the fisherman's home. The villagers contend that the families which worship such *ebisu* stones in their houses enjoy abundant catches (Sakurada 1968:206-8).

Sakurada reports of a fisherman who has been worshipping a *sake* bottle he had taken from the sea. The man of a fishing village in Oshima, Yamaguchi Prefecture, found a *sake* bottle drifting in the open sea, but returned home without picking it up. Next morning when he went to the beach, he was surprised to see the same *sake* bottle on the seashore. He took it to his house. Since then, it is said, he was always lucky in catching fish and eventually became one of the wealthiest persons in the island. For this reason he has continued to worship the *sake* bottle that, like a stranger, brought good luck when it was well treated (Sakurada 1968:214).

Fishermen in Misaki, Kagawa Prefecture believed that a drifting Noh mask taken out of the sea brought them good luck (Utsumi 1951). Initially, they could not catch any fish after picking up the drifting Noh mask, so the captain of the boat went to a diviner to find out what was wrong. He was told that although the mask become angry with a crew member who criticized the idea of picking up the mask. The captain properly enshrined the mask in the *kami-dana* (small shrine) in his house and after that, to his satisfaction, he was able to first catch lots of sardines and then a large catch of tuna using the sardines at bait (Utsumi 1951).

Along with stones, shells, bottles, masks, drifting corpses, and other drift materials from the sea, whales, dolphins, and sharks are often called Ebisu. They are worshipped as such in many fishing villages, in the belief that they will bring good catches.

In picking up a drifting corpse from the sea, fishermen must follow certain rules. For instance, in many villages corpses must always be taken up on the starboard side of boat, never from the port side, although in certain villages in the Koshiki Islands the sides the reversed. While the side of a boat deemed proper for taking a corpse aboard varies locally, taking a corpse on board is almost always contrasted to the procedure for enshrining the *funa-dama* or guardian spirit in the boat at the launching ceremony. Specifically, in villages in Kabashima, Go to Islands, Nagasaki Prefecture, and in fishing villages in Fukuoka and Yamaguchi Prefectures, it is said that since the *funa-dama* goes on board from the port or left hand side of the boat, a corpse must be picked up from the starboard side and taken ashore from the port (Yanagida 1975:74).

According to a report by Yoshikawa (1951), in Kozu-shima, south of Izu Peninsula, a chief carpenter gets on board always from the port side to enshrine the items of the *funa-dama,* whereas fishermen take a drifting corpse on board from the starboard side. In many other villages at the launching ceremony the chief carpenter gets on the boat from the port side of the boat to enshrine the items (a woman's hair, lady's powder, lipstick, comb, mirror, dice made of willow wood, grain, and so on) for the *funa-dama.* The items for the *funa-dama* often include, besides those mentioned a couple of male and female dolls made of folded paper. As some of the items imply the *funa-dama* is usually perceived to be a female deity throughout Japan. In villages on Miyake Island the boat-owner's wife is responsible for the worship of the *funa-dama.* When the boat returns to port, she always goes on board from the port side and never from the starboard (Kurata 1949:291).

In Kanegasaki, Fukuoka, in picking up a drifting corpse, fishermen always take it into their boat from the starboard side and place it in the bow. This, they explain, is because the front part of the vessel is outside the domination of the *funa-dama,* who is considered to control only the stern and is facing astern (Yanagida 1975:74-5). Fishermen of Katsumoto-ura, however, contend that since the *funa-dama* resides in the bow, a corpse must be taken aboard from the portside of the stern, placed in the stern, and removed from the portside upon their return to port. It is for this reason that they urinate only from the stern and never from the bow. While fishing in the open sea, fishermen from other villages of Iki Island urinate only from the starboard and never from the port side, as the port side is considered to be the passing way of the *funa-dama* (Yamaguchi 1934:232).

While the symbolic associations of the port side of a boat with the sacred *funa dama* and of the starboard side with pollution can be found in many instances (Yanagida 1975:74), the symbolic meaning of the parts of a boat may differ according to each village. Yet the association of the one side or part of a boat with the sacred and of the other side or part of a boat with the polluted obviously exists. In other words, the dual symbolic divisions of the boat into the sacred and the polluted, and the use of these divisions to deal with sacredness and pollution, are essentially and same.

Visiting gods coming from far beyond the sea bringing good luck to people are worshipped today in the Amami and Ryukyu Islands. The "other world," from which visiting gods come to visit people to bring about abundant crops and good fortune, is called *neriya* or *niira* in the Amami chain, and *nirai* in Okinawa. It is seen as a place beyond the sea, at the bottom of the sea, or deep under the ground. Significantly, *nirai* is not always thought of as a world of paradise or of abundance, but occasionally it is considered to be a world of evil. Accordingly, visiting gods are believed to be capable of bringing illness to the inhabitants. There is no evidence to indicate that the notion of *nirai* as a world of evil is historically either older, or more recent, than that of *nirai* as a world of abundance (Sumiya 1963; Ushijima 1969; Hika 1971; Kreiner 1971; Miyara 1973). It seems clear that the other world has been conceived all along to have both good and evil aspects, depending upon specific contexts.

In a similar fashion Ebisu is not always a benevolent deity. Occasionally he sends *tatari* (mystical retribution) to people. It is reported by Taro Nakayama that there is an Ebisu Shrine where there are two Ebisu statues. Because an Ebisu statue was once stolen from the shrine, the people made another one. The man who had stolen the original statue became so ill as a result of Ebisu's mystical retribution, however, that he returned it to the shrine; consequently the shrine was endowed with two Ebisu statues (Nakayama 1941:228; Nakayama 1976:285-6). In some places bogies (*bakemono* or *yokai*) in the sea are called "Ebisu" (Yanagida 1963:406). There is also a case in which the god Ebisu is believed to have caused in anger a larger tamboo grove to wither (Nakayama 1941:288). Evidently

Ebisu has both a benevolent and a malevolent character.

Interestingly, in many villages the god Ebisu is often perceived to be one-eyed, deaf, hunchbacked, or left-handed. It was considered to be hermaphroditic in Uji Yamada, Wakayama Prefecture (Nakayama 1941; Yanagida 1963:406; Nihon Kokugo Daijiten Vol. 3, 1973). The deformity or anomaly of Ebisu is related to the notion that Ebisu belongs to, or comes from, the "other" world. The meaning of the word *ebisu* itself carries the connotation of deformity and abnormality; for example, *ebisu-buna* means a malformed crucian carp, and *ebisu-zen* means abnormally arranged dishes on the table (Nihon Kokugo Daijiten Vol. 3, 1973). The notion that Ebisu is both man *and* woman at the same time seems related to an aspect of Ebisu as a mediator between the "other" mystical world and the world of humanity. As Leach (1976:72) contends, the mediator, whether he is a "real" human being (e.g., a shaman) or a mythological god-man, often takes on liminal attributes.

Conclusion

Why is it then that strangers, visitors, and even drift materials are imputed to have mystical power?

The association of the Japanese notion of "stranger" with animal spirit holders is undoubtedly related to the Japanese villagers' conception of the "outside" *(soto or yoso)* or "others" as distinguished from the "inside" *(uchi)* or "we" (Nakane 1970: Chapt. 2). In Japanese villages strangers known as "tabi" or "tabibito" are much feared and treated with great caution. They do not share the basic values and assumptions of the village concerned (cf. Schutz 1971:96). While people belonging to the inside are classified into various categories, outsiders and strangers are undifferentiated. They are unknown and unclassified. How they fit in is not determined. Therefore, when they enter uchi *(inside)* space they are considered potentially dangerous, both in physical and a mystical sense.

It is not unique to Japan that strangers coming from the outside world often are regarded as malevolent and harmful. It is common to read in ethnographies from Africa and elsewhere that strangers whose past is unknown often are suspected of witchcraft (e.g., Middleton 1966;242). In many parts of the world (e.g., modern Greece, the Near East, and Ethipia), where the belief in the evil eye exists, strangers often are suspected of being the vehicles of the evil eye (Maloney 1976).

In Ethopia "the buda *(evil eye)* people are `strangers' to the land of the Amhara. Originating from, a different region, they are landless and make a living with their manual skills of smithing, taming, weaving, and pottery making" (Reminick 1974:289-290). In contrast with the rega people whose ancestry is well known, or of "clean bone," the buda are of a different ethnic origin, and their ancestry or kin are unknown (Reminick 1974:280-81). In Mexico the evil eye is usually referred to as mal de ojo, mal ojo, or simply ojo. According to Kearney (1976:175, 182), "Mal ojo, is, however, specific to human threats....But of all humans, potentially the most dangerous are strangers or other anonymous people who are likely to be unidentifiable or absent when symptoms develop." With respect to withcraft in modern Greece "the people most often gossipped about are those who are outsiders" (Dionisopoulos-Mass 1976:53). In a Tunisian village "prying strangers and marginal persons or deviants are often considered possible users of the *(evil)* eye and hence should be avoided, especially by women and children" (Teitelbaum 1976:64). Among the Lugbara, according to Middleton (1966:242), "strangers whose past is unknown" and "the smiths, who are almost always Ndu who have entered Lugbara individually to practice their craft, which is much feared, are often suspected of witchcraft." This reminds us of the Japanese blacksmiths in the San'in region, as described above, who are usually strangers having mystical abilities to possess people, causing them to become mentally deranged.

Nevertheless, as we have seen, strangers, visitors, and drift materials coming from far away or from the other world can bring good luck to people. This positive side of the notion of stranger also can be found in other cultures. In ancient Greece it was believed that the gods take the appearance of strangers, and visit various cities to inspect human conduct. A passage from Homer's (XVII:485-488) *Odyssey states*, "Aye, and the gods in the guise of strangers from afar put on all manners of shapes, and visit the cities, beholding the violence and righteousness of men." The *Ordinance* of Manu of ancient India indicates that the hospitable treatment of noble visitors will bring about wealth, fame, long life and heavenly welfare (III:106). Peoples in Arabia, the Maoris of New Zealand, and other ethnic groups treat strangers and visitors hospitably, for they believe that strangers will bring rain, food, and happiness to them (Wastermarck 1906 Vol. I: 582, 592, 593 et passim).[5]

For the Balinese, the island of Nusa Penida off the eastern coast of south Bali is the source of all evil forces, epidemics, and troubles. There reigns "the great lord with the fangs" called Ratu Gede Mecaling, who is believed to make a regular visit with once a year when the rainy season is about to begin (November and December), i.e., during the *liminal* period between the rain and dry seasons, to spread illness among the Balinese. However, this "lord" also has a positive function. A female sadag (spirit medium) called Batur Sari told me that Ratu Gede Mecaling has strong, efficacious power to cure illness. A stone statue representing Ratu Gede Mecaling rests in the shrine of her compound. The power of the "lord" can be utilized for positive purposes.[6]

Whether supernatural powers associated with strangers and visitors are malevolent or beneficial seems to be determined by the context as well as by certain beliefs in visiting gods or the god Ebisu. A dead corpse on land is ritually unclean and polluting to people, yet it brings good luck if picked up drifting in the sea. Dolphins are normally fishermen's enemies, for they are after the same fish, yet they are believed to bring good luck as Ebisu when they are perceived as coming from far away. At this point we agree with Lévi-strauss' (1950:XLVII) statement: "C'est dans ce caractére relationnel de la pensée symbolique que nous pouvons chercher la réponse à notré probéme (It is in the relational character of the symbolic thought that we can search for the answer to our problem)."[7] While strangers and visitors and regarded as potentially dangerous in ordinary contexts, when there is a release from calamity or unusual good fortune, strangers may be credited for having brought about the happy turn of events. When the catch is large, for example, strangers are treated with hospitality, as Ebisu, by the fishermen.

It seems that strangers, visitors, and flotsam not only represent the mystical "other world," but they are also the marginal, "liminal" figure or things which mediate between the world of uchi (inside) and the world of yoso (outside), between men and gods, between the ke (secular) and the hare (sacred), or between "this world" and the "other world." Strangers who have recently settled in a village are neither full members of the village nor total strangers entirely unrelated to the rest (cf. Yamaguchi 1975:81-90). A corpse adrift on the sea is regarded as highly ambiguous by fishermen, because for them and for the Japanese in general a floating corpse on the sea is not regarded as totally dead until it is buried with a proper funeral ceremony. (Namihira 1978:353). The merebito, visitors or visiting gods, and men or things perceived as Ebisu, all bringing good luck to people, are obviously the mediators between men and gods, and between the world of humanity and the world of divinity. In view of the fact that the festivals for the god Ebisu are often performed at both the beginning and the end of the year (Miyata 1972:115), the liminal nature of the god is evident in temporal terms as well (cf. Turner 1969:96; Leach 1977:72). Moreover, according to Yanagida, ebisu doki (ebisu time) denotes the time between day and night, or the dusk of the evening. Twilight or dusk is traditionally regarded as a mystically dangerous time because supernatural monsters are about (Yanagida 1938:78). The evening, just before night falls, is called ouma ga doki, which means the time when one encounters demons.[8]

Related to this mediating nature, the strangers and visitors are usually seen as gods and men at the same time. This is exemplified in the rituals of the Yaeyama Islands, Okinawa Prefecture, reported by Seiichi Muratake. Two young men disguised as the god Akamata and the goddess Kuromata, wearing red and black dresses respectively, appear from a cave outside the village at sundown. They visit all the houses of the village to bring them good luck and then return to the cave before daybreak. The cave is believed to be connected to the bottom of the sea, where the world of paradise, or of the death, or the other world, is located. In the sense that the two gods are portrayed by mortal men, they are half men/half gods during the ritual (Muratake 1975:228-237). There exist ethnographic parallels in other cultures where things or creatures regarded as mediators between two categories (e.g., men and gods, and animals, culture and nature, this world and the other world, etc.) are often charged with mystical power (cf. Leach 1964:39).

While it is necessary to take into account historically derived beliefs and concepts such as marebito, Ebisu, and visiting gods, to help us account for the two opposing aspects of the Japanese notion of stranger, it is also useful to recognize that strangers, visitors, drifting corpses and other drift materials are the mediators between this world and the other world, and their mediating nature itself provides them with mystical powers. The ambiguity of the Japanese attitude toward foreigners stems from a very basic set of cultural concepts similar in its essential structure to notions of "stranger' found in other cultures.

Reference

1. A summarized form of this paper was presented at the 76th Annual Meeting of the American Anthropological Association, Houston, Texas, November 29-December 4, 1977. I am grateful to Mary Sanches for her invitation to the session, "Japanese Studies: New Models and Directions." I wish to thank Thomas P. Rohlen, John L. Fischer, and Geoffrey Eisen for revising the English style and supplying helpful comments which are incorporated in this paper. I also wish to thank Hitoshi Ueda, Kazuto Matsunaga, Koichi Maruyama, Fujiko Ueda, Kazukimi Ebuchi, Emiko Namihira, Jun Katada, Sakumi Itabashi and others who participated in fieldwork in Japanese villages and helped me a great deal. The material based on fieldwork was financially supported by grants from the Wenner-Gren Foundation, the Scientific Research Fund of the Japanese Ministry of Education, and the Scientific Research Fund of the Japanese Ministry of Education, and the Scientific Research Fund of the Research Institute of Comparative Education and Culture. Kyushu University. Grateful acknowledgement is made to those institutions.
2. The names of individuals, Murata and Nakao, and of villages, Tagawa and Sato, are fictitious.
3. This was when I travelled with Professor and Mrs. Claude Levi-Strauss in the Oki Islands in November, 1977.
4. In this regard I am much instructed by Turner (1969:94-III).
5. As to the examples from the Odyssey, the Ordinance of Manu and Westermarck (1906) I was instructed by Matsumura (1930:360;380). According to Benveniste (1969, I:361), in Greek *xénos* means "stranger," and the verb *xenízo* "the act of hospitality."
6. This material is based on my fieldwork in Bali in 1974-75. The name of the village where this information was collected is Desa Adat Intarian, Desa Sanur. The research was supported by a grant from the Scientific Research Fund of the Japanese Ministry of Education. See also Swellengrebel (1960:38).
7. This is my translation from French. With respect to the dual symbolic classification I was instructed by Needham (1973, 1978: 17-19).
8. There is a country-wide belief that sunset is the hour when

demons *(ma)* and supernatural monsters *(yokai)* are most likely to appear and attack people. Children are often called indoors at this time to protect them from mystical dangers. This liminal time between day and night is called *"mou mou doki"* in Shimane Prefecture and in Tsushima Islands, Nagasaki Prefecture. The [illegible], and doki means time. this time is deemed mystically dangerous (Yanagida 1956:404). During my childhood, when it got dusky, I was also called indoors by my grandmother because of the danger inherent at the time of day.

BIBLIOGRAPHY

Benveniste, E. 1969. Le Vocabulaire des institutions indo-éuropéennes. (2 vols.) Paris.

Dionisopoulos-Mass, R. 1976. The Evil Eye and Bewitchment in a Peasant Village (Greece).

The Evil Eye, ed. C. Maloney, pp. 42-62. New York.

Fujiwara, M. 1949. Naya Buraku no Gyoro-soshiki to Shinkó Keitai. (Fishing System and Belief System in Naya Village). Minkan Denshó (Folk Tradition) 13:27-31.

Hika, M. 1971. Ryukyu no Saishi to Sekaikan no meguru Mondai (Problems Centering Around the Ritual and World View of the Ryukyus). Okinawa Bunka Ronsó (Essays on Okinawa Culture) 2, eds. T. Oto and T. Ogawa, pp. 461-467. Tokyo.

Homer. 1919. Odyssey (translated by A.T. Murray). The Loeb Classical Library. London.

Kearney, M. 1976. A World-view Explanation of the Evil Eye. The Evil Eye, ed. C. Maloney, pp. 175-192. New York.

Kreiner, J. 1971. Nansei Shotó ni Okeru Kami Kannen (The Concept of God in Southwestern Islands). Okinawa Bunka Ronso (Essays on Okinawa Culture) 2, eds. T. Oto and T. Ogawa, pp. 448-460. Tokyo.

Kurata, I. 1949. Fune ni Kansuru Shiryó (Materials on Boats). Kaison Seikatsu no Kenkyu (Studies on Life in Fishing Villages), ed.

K. Yanagida. Tokyo.

Leach, E. 1964. Anthropological Aspects of Language: Animal Categories and Verbal Abuse.

New Directions in the Study of Language, ed. E.H. Lenneberg, pp. 23-63. Cambridge.

—1976. Culture and Communication: The Logic By Which Symbols Are Connected. Cambridge.

Levi-Strauss, C. 1950. Introduction a l'oeuvre de Marcel Mauss, Sociologie et anthropologie. Paris.

Mabuchi, T. 1980. Space and Time in Ryukyuan Cosmology. Asian Folklore Studies 39:I-19.

Makita, S. 1966. Umi no Minzoku-gaku (Folklore of the Sea). Tokyo.

Maloney, C. (ed.) 1976. The Evil Eye. New York. matsumura, T. 1930

Minzoku Gaku Ronko (The Study of Folklore). Tokyo.

Middleton, J. 1960. Lugbara Religion. London.

Miyara, T. 1962. Yaeyama Guntó ni Okeru Himitsu Kessha ni Tsuite (Secret Societies in the Yaeyama Islands). Minzokugaku Kenkyu (The Japanese Journal of Ethnology) Vol. 27:13-18.

—1973. Yaeyama Guntó (Yaeyama Islands). Nihon Minzoku Gakkai (The Japanese Society of Ethnology), Okinawa no Minzokugaku Teki Kenkyu (Ethnological Studies of Okinawa). Tokyo: Minzokugaku Shinkokai (The Japanese Society for the Promotion of Ethnology).

Miyata, N. 1972. Kinsei no Ryúkó Shin (Popular Deities in Modern Era). Tokyo.

Murataka, S. 1975. Kami Kyódótai Hójó (God, Community, and Fertility). Tokyo.

Nagano, Y. 1973. Ijin Kantai (Hospitality to Stranger). Shúkyógaku Jiten (Dictionary of the Science of Religion), eds. I. Oguchi and I. Hori. Tokyo.

Nakane, C. 1970. Japanese Society. Berkeley.

Nakayama, T. 1941. Nihon Minzokugaku Jiten (Dictionary of Japanese Folklore). Tokyo.

—1977. Nihon Minzokugaku (Japanese Folklore). Tokyo.

Namihira, E. 1978. Suishitai wo Ebisu to Shite Matsuru Shinkō: Sono Imi to Kaishaku (Ebisu: A Liminal Deity in Japanese Folk belief). Minzokugaku Kenkyu (The Japanese Journal of Ethnology), Vol. 42:334-355.

Needham, R. 1973. Right and Left: Dual Symbolic Classification. Chicago.

—1978. Essential Perplexities. Oxford.

Nihon Kokugu Daijiten (Dictionary of the Japanese Language). 1972. vol. 20. Tokyo.

Okada, A. 1955. Krishitan Bateren (Japanese Catholics). Tokyo.

Okano, H. 1960. Marebito (Visiting God). Nihon Shakai Minzoku Jiten (Social and Ethnographical Dictionary of Ethnology) 4, ed. N. Minzokugaku Kyókai, pp. 1364-1366. Tokyo.

Origuchi, S. 1975a. Origuchi Shinobu Zenshú (Complete Works of Origuchi Shinobu). Vol. I. Tokyo.

—1975b. Origuchi Shinobu Zenshú (Complete Works of Origuchi Shinobu). Vol. 2. Tokyo.

—1976 Origuchi Shinobu Zenshú (Complete Works of Origuchi Shinobu). Vol. 7. Tokyo.

Reminick, R.A. 1974. The Evil Eye Belief among the Amhara of Ethiopia. Ethnology 13:279-291.

Sakurada, K. 1968. Gyoson no Dentó (Tradition of Fishing Village). Tokyo.

Schutz, A. 1944. The Stranger. American Journal of Sociology 49:489-498. Reprinted in A. Schutz, 1971. Collected Papers II: Studies in Social Theory. The Hague.

Seki, K. 1960. Namahage (Masked Dance). Nihon Shakai Minzoku Jiten (Social and Ethnographical DIctionary of Japan), ed. N. Minzokugaku Kyókai (Japanese Society of Ethnology) 3:1071-1073. Tokyo.

Sumiya, K. 1963. Amami Oshima Kunnaka no Kami Matsuri (Ritual of Kunnaka, Amami Islands). Shakai to Denshó. Vol. 7 No. I.

Swellengrebel, J.L. et al. *1960. Bali: Studies in Life, Thought and Ritual. The Hague.*

Takeuchi, T. 1960a. Kojiki (Beggar). Nihon Shakai Minzoku Jiten

(Social and Ethnolographical Dictionary of Japan), et. N. Minzokugakù Kyókai (Japanese Society of Ethnology) 1:413-415. Tokyo.

—1960b. Yosomono (Outsider). Nihon Shakai Minzoku Jiten (Social and Ethnographical Dictionary of Japan), Vol. 4:1942-1945.

—1960c. Ebisu. Nihon Shakai Minzoku Jiten (Social and Ethnographical Dictionary of Japan). Vol. I:91-92. Tokyo.

Teitelbaum, J.M. 1976. The Leer and the Loom-Social Controls on Handloom Weavers (Tunisia). The Evil Eye, ed. C. Maloney, pp. 63-75. New York.

The Ordinance, of Manu. Translated from the Sanskrit, completed and edited by E.W. Hopkins. London, 1884.

Turner, V.W. 1969. The Ritual Process. Chicago.

Ushijima, I. 1969. Ryukyu Miyako Shoto no Saishi Kozo no Mondai Ten (Problems on Ritual Organization of the Miyako Islands, Ryukyu). Shichó 106:85-100.

Utsumi, N. 1951. Misaki no Ryóshi (Fishermen of Misaki) Minkan Densho 13:27-31.

Westermarck, E. 1906. The Origin and Development of Moral Ideas. Vol. I. London.

Yamaguchi, A. 1934. Ikitó Minzokushi (Ethnography of Iki Island). Tokyo.

Yamaguchi, M. 1975. Bunka no Ryógisei (Ambiguity of Culture). Tokyo.

Yanagida, K. 1938. Kinki Shúzoku Goi (Vocabularies of Taboo Customs). Kokugakuin Daigaku Hogen Kenkyukai (The Society for studies of Dialect, Kokugakuin University). Tokyo

—1956. Sógó Nihon Minzoku (Goi Japanese Synthetic Folk Vocabularies). Tokyo.

—1963a. Minzokugaku Jiten (Dictionary of Folklore). Tokyo.

—1963b. Bunrui Saishi Shuzoku Goi (Classified folk Vocabularies and Rituals). Tokyo.

—1975. Bunrui Gyoson Goi (Classified Folk Vocabularies of Fishing Village). Tokyo.

Yoshida, T. 1967. Mystical Retribution, Spirit Possession, and Social Structure. Ethnology 6:237-262.

—1972. Nihon no Tsukimono (Spirit Possession in Japan). Tokyo.

Yoshida, T., and H. Ueda. 1968. Spirit Possession and Social Structure in Southwestern Japan. Proceedings, VIIth International Congress of Anthropological and Ethnological Sciences, Science Council of Japna 2:377-378. Tokyo and Kyoto.

Yoshida, T.,K. Maruyama, and E. Namihira. 1974. Technological and Social Changes in a Japanese Fishing Village, Journal of Asian and African Studies 9:1-16.

Yoshikawa, Y. 1951 Kózushima no Minzoku (Folk Customs of Kózu Island). Minkan Denshó (Popular Tradition) 15:33-36

Chapter-8

THEMES IN THE SYMBOLISM OF NDEMBU HUNTING RITUAL*

By Victor Turnel

Chapter-8

Fon the Ndembu tribe of Zambia the hunt is more than a food quest; it is a religious activity. It is preceded and followed by the performance of rites and is believed to be beset with perils of an ultrahuman order. I have discussed the social importance of hunting among the Ndembu in a number of previous publications (1953, 1957, 1961), and will therefore confine myself to repeating that this importance does not derive from the objective contribution to the food supply made by the chase. It arises partly from the high ritual status of the hunter and partly from the fact that, for the Ndembu, hunting epitomizes masculinity in a society jurally dominated by the principle of matrilineal descent. In agricultural production (mainly the cultivation of cassava, finger milter, and maize), and in the preparation of food, women's work has major importance, though men today are increasingly drawn into the cultivation of crops for cash while hunting declines with the shorting out of game.

Ndembu recognize two main branches of hunting: (1) *Wubinda*, which includes every recognized technique for killing animals and birds - firemans, bows and arrows, spears, snars, traps, pitfalls, nets, the use of birdlime, etc.; (2) Wuyanga, the skilled use of guns. Although women and children *snamre* small animals and birds, this activity is not described as Wubinda; the term is reserved for the kiling or catchng of bigger game. Forest game is hunted all year round, except at the height of the rainy season, but animals are hunted on tile plains which stretch around tile upper reaches of rivers most of the Ndembu territory in Mwiniglunga District in north western Zambia lies on the Congo-Zambezi watershed and is therefore an area of river sources mainly when the grass has grown long enough to give the hunter adequate cover.

During the period of my field research, guns were by no

means plentiful among the Ndembu. According to the 1951 District Report (kindly made available to me by Mr. R. C. Dening, then District Commissioner), 68 breech loading guns and 1,154 muzzle loading guns had been registered at District Headquarters. These figures refer to the whole of Mwinilunga District, which includes not only 18,346 Ndembu, but also 13,107 Kosa people. The total taxpaying population of adult males was recorded as [illegible]. The ratio of approximately one gun to nine adult males is probably not incorrect. Quite a high proportion of the guns are ancient flintlocks, used as currency in the nineteenth century slave trade, and are inefficient and dangerous to use. Thus few men can hope to possess guns, and of these, fewer still become really proficient hunters.

To the two main branches of hunting correspond two cults, also called *Wubinda* and *Wuyang'a*, and the latter has many of the characteristics not merely of a profession but even of a vocation. The gun-hunter (*chiyang'a*) is often a solitary adept who spends much of his time alone or accompanied by a single apprentice (who is also a candidate for admission to the cult) — in the wild bush with all its visible and invisible dangers. He is assisted by the guardian shade of a deceased hunter kinsman and by magical charms, he performs rites to propitiate the shades of hunter-dead before he ventures into the bush, and he is believed to encounter there the inimical powers of witches, sorcerers, ghosts, werelions, and persecuting ancestors.

A *chiyang'a* is also a *chibinda* (a hunter with bows and traps), but not every *chibinda* is a *chiyang'a*. *Wubinda* is the older cult and is said to have come with the forbears of the Ndembu when they migrated from the kingdom of Mwantiyanvwa, the great Lunda chief in Katanga, more than two centuries ago. *Wuyang'a* is believed to have been introduced, along with the first muzzle-loading guns, by Ovimbundu traders who came regularly from Kasanji and Bihe in western Angola to purchase slaves and beeswax in the mid-nineteenth century. It shares many features of its symbolism with *Wubinda* on which it must have been speedily grafted.

Ritual of Affiction

Wubinda belongs to the category of Ndembu ritual that I have called "ritual of affliction" (see pp. 9-10). The rites belonging to this category are performed to propitiate or exercise ancestor shades that are believed to bring misfortune, illness, or reproductive disorders. The victims are their living kin. The alleged motives for afflicting vary, but it is commonly said that the victim has neglected to make offerings to the shade at its shrine or has forgotten the shade "in his heart." Affliction is conceived to be a sharp rebuke for such negligence. In almost every case I have been able to observe of illness or misfortune treated by ritual of affliction, there has been an additional factor of social disturbance. The victim has here been afflicted as a representative of a quarrel-ridden social group (a village, matrilineal descent group, or extended family), even if he or she is not held to be personally blameworthy. I have heard it suggested that such affliction is "good" (*wahi*) because the ritual to remove it "brings to light" (*ku-solola*) and so dispels the quarrels (*madombu*) and grudges (*yitela*) in the group.

There are various modes of affliction. Women, for example, are afflicted by ancestor shades (*akishi*, singular *mukishi*) with a number of clearly defined reproductive troubles, each kind corresponding to a named mode of affliction. For example, an ancestress "coming out in (the mode of) *Nkula*"(as Ndembu put it) afflicts her kinswoman (nearly always in the matrilineal line) with menstrual disorders. The rites to propitiate such shade manifestations might be termed "gynecological" rites. Hunters, too, are afflicted with different kinds of bad luck in the chase by dead hunter kinsmen (patrilateral as well as matrilineal).

To each mode of manifestation there corresponds a curative rite which bears its name. Thus "*Nkula*" is performed to cure a patient "caught" by the "*Nkula*" manifestation, *Nkula* cult members are recruited from those who have been its former patients. The patient is thus also a candidate for admission to the cult association, while the doctor is simultaneously as adept. Such associations of adepts cut across corporate groups with a kinship or local basis and across one another. They are called into transient being and action by a diviner's verdict. The divination seance itself may be regarded as a phase in a social process: (1) the beginning of a person's illness, reproductive trouble, or misfortune at hunting; (2) informal or formal discussion in the local community as to what is to be done; (3) representatives of the community are sent to a diviner; (4) a seance terminated by the diviner's diagnosis of the nature, cause, and agency of affliction and his recommendation that a certain type of rite should be performed; (5) the actual performance of that rite.

Wubinda

The cult of *Wubinda* is an assemblage of five rites called respectively: *Mukala, Chitampakasa, Kalombu, Mundeli* and *Ntambu*. Each of these names denotes a specific manifestation of a hunter ancestor, and much of the symbolism of the propitiatory rite is expressive of the attributes of that manifestation. Thus the senior adept in the *Mukala* rite makes whistling noises and at one stage wears strips of hide, each with a ridge of fur, because the *Mukala* manifestation is thought to whistle game away from the hunter and to wear thes "*mazang'a*," part of the garb of hunters in bygone times. *Mukala* may be performed for a young man who has just started to hunt seriously, though spirits may manifest themselves in this mode, so Ndembu think, to established hunters as well. The other modes of affliction affect only experienced hunters who have already been accorded cult names.

Wuyang'a

The cult of *Wuyang'a* differs from *Wubinda* in that it consists of a graded series of four rites, each of which indicates the attainment of a certain degree both of proficiency in killing animals and of esoteric knowledge of the cult mysteries. These grades of initiation into *Wuyang'a* are as follows. (1) *Kuwelesha*, "causing to be washed" in this case with pounded leaf medicine (*nsompu*). Here the novice or apprentice in "huntsmanship" (as *Wuyang'a* might be termed), having enjoyed a measure of success in shooting animals with an inherited or borrowed gun, is deemed worthy of being washed with a decoction of bark-scrapings and leaves taken from a number of tree species, each of which is thought to impart some aspect of "huntsman-ship" to the would-be hunter. (2) If the young hunter has demonstrated his prowess he undergoes *Kusukula*, "initiation (into hunts-manship)." At the end of this rite he takes a special hunter-name from a collection of names reserved for initiated hunters. (3) *Kutelekesha*, "causing to cook (meat)": this is both a celebration of the hunter's skill and success over a long period and a feast in honor of his guardian ancestor spirit who had provided him and through him his dependents and fellow villagers – with a regular supply of meat. In the course of this rite much meat is given by its sponsor to hunter adepts and to the general public. (4) *Mwima*, "ripeness" (from *Kwim*, "to bear fruit"): this is the *dernier cri* in praise and self-praise for a gun hunter. Only the greatest hunters are bold enough to hold *Mwima* which is a sign that a man has "finished huntsmanship". Incidentally, the term *mwima* is also applied to the forked branch shrine planted in honor of a hunter's shade. We shall shortly discuss this structure in detail, but it is worth mentioning in passing that the "fruit" borne by it are trophies of the chase, the heads and entrails of antelope and other game. In all this an important analogy is made by Ndembu between what they consider is woman's dominant role, the bearing of children, and man's which is the bringing home of carcasses from the hunt. In hunter's and a women's rites of affliction the same symbols stand respectively for a multiplicity of kills and a multiplicity of children. Women do not posses a *mwma*, and indeed their reproductive powers are endangered by close contact with "the things of huntsmanship," but the values associated with *mwimu* are those which assert a parallel between the many kills desired for a male hunter and the many new lives desired for a mother.

Hunting Rites

Since space is limited I can do little more here than indicate a few of the main themes running through the symbolism of *Wubinda* and *Wuyang'a* and of the mortuary rites of professional hunters. I have discussed already the semantic structure and properties of some of the principal symbols found in Ndembu ritual and there distinguished between three "levels" or "fields" of meaning possessed by such symbols. I pointed out that many ritual symbols are multivocal or polysemous, that is, they stand for many objects, activities and, relationships — there is not a one-to-one relationship between symbol and referent but a one-to-many relationship. Each major symbol has a "fan" or "spectrum" of referents (*denotata* and *connotata*), which tend to be interlinked by what is usually a simple mode of association, its very simplicity enabling it to interconnect a wide variety of referents. Some of symbols we shall shortly consider have this polysemous character. I shall consider them first on the level of their exegetical meaning secondly in their operational meaning and thirdly in their positional meaning. The first level, briefly, represents the interpretations of my Ndembu informants in this case of hunter adepts—the second results from equating a symbol's meaning with its use, by noting what Ndembu do with it, and not only what they say about it, while the third level of meaning consists in examining a symbol's relationship to others belonging to the same complex or *Gestalt* of symbols. I hope to show that this set of methodological tools has its uses in exposing to view the deeper layers of a society's system of values.

Simply because each ritual symbol is so dense with significance, the task of presenting, classifying, and analyzing the referents of even a few interrelated symbols is necessarily a long one. For ritual, in one important aspect, is quintessential custom; what is distributed through many fields and situations of secular life is condensed into a few symbolic actions and objects. For every kind of hunting rite, itself an epitome of a whole sector of Ndembu culture, a quintessential feature is the temporary shrine erected to the hunter ancestor, who is either afflicting his living kinsman with bad luck or has already been propitiated and is regarded as the source of his good fortune in killing game. This shrine typically has three main components and may be associated with further symbolic units according to the specific rite that is performed. These three components are (i) a forked branch known as *chishing'a, muchanka*, or, as we have seen, in the case of a supreme hunter, *mwima*; (2) a small piece of termitary earth trimmed into a square of rectangular shape and laid at the base of the forked branch, which is firmly planted in the ground, facing the ritual assembly or "congregation"; (3) a braid of grass, of the *kaswamang'-wadyi* species, which grows to a considerable height on the plains.

The Exegetical Meaning of Chishing'a

Each of these components is a complete system of meaning and may be analyzed at the three levels of interpretation discussed earlier. Let us, then, consider the forked branch at the level of indigenous exegesis. In explaining what a symbolic object stand for, Ndembu normally look to two of its characteristics, its name and its natural properties, as the *fons et origo* of interpretation. Let us then consider the name *chishing'a*, commonly applied to these shrines. My informants are in general agreement that the term is derived from the reflexive form of the verb *ku-shing'a* or *ku-shing'ana*, "to curse," namely, *kudishing'a*, which means "to curse one another." This may well be an instance of fictitious etymologizing (see Turner 1961, 57), but fictitious eymology, like homogony (i.e., increasing the senses possessed by a word by adding to them those of a word of the same form but different derivation), is a device whereby the semantic wealth of a word or symbol may be augmented. Whether this is the case or not, my informants are also in agreement in stating that "meat (*mbiji*) is a cause of quarrels (*madombu*), and in quarrels people curse one another" with implications of the use of sorcery.

"Meat is a cause of quarrels" in two basic situations. In the first place, hunters often conceal from their fellow villagers that they have made a kill, pleading dolefully that they have had no luck. Meanwhile, they have divided the meat secretly among the members of their elementary family and personal friends, instead of distributing customarily specified joints among the members of their village matrilineage. If this is later discovered, grudges (*yitela*) will develop, leading to the invocation of ghosts to kill the hunter, if the situation is not remedied. Such an invocation is known as *ku-shing'ana*, a "curse." In the second place, even when the meat is distributed in public, villagers tend to quarrel about the amount given to them, for example, a classificatory mother's brother will demand an equal share with a full mother's brother. Thus jealousy (of the hunter's prowess), envy over the distribution of meat, hatred of the hunter by those who have been cheated, and quarreling between individuals and factions over amounts (quite a bunch of deadly sins, not to mention greed!) are regularly associated with the hunter's role. One informant told me a hunter eats good meat while others starve, and they say that he ought to find bad luck because he (does not give them meat." Another said that "Hunting is sorcery (*Wuloji*), for hunters have snake-familiars (*malomba*) which kill their relatives to increase their (the hunters') power." For each tuft of the victim's hair the hunter is said to acquire the power (*ng'ovu*) to kill an animal. Far from feeling shame on account of their bad reputation, hunters, like big businessmen, seem often to rejoice in being known as "hard guys" and in song and invocation to hunter spirits refer to themselves by terms normally considered opprobrious, such as "adulterers who sleep with ten women a day" and "great thieves." They take ride in the envy directed against them for they say that only those who are successful are envied. To be "cursed" is part of what they term their "pride" or "dignity" or "self-praise of huntsmanship" (*kudilemesha or kudivumbeka kwawuyang'a*). Yet there is ambivalence in Ndembu society's attitude towards the hunter for he is, when all is said and done, the provider of the most prized food of all.

There was no agreement about the meaning of the word *mu-chanka*. One informant said that it was "an old word for the way animals move when a hunter is chasing them." *Mwima*, as we have seen, means "ripeness" or "bearing fruit," and this may refer to the skulls of buck and other trophies "borne" by the forked branch.

The name *chishing'a*, then, is heavily charged with the irony of huntsmanship. The meaning of the hunter as provider of blessings is expressed by language of quite opposite tendency. Let us now consider the natural properties of the forked branch. These provide further sources of meaning. They may be subdivided into two aspects: the species of trees used for the *chishing'a* and the shape of the *chishing'a*.

Trees, bushes, and herbs play the important part in Ndembu ritual that they play in the ritual of other forest Bantu. Each species is thought to have its own virtues, both for treating illness and in religious rites, but there is a crucial distinction to be made between these two major uses. When trees are used in the empirical treatment of illness, usually in the form of pounded leaves, scrapings of bark, and sliced roots mixed with hot or cold water, emphasis is laid on their directly physical effects on the senses. Thus in the treatment of pyorrhea, "medicine" (*yitumbu*) made from the sliced roots of various trees is heated and the patient is made to rinse his mouth with it. The aim of the treatment is "to remove pain so that the bad teeth will fall out by themselves." Among the ingredients are the roots of the *mwalu* tree, which is used "because it is bitter and can kill the disease." (*Musong'u*, a "disease," has certain animal and human characteristics; it can "move," "curl up," "think," "go away, "die.") *Musosu* is used because it is rather "sweet" and deadens pain.

Kambanjibanji is "hot" (*yeya*) and drives off the disease. *Kapepi* is used "because it sets the teeth on edge by its bitterness (*wukawu*), so that the bad ones drop out."

Now the same term, *yitumbu*, is applied to pounded vegetable medicines used as potions and lotions in religious rites, but the nature of the association shown in these rites is quite different. Here certain selected natural properties of the tree are regularly connected with values, moral qualities, principles of social organization, and with religious beliefs. I have many statements from informants that actually identify the *Yitumbu* in a rite of affliction with the mode of affliction in which an ancestor spirit has "emerged." Thus, the leaves of trees that secrete red gum or have red wood or roots are used in the "medicine" with which a woman patient is washed in the *Nkula* rite. An ancestress who "comes out in *Nkulu*," as Ndembu say, afflicts her victim with menorrhagia and other periodic disorders involving the loss of blood which, so the people think, should cohere around the implanted "seed of life" (*kabubu kawumi*) to form an infant. The patient is exposed to a hot fire so that fragments of leaces should adhere to her when the medicine has dried. These fragments are said to be a "symbol (*chinjikijilu*) of the shade (*mukishi*) in Nkula." The "red" properties of this mode of affliction are here represented by the green leaves of trees that are ritually standardized as "red" (*-chinana*). "Redness" is a complex concept in Ndembu ritual, and in *Nkula* alone it stands for (1) menstrual blood; (2) maternal blood, "that is clear and good and shown at parturition"; (3) the principle of matriliny itself — a matrilineage is called *ivumu*, "a womb"; (4) the *Nkula* cult; (5) the historical continuity of the Ndembu with the great Lunda empire, whose foundress, Luweji Ankonde, suffered from menorrhagia and was cured by the first *Nkula* rite. In the hunting cults, "redness" has a further "fan" of referents, associated mainly with the shedding of the blood of animals. The forked branch shrine, though it is frequently splashed with offerings of blood, is not a red symbol but, in terms of its color symbolism, a white one. It is made from five species of trees. These are not used interchangeably, but the kind of rite determines the kind of shrine tree. The same species also provide ingredients for hunting "medicines," of the ritual type we have just been discussing. Whether these species are used for medicines or shrines their referents remain the same.

The five species are: *Musoli* (*Vagueriopsis lanciflora*); *Museng'u* (*Ochna sp.*); *Kapwipu* (*Swartiza madagascarienisis*); *Kapepi* (*Hymenocardia mollis*); *and Mubula* (*Uapaca sp.*).

Musoli

Musoli is employed as "medicine" in rites to restore female fertility as well as in hunting rites. This tree has edible yellow fruit, much appreciated by duiker and other woodland buck during the early rains. Snares are set beneath musoli trees to trap these animals. Ndembu say that the name musoli, derived from *ku-solola*, "to make visible" or "reveal," is connected with the capacity of the tree to draw forth animals from their hiding places in the bush and make them visible to hunters. This is a "natural" capacity of the tree, as we would say, but Ndembu see in it something more. It is for them a particular instance of a power underlying all life, the power of "making visible." Thus, *musoli* medicine is given to a barren woman so that she will "make children visible" (*ku-solola anyana*) and to a hunter "to make animals visible" (*ku-solola anyana*) for him. *Musoli* has the further sense in the hunting rites of "producing to view a large gathering of people" (*ku-solola luntu lweneni* or *chipompelu cheneni*). The reasoning behind this is that just as the many fruits of the *musoli* bring out of hiding many animals, so will its ritual use bring many people to praise the hunter who has sponsored the rite, and who (it is implied) has killed many animals. The *musoli* tree, therefore, represents the prowess of the hunter at his profession and the fame (*mpuhu*) it confers on him.

Museng'u

The Ndembu derive the name of this species from *ku-sen g'uka*, "to multiply." The tree bears a great number of tiny black edible fruits, and informants connect this prolificity with its name. It is also connected with the term *ku-seng'ula*, "to [illegible]" in practice by blowing "medicine" in the ears. Like *musoli*, museng'u is used in both hunting and "gynecological" rites; in the former it represents "a multiplicity of kills," in the latter "a multiplicity of offspring."

Kapwipu

This tree is also known as *mutete*, and it is from this ritual usage that Ndembu normally commence its exegesis. *Mutete* itself is the first word of a phrase *mutete 'manyangi wuta wachashi*, literally, "the one who cuts huntsmanship" (i.e., "cuts up and distributes meat"), "the empty gun," or "the gun that misses its aim." In explanation of this phrase an informant told me:" A hunter was in the habit of killing many animals, but then he missed his aim once or twice. Others told him to hold his gun correctly, for the shaking of his mind caused him to miss. They played a hunting drum (i.e., performed *Wuyang'a* or *Wubinda rites*) for him and instructed him to shoot properly. After this, he never missed. So he praised himself thus: 'At first I killed animals, later I failed to do so, then after missing I killed again."

The *mutete* tree, then, epitomizes the whole process of *Wubinda*—hunting as a set of rites of affliction. Good luck depends on the favor of hunter ancestors, and they will withdraw their assistance from you, sometimes to punish you for disturbing meat unfairly, sometimes because a ritually impure person such as a woman or an uncircumcised boy has eaten the sacred portions of meat (head, lungs, entrails), called *yijila* ("tabooed things"), reserved for the hunter. This withdrawal, and even active persecution, is something other than merely punitive. For the Ndembu have the notion that affliction is also a sign of election. The afflicting ancestor shade wishes to become "your shade" (*mukoshi weyi*), in other words your guardian or patron shade. First, however, you must do something for him; you must perform rites for him, both private and public, and demonstrate that you have "not forgotten him in your liver" (the seat of the emotions in Ndembu belief), by making offerings either on his grave, if it can be found, or on a *chishing'a* specially planted to him. The identity of the hunter shade is established by divination, as also is the mode in which he is manifesting his displeasure. At the public phase of the rite, it is considered pleasing to the shade to mention his name often in invocationsand praises. This is considered a form of ku-solola, of "revelation." If the shade has been placated he will "help you to kill many animals" and so contribute to your eventual fame as a great "*Mwima*" hunter. The motto of the Ndembu might well be "you must suffer to succeed." It is this theme that is so signally represented by the *kapwipu* or *mutete* tree. In this case, it is the "name only" (*ijina hohu*) that determines the chain of associations, not the properties of the species, but we shall see that *kapwipu* shares certain physical properties with the other species mentioned which make it suitable for use as a "*chishing*'a"

Kapepi and Mubula

I must discuss these species briefly, owing to shortage of space, and say that kapepi is connected with terms meaning "wind" and "breath" and stands for the desired invisibility and ubiquity of the hunter. *Mubula* another fruit tree, is etymologically connected with *ku-bula*, "to make fire by steel, flint and dry-moss tinder" as hunters do in the bush; it also refers to the firing of their flintlocks.

The Shape of Chishing'a

A *chishing'a* is a branch forked in one or more places, stripped of all its leaves and bark. The species I have mentioned are said to be termite-resistant and to have a "strong wood," representing the "strength" (*wukolu*) of huntsmanship. It has been said to me repeatedly by Ndembu hunters that string cannot be made out of the bark of any of the trees used for these shrines. "If they were string-trees, they would tie up (*ku-kasila*) the huntsmanship of the candidate." In just the same way, string bearing trees may not be used in gynecological ritual for fear of "tying up" the fertility of the patients.

The prongs of the extremities of the branches are sharpened by the knives of hunter adepts. This is to represent the "sharpness" or "keen-ness" (*ku-wambuka*) of huntsmanship. As informants said: *Wuhinda wawambuka nang'ovu*" ("huntsmanship is sharp with power"). The causative form of *wambuka, wambwisha*, means "to whet a knife," and it is as though the hunters were trying to "whet" the candidate's huntsmanship. Forked-branch shrines are common throughout Africa, and they are by no means always associated with hunting cults. What is interesting in the present context is that Ndembu ascribe to such shrines senses that express the values of their hunting culture. One of the marks of a viable ritual symbol may be said to be its capacity to move from society to society without marked change in form but with many changes in meaning. Though referents are lost in transference, new referents are readily acquired. Certain symbols arouse an almost universal response, much as music does. This is a problem that would repay investigation in terms of a detailed comparative study.

The whiteness of the exposed wood in each species of *chishing'a* is also held to be significant by Ndembu informants. Whiteness (*wu-tooka*) in Ndembu ritual has many connotations. These include: strength, health, good luck, ritual purity, authority, good will between tile ancestors and the living, the clear and known as opposed to the obscure and unknown, life, power, breast milk, seminal fluid, the whiteness of cassava meal and roots. In the context of hunting ritual the qualities of health, strength, toughness, luck at the hunt, virility, and a state of *bon rapport* with the ancestors tend to receive special stress among the "white" senses.

The Operational Meaning of Chishing'a

The way a symbolic object is used, I have suggested, forms an important part of its meaning. Before we can fully appreciate what the *chishing'a* "means" to Ndembu, therefore, we must enquire how it is collected, set up, and thereafter utilized. A *chishing'a* may be cut: (1) by a solitary hunter: (2) by a hunter and the "great hunter" who is training him, known as his "mother of huntsmanship" (*mama daWuyang'a*) - for among the matrilineal Ndembu the term "mother" refers to one who nourishes with knowledge as well as with milk and is used metaphorically of male authority figures and teachers; and (3) by a group of hunter adepts. When the latter collect a *chishing'a* one hunter lays his ax to the root while the others seize hold of the branches and bear down on them while they sing the melancholy, nostalgic songs of their cult. A hunter adept explained this as follows: "the hunters pull down the tree together to prevent it falling by itself - if it fell of its own accord the huntsmanship would be lost." Here again we find "huntsmanship" (*Wuyang'a or Wubinda*) being regarded almost as though it has physical properties, like a fluid that may be spilled, or a charge of electricity that may be carelessly expended.

The operational level of meaning is the level on which we may observe most clearly the sociological concomitants of ritual symbolism, for we observe not only what is done with the symbol but who does it. Here the unity and exclusiveness of the hunters' cult association is clearly portrayed. This is further exemplified in the setting up of the *chising'a* in some of the rites. For example, in *Mwima*, the celebration of a great hunter's prowess, the hunters excavate a hole with their gun butts, then lift up the *chishing'a* collectively by means of their gun barrels, place it in the hole, and tamp it in firmly all together with their hands.

The *chishing'a* and indeed the *ayishing'a* (the plural form) of all *Wuyang'a* rites, is planted in the hunter's village near the shrine trees planted to his matrilineal ancestors. But for many of the rites of *Wubinda*, the generic cult, the ayishing'a are inserted in large termite hills in the bush. *Ayishing'a* are also inserted in hunter's graves located at the fork of two paths leading from the village. It is at these *ayishing'a* that Ndembu say. "*Chishing'a* is the first place to which a hunter brings meat when he has made a kill. It is a *mutulelewa*, a place where meant is put. The whole carcass is put there before the hunter takes it to village to be eaten." The sacred portions of the animal, mentioned above, are placed on the *chisliing'a*, as an offering to the hunter ancestor in the *Mlukala* rite, for example,' when a hunter has made a kill, he washes the *chish'ng'a* with blood, impales pieces of *yijila* on the prongs, and expresses his gratitude to the patron spirit who has manifested himself in the form of *Mukala*, a mischievous entity which drives and whistles the game away from the hunter until propitiated. When the hunter, on learning from a diviner that he is being afflicted by an ancestor in the form of *Mukala*, first sets up a *chishing'a*, he chooses one of *musoli* wood, plants it, and invokes the shade manifestation as follows: "You, my kinsman who have already died, if you are the one who has come out in *Mukala*, now listen to me. Tomorrow, when I go into the bush to look for animals, you must cause me to see them quickly. I must kill animals by gun or trap." He then puts some powdered white clay (*mpemba or mpeza*) in his mouth and draws a line with the moistened clay from the *chishing'a* towards himself, places some on his temples, down the center of his brow, spits some on his shoulders, and draws a line of white upwards from his navel. "He puts it on his temples, beside his eyes," an informant said, "to see everything perfectly clearly (to spot animals in hiding or at a distance), on his brow that his face should be white or lucky, on his shoulders because he carries his gun and meat on them, and on his stomach, that there might be food in it." Then the hunter spits white powder on the *chishing'a*.

The hunt that follows may be regarded not merely as a utilitarian food quest but as some sort of a rite of sacrifice. It is not strictly comparable to the sacrifice of pastoral peoples, who give to the Deity or the ancestors a valuable animal as a token of their homage, penitence, and atonement, for the hunter has no animal to offer. The animal must first be given to him by the hunter shade, and this is already a sign of partial reconciliation, of the shade's provisional approval of the hunter's worthy intention. Nevertheless, until the hunter has made his offering of the blood and *yijila* at the *chishing'a* shrine he has not fully demonstrated his intention to propitiate and revere his ancestor. It is as though the shade, in giving him an animal, were putting his expression of good will to the test. Moreover, there is an element of gift exchange, of transaction, about the relationship between shade and hunter that contrasts with the attitudes of submission and adoration found in fully developed sacrifice to a deity.

Among the Ndembu, the ancestors do not represent or embody the moral order so much as continue after death to interact with their living kin, in terms of their human likes and dislikes. In most ritual contexts, not remote ancestors but the spirits of the comparatively recently dead are involved, and these shades are believed to afflict the living not only in punishment for wrongdoing but also because they themselves still harbor ill will against them on account of quarrels they took part in when they were alive. For the Ndembu, the moral order is felt to transcend both the living and their deceased kin, to be in fact something axiomatic in terms of which both the living and the spirits of their ancestors must seek to become reconciled (see above pp. 49-50). The mutual bargaining that for Ndembu characterizes the dealings of dead with living has a severely practical aspect. If the dead use their powers of invisibility and panic making to drive animals towards the hunter, he will feed them with blood and cause their names to be remembered among men. For the dead depend on the living - to be sustained by food, offerings, and memories - and the living depend on the dead - for strength, health, fertility, fame and good fortune. The moral order that decrees piety to the dead and comparison for the living is felt to be higher than both and in some obscure way to be connected with the high God *Nzambi* or *Shakapang'a Nzambi* is not directly worshipped; "He is so far away," the people say.

The Positional Meaning of Chishing'a

A major—one might even call it nuclear—symbol like *chishing'a* is nearly always found in regular association with other symbols which, like adjectives in language, qualify or extend its meaning. I have mentioned earlier that a hunter's shrine typically consists of a *chishing'a* together with a small piece of termites nest and a braid of *kaswamang'wadyi* grass. Small termitaries, known as *mafwamfwa* (singular, *ifwamfwa*), domed or finger-shaped, are a familiar feature of the Ndembu woodlands and plain margins. In circumcision and funerary rites they have an explicitly phallic significance. The swarming life within them is pointed out as a sign of "procreation" (*lu-semu*). In hunting rites, the *ifwamfwa* is usually shaped into a cube and is either placed just in front of the *chishing'a*, or the branch is inserted in a hole in it (e.g., at *Kusukula*). Such a cube is called *katala kamukishi*, "the little hut of the ancestor shade." The shade is thought to visit its "hut" during and after the rite. The small termitary also represents in hunting rites the large termite hills (*tuwumbu* singular *kawumbu*), sometimes fifteen feet or so in height, which stud the Mwinilunga bush. Informants say: "A termite hill is a favored site for hunter shades, who like to live on high places and, like lions, climb up them to see if there is game about." It was also pointed out to me that hunters hide themselves behind termitaries, large and small, when they stalk their quarry. Finally, in some *Wuyang'a rites* (such as *Mwina*) the termitaries are called *mibhumba*, a term that represents a dome-shaped cover of molded moistened earth raised on graves. The same term is applied to small termitaries placed in a ring round a dead hunter's head, which is allowed to appear above the surface of his grave. Hunters are buried, sitting upright, "like alert lions," and an opening is made in the ring of termitaries, "so that they may see clearly." Thus the symbolism of the termitary includes in its exegetical meaning references to burial practices peculiar to hunters, to the hunter's stealthy pursuit of game, to his vigilance, to his leonine traits (indeed the very name of the rite *Ntambu* signifies "the lion"), and to the feeling that his proper "home" is in the bush (represented by the termitary "hut") rather than in the village. Besides these senses there are overtones of fertility and virility from other rites in which termitaries represent these qualities.

The braid (*chibaba*) of *kaswamang'wadyi* grass is placed underneath the first fork (*mpanda*) of the *chishing'a*. Its name is derived from *ku-swama*, "to hide," and *ng'wadyi*, "the bare-throated francoin." At *Kutelekesha*, in the course of invoking hunter ancestors, the hunters say: "Today this grass is *kaswamang'wadyi* where all the animals and birds in the bush conceal themselves. If an animal is hidden in the grass, may we hunters be quick to see it, that we may shoot and kill it and be well pleased. May we carry it back and eat its meat. Do not hide it from us. It must appear, you must reveal it quickly (*muyisololi swayiswayi*)." The familiar theme of "making visible" (*ku-solola*) is again exemplified. Ndembu believe that the use of this grass in ritual will make the hunter invisible to the game he stalks.

The twist of grass divides the *chishing'a* into two sections. This division has meaning for the Ndembu. Below the grass, ancestor spirits come "to drink blood." On the forks, trophies of the chase are hung. "The hunter must resemble the ancestor shades," I was told, "the animals will not see him on account of the grass." The prongs of the divided branch may be said to represent the hunter's power to kill animals, power that he obtains from the ancestors by feeding them with blood. The shades are believed to "emerge" (*kw-idikila*) from the earth in which they have been buried, into their "grave-hut," and ultimately into the chishing'a itself.

Features of the topography that have importance for hunters are thus represented in combination: *chishing'a* = forest; *ifwamfwa* = termitaries; and *kaswamamng'wadyi* = grass plains. Here we have the familiar ritual principle of association by *pars pro toto*. When we consider these three symbols together, we must also not the important division between the visible animals and the invisible shades, whose property of invisibility is desired by the hunter so that he may approach and kill the game. These conjunctions and divisions are aspects of the positional meaning of *chishing'a.*

The Semantic Morphology of Chishing'a

Although the *chishing'a forked* branch shrine is an important element of Ndembu hunting ritual, there are hundreds of other symbols in the system, some of which are full or partial expressions of the same basic themes, while others represent different themes. Each of the *Wubindia* rites, for example, has its own ritual "plot" and idiosyncratic character. *Chishing'a* may fairly be said to typify the hunting symbol, since it is found in every hunting rite.

Starkly simple in outward form, a mere forked stick bare of bark, it is, as we have seen rich in meaning. Let me try to express this semantic wealth diagrammatically, so as to bring out the semantic structure of this symbol. (See Diagram 9).

The following may be said to comprise part of the "meaning" of a *chishing'a:*

(1) Social Relationships

- (a) Between hunters and nonhunters;
- (b) Between hunter's elementary family and matrilineal kin;
- (c) Between full and classificatory matrikin of hunter;
- (d) Between hunter and "his" hunter ancestor shade (most

frequently the mother's brother or father);

(e) Between hunter and his instructor in "huntsmanship";

(f) Between fellow members of the hunters' cults.

(2) Values

(a) Toughness of mind and body;

(b) Efficiency in providing meat;

(c) Piety towards the hunter ancesotrs;

(d) Making known or visible what is unknown and hidden;

(e) Fertility (multiplicity, fruitfulness);

(f) Hunters, skill in concealing themselves from animals;

(g) Fairness in meat distribution;

(h) The sacredness of age and sex distinctions (taboos against eating of *yijila* by women and uncircumcised boys);

(i) Suffering that good may come of it;

(j) Acuity of hunter's responses;

(k) Skill in the use of weapons.

(3) Topographical Features

(a) Forest;

(b) Plains;

(c) Termite hills and nests;

(d) Burial sites.

All these referents,[2] merely at the level of Ndembu exegesis, are possessed by a piece of stick, a bit of grass, and a fragment of termitary. This is but a single example of the mighty synthesizing and focusing capacity of ritual symbolism. It might almost be said that the greater the symbol, the simpler its form. For a simple form is capable of supplying associative links of a very generalized character; it displays a feature or features that it shares, literally or analogically, with a wide variety of phenomena and ideas. Thus, the whiteness of *mpemba* clay recalls the whiteness of milk and of cassava meal and, more than these, such abstract ideas as freedom from impurity, goodness "without spot," and the like.

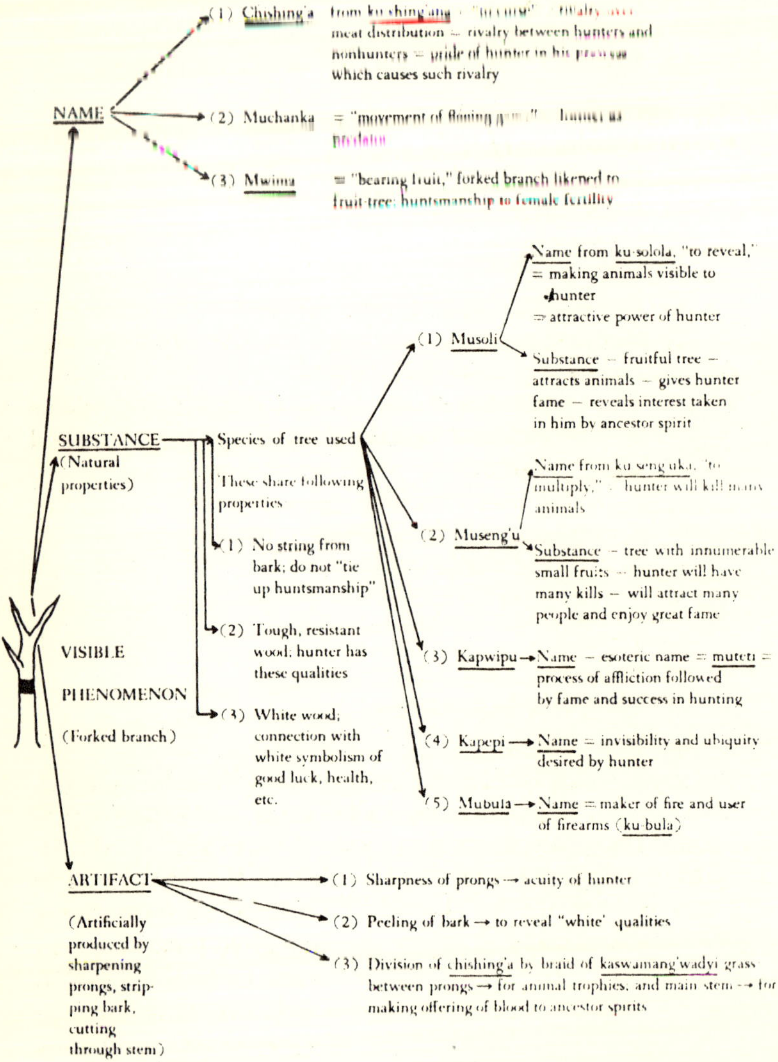

Diagram . Symbolism of Chishing'a

Finally, it must be stressed that the *chishing'a* is regarded by Ndembu not as an object of cognition, a mere set of referents to known phenomena, so much) as a unitary power, conflating all the powers inherent in the activities, objects, relationships, and ideas it represents. What Ndembu see in a *chislti'zg'a*, made visible for them in its furcate, ambivalent, and awe-inspiring nakedness, is the slaughterous power of *Wubinda* itself.

BIBLIOGRAPHY

Turner, Victor W.. 1953. *Lunda Rites and Ceremonies* (Occasional Papers of the Rhodes-Livingstone Museum, N.S. No. 10). Living stone: Zambia.

______, 1957. *Schism and Continuity in an African Society: A Study of Ndembu Village Life*. Manchester University Press.

______, 1961. *Ndembu Divination: Its Symbolism and Techniques* (Rhodes-Livingstone Paper 31)/ Manchester University Press.

NOTES

1. The Anthropological Quarterly, XXXV, No.2 (1962).
2. Some informants have told me that the *Kabalabala* tree is also made into a *chishing'a* but I have no detailed information on this point.
3. And others - implicit in those aspects of the symbolism which connect it with such sectors of the ritual system as life crisis ritual, gynecological ritual, venetration of village ancestors, antiwitchcraft ritual, divination procedures,.etc.

---

* *The Anthropological Quarterly*, xxxv, No. 2 1962.

Chapter-9

Spear Symbolism in Nuerland

By E.E. Evanspritchard

Chapter-9

When I think of the sacrifices I have witnessed in Nuerland there are two objects I see most vividly and which sum up for me the sacrificial rite: the spear brandished in the right hand of the officiant as he walks up and down past the victim delivering his invocation, and the beast awaiting its death. It is not the figure of the officiant or what he says which evokes the most vivid impression, but the brandished spear in his right hand.

We have noted that the *lam* or invocation states the intention of the sacrifice. Its words are a projection of the will and desire of the person as he turns towards Spirit; and an essential part of the action is the brandishing of the spear. As the officiant walks up and down delivering his oration the movements of the spear in his right hand emphasize his words; opening and closing his fingers on it, poising it in his hand, raising it as though to strike, making little jabs with it into the air, pointing it towards the victim, and so on. These movements are an integral part of the expression of intention, and there is more in the action than meets the eye.

In Nuer ritual the meaning of symbolism is generally at once evident to ourselves, at any rate in its main import, for there is an intrinsic relation between the symbol and what it stands for. When an animal is cut in half in cases of incest, to allow intermarriage between distant kin, before a man takes his dead brother's wife in leviratic union, at the closing of an age-set, in mortuary ceremonies, and on other occasions, we can at once perceive how the purpose of the rite is expressed in the severing of the carcass. A relationship of one kind or another between persons is being severed. Likewise the symbolism of the rite, common among primitive peoples, of putting out fires and relighting them at a man's mortuary ceremony, and in the case of the rehabilitation of a homicide the relighting of them with fire-sticks, is at once evident for us. The past is finished with; one begins anew.

The shaving of the head of a bride at her marriage of a boy at his initiation, of a kinsman at a mortuary ceremony, and of a homicide at the settlement of a feud expresses, and brings about, the passing from one state to another as obviously for us as for Nuer. Again, we can see immediately also the appropriateness of the action to the situation and purpose in the ritual making of a line or boundary (*kogh*). A leopard-skin priest cuts a line between opposing factions to forbid combat. The dominant lineages of the Gaagwong and Leek tribes may not, for a mythical reason, tether their cattle in a common kraal, but if they cannot conveniently avoid doing so a line of earth is thrown up between the sections of the Kraal occupied by each. On the other hand, whilst there is generally a ridge of raised earth dividing adjacent gardens of neighbours this is absent when the owners of them are members of the same *ric* or age-set. When in certain ceremonies Nuer throw ashes into the air or asperse their bodies we do not have difficulty in perceiving that they are expressing the idea of evil being blown or washed away. Another, and final, example is that of a man who leaves the tribal territory where he was born and brought up to reside in the territory where he was born and brought up to reside in the territory of a different tribe. He may then – it may not be a regular practice, though I was told that a man might die of *nueer* were he not to take the precaution–take a pot of earth from his natal territory and mix it in infusion,with earth from the territory of his adoption, and drink the infusion, on each occasion adding more of the new earth and less of the old, thereby slowly making the transference from his old to his new home. We have no difficulty at all in understanding and entering into this symbolism. Likewise we readily understand the imagery of various rites I have described in this book, such as the bending of a bracelet to close the jaws of crocodiles, the placing of the corpses of infant twins on branches of trees, and many other rites.

Since we at once perceive the meaning of the symbolism of the ritual action we may suppose that Nuer also perceive its logical fitness to its purpose; and, indeed, it is often certain that they do so, for if asked to explain what they are doing they interpret the symbolism of a rite in terms of its purpose. The symbolism is manifest to them, as it is to us. But there is a deeper symbolism which is so embedded in ritual action that its meaning is neither obvious nor explicit. The performer may be only partly aware or even unaware that it has one. Interpretation may then be difficult for a person of alien culture, and the door is open for every kind of extravagant guesswork to enter. Nevertheless, if it be rash in such circumstances to put forward symbolic interpretations of ritual acts, or features of them, we are sometimes compelled to make the attempt, as in this excursus on the spear, by the very emphasis given to them by the culture we are trying to understand.

Since we have no spears ourselves and nothing which takes their place in our lives it is difficult for us to appreciate their importance for Nuer. Nuer have no knives, other than that (*ngom*) used for cutting the marks of manhood at initiation, so that their fighting spears, besides their use as weapons, have to serve where other peoples use knives.[1] A man's fighting-spear (*mut*) is constantly in his hand, forming almost part of him-when he is fighting, hunting, travelling, herding, dancing, displaying himself with his oxen, playing with his comrades, and so on and when he lays it down it is within his reach; and he is never tired of sharpening and polishing it, for a Nuer is very proud of his spear. In writing a preliminary account of Nuer age-sets many years ago and without reference to symbolic significance of the spear I wrote that 'one is surprised at the real feeling a Nuer expresses for his spear, almost as though it were animate and not a mere weapon'. Later I came to realize better that in a sense it is animate, for it is an extension and external symbol of the right hand, which stands for the strength, vitality, and virtue of the person. It is a projection of the self, so when a man hurls his spear he cries out either 'my right hand' or the name of the ox with which he is identified.

The spear,being an extension of the right hand, stnds for all that the right hand stands for, for what is strong, virile, and vital, and consequently for masculinity and hence for the paternal kin and lineage. Therefore during the discussions about bridwealth in the byre of the bride's home on her wedding day the bridegroom people sit on the right side of the byre and the bride's people on the left side. Therefore, also, when the carcasses of oxen sacrificed at marriage ceremonies are divided among the kin, the right fore and hind legs are the portions of the father's brothers and sisters and the left fore and hind legs are the portions of the mother's brothers and sisters. The left side symbolizes evil as well as femininity; and there is here a double association, for the female principle is also associated with evil directly, as it were, and not merely through the convergence of femininity and evil in the concept of the left side. Thus we have two opposites, the one comprising th4e left side, weakness, femininity, and evil, and the other comprising the right side, strength, masculinity, and goodness.[2]

That the right side is the good side and the left side the evil side may have been noted in various places in this book. When a fruit or animal is cut in two at sacrifices the left half may be either thrown or given away and only the right half be consumed by the people of the home. It is propitious for a sacrificial ox stabbed with the spear to fall on its right side and unpropitious for it to fall on its left side. A dead man is buried to the left of his hut or wind-screen, the side of misfortune. A woman is said to warn her son that when he visits he bride to cohabit with her she may crouch to the right side of the entrance to the hut so that he has to enter by the left side. If she does this he must order her to the other side lest some ill come to him.[3]

When I was in Nuerland I was only half aware of the significance of left and right for Nuer. When writing this book I found therefore that in several respects my observations, or at any rate what I had recorded, were insufficient to answer certain questions that arose from a further consideration of the left-right polarity. It occurred to me that if the representations were as I supposed them to be then, for example, when Nuer deform the horns of their favourite oxen with which they identify themselves, it should always be the left, and never the right horn which is trained downwards. Or again, when Nuer erect the sacred pole, associated with God, the spirits of their lineage, and also with its ghosts, at the entrance to their windscreens, which is their practice, it should always be to the right of the widnscreen (taking, in this case, bearings from within it). My recollection confirmed to some extend by the evidence of my photographs[4] supported these conclusions, but I asked Dr. Lienhardt and Dr. Howell to verify them, which they have been able to do. It should follow also that a husband sleeps on the right side of the hut and his wife on the left side, and here again Dr. Lienhardt has been good enough to confirm that this is the invariable practice. He has made a further and important observation. I was aware that the the west is associated with death and the east with life, but I did not know, till he told me, that east is identified with right and west with left, thus bringing into the left-right polarity the polar representations not only of life and death but also of the cardinal points east and west. I am indebted to Dr. Mary smith for the further observation that Nur speak of 'right-handed peace' ('*mal me cuec*'). They would never speak of left-handed peace.

It is in accord with what we have learnt of the associations with left and right in Nuer thought that Nuer youths should emphasize the contrast between the two hands by putting the left arm out of action altogether for months or even a year or two. This they do by pressing a series of metal rings (*thiau*) into the flesh of the left arm from the wrist upwards so tightly that sores and great pain result and the arm is rendered useless for any purpose other than the display of fortitude and as a passive instrument for the right hand to play upon. A ring on a finger of the right hand is rubbed up and down the discs on the imprisoned left arm to accompany the compliments and endearments of courtship. Such a mutilation is only fully intelligible in terms of symbolic associations. Here the fact that it is only the left horn of favourite oxen which is debased (if the right is trained at all it is trained upwards) is of great significance, for, as will be seen, a man and his favourite ox are identified. What he does to the ox he does to himself.

It is perhaps important to add that Nuer do not think of the left hand as being in a material sense evil. Left-handed persons suffer no disabilities at all and are not considered in other respects as different from other people. Nuer do not, in my experience, attach any importance to the matter, but simply say of a left-handed man that his left hand is right hand. It is the quality of leftness, not the thing that is left, the hand itself, which is significant for them. Similarly, the left half of the severed carcass of a sacrificial animal is not intrinsically evil. It is always eaten by someone. It is bad symbolically, not in itself, and symbolically only in certain contexts or for certain people.

Fig. 4 Instrument and in wedding invvecation

It is suggested that the spear as a projection of the right hand symbolizes the vitality of man, the manhood of man with the associations of lineage values that go with it. It is within the logic of the representation that we speak only of men. The spear stands for masculinity. Women do not bear fighting-spears. The spear does not go with femininity. Hence also boys do not bear fighting-spears till at their initiation to manhood they are given them by their fathers. Before this event they are something in between men and women, and this is shown by the fact they milk the cows, a feminine task that men may not undertake. That neither women nor boys bear spears means that they do not go to war and also that they do not sacrifice. It is not just that a woman may not slaughter the sacrificial victim—it is not, in any case, important who slaughters it—but that, not being able to bear the spear, she cannot make the sacrificial invocation, which is made by the spear in the right hand as well as by the mouth. She can indeed address Spirit at sacrifices, but if she does so she prays (*pal*); she does not invocate (*lam*). This is understandable when we think of the spear as an extension of the right hand and hence as representing strength, masculinity, and goodness. Sacrifice, like war, belongs to that side of life, what we ourselves call the spear-side.[5]

It is important here, and before we proceed further with the argument, to note that the spear we concerned with is the *mut*, the metal fighting-spear (or, in a more restricted sense, spear-head), the only spear used in sacrifice. It is not a *bidh*, a metal fishing-spear, and it is not a *giit*, a fighting-spear fashioned out of substances other than metal. We have further to bear in mind that though spears are now easily obtained by purchase from Arab traders this is a very recent development. There is no iron in Nuer-land, and what metal spears the Nuer used to possess were procured in one way or another from neighbouring peoples, and it is certain that till recently there were very few of them. Nuer made up for the deficiency by fashioning spears from horn and bone and hard wood. Spears fashioned from these materials were still plentiful when I was living in Nuerland, though they were taking on more and more a purely sentimental and ceremonial value, being often used in dances but seldom for fighting and hunting. Since, however, the spears of the ancestors, the names of which are cried out ininvocatios, were iron fighting-spears, and since Nuer could not have done without some of these cutting blades, there must always have been a certain number of them, and also a certain number of iron fishing-spears (for which horn, bone, and wood substitutes are unsuitable), but, as Dr. Howell has pointed out, they were few in number, this accounting, in his opinion, for the high value—several head of cattle—placed upon them.[6] I agree with him that it must have very rare for a man to have had more than one *mut*, the *giit* spears being regarded as supplementary to it. This must consequently have been a very valuable possession and, if lost, most difficult to replace; and it was not just a private possion but a family heirloom passed from father to son down the generations. This does not mean that it was a relic. It was for practical use and therefore when worn was presumably replaced; otherwise one would see these ancestral spears today. However, the age of a spear has no great significance for Nuer. For them even if the spear a man's father gives him at his initiation has been bought from an Arab merchant, and is not in fact the spear the father received from his father and the father's father from his father, it is ideally so regarded and thus serves as a symbol of filiation. The spear is thus a point at which two complex social representations meet, that of the person and that of the lineage. Consequently I do not think that the high assessment of spears in cattle can be assigned to scarcity alone or even that scarcity was at any time the primary consideration. Spears, both fighting- and fishing-spears, were something more, and fighting-spears something much more, than weapons of war or of the chase. They were almost parts of the person. I have seen Nuer enraged when neighbours have borrowed their spears without permission, especially if they have lost them, their anger being out of all proportion to the offence if we think of the matter solely in terms of economic value, for the economic value of spears is negligible at the present day. It is the audacity and the insult which outraged the owner, as though someone had taken, and perhaps lost, part of his person; and all the more so in the case of the fighting-spear, with which are bound up his manhood and his participation in his lineage,as we see from the manner of his receiving it at his initiation.

I have discussed elsewhere[7] the ritual of intiation and I do so again in connexion with the role of cattle in Nuer religion. All that need be said here is that when a boy is initiated into manhood and takes on the full responsibilities of that status he is presented by his father with a *mut*, a metal fighting-spear, and an ox—the two objects in which, as I have said, the whole drama of sacrifice is centred. I discuss here only the spear. A boy may before initiation possess a fishing-spear, but even today he is most unlikely to own a fighting-spear. Even should he do so, he would still be presented with a spear by his father at his initiation, for it is a ceremonial gift expressing formal recognition of his manhood and all that that means in the social life of the Nuer, and also the handing over by one generation to another. It is not just a spear, but a new status also that he is being given. The boy is now boy no longer but man and warrior and soon to be husband and father. He takes part in feuds and wars, and raids. He also for the first time engages in dances and displays with oxen, both of which among the Nuer are martial exercises as well as play intimately associated with courtship; and also in the pursuits of herding and hunting. All these activities require the use of the spear, but it is important that we recognize that it is not the acquisition of a weapon, whatever its economic value might have been in the past, nor even its utility, great though that may be, that gives a crucial significance to the gift of a spear at initiation. Its significance is moral, not merely utilitarian. It is not the spear itself, nor its possession, which is stressed but the activities associataed with it: war and raiding, dancing and display, and herding. The uses of the spear itself and the evaluations of its uses as an index of social personality are blended, so that the spear is not just a weapon but also something which stands for a very complex set of social relations.

But the investment of a youth with a spear at his intiation would seem to be something more, for, as we will see in discussing the sacrificial role of cattle, initiation is not only into the social life of adults but also into a new relationship with the cattle which has an important religious side to it. There is now established an identification, deriving from the sacrificial situation, between the initiates and cattle and, looked at from this point of view, the rites of initiation may be said to have a sacramental character. The boy enters into communion with the spirits and ghosts of his lineage through the cattle. 'The spear of the cutting (initiation)' is thus a symbol of a sacramental change as well as of a change in social status. In both symbolic aspects it is an extension of, and stands for, the right arm and represents strength, strength of the soul as well strength of the body of the person; and, as I shall attempt to show, in both the symbolism is also a representation of the collective strength of the lineage to which the person belongs.

I have suggested that the fighting-spear has a symbolic meaning for Nuer besides what it means for them as weapon and tool—that it is a projection of the self and stands for the self. This is most important for an understanding of Nuer sacrifice. Its manipulation in the most common, and for a study of religion the most significant, sacrifices, the personal and piacular ones, expresses, if our interpretation is right, the throwing of the whole person into the intention of the sacrifice. It is not only said but also thought, desired, and felt. Not only the lips make it but also the mind, the will, and the heart. This interpretation makes the miming with the spear intelligible for, as an extension of the right arm, it stands for the whole person.[8] It is for this reason that a spear must carried during the invocation and not in order to slay the animal at the end of it. Other invocations by other men may follow before that is done, and the quick dramatic thrust into its heart which concludes the rite may be made by anyone, and not necessarily by a man who has made an invocation or by a spear used in the invocation.

But we have also to note that on many sacrificial occasions—those of a collective kind held in structural situations—when a man makes an invocation he does so as the representative of his clan (where 'clan' is used in this context 'clan or lineage' is to be understood—a man may be speaking in reference to his maximal lineage). He identifies himself with the clan by identifying his spear with that of the ancestor of the clan. It is his own spear which he brandishes but the name of the spear he shouts out as he does so is that of the spear of the ancestor of the clan, the clan spear-name. This is characteristic of sacrifices of the collective type, and it is towards them that the discussion is now directed.

Each of the Nuer clans has a spear-name and sometimes a

large lineage of a clan has secondary name which is different from that of another lineage of the same clan. This spear-name is shouted out by a representative of the clan while he brandishes a spear in his right hand, in war, at weddings, and on other public occasions when the clan as a whole is concerned—ideally, that is, and never actively and corporately. It is especially shouted out as an exordium to sacrificial invocations on occasions of collective significance (pp.288-9). It is '*mut gwara*', 'the spear of our fathers'. On such of these occasions as require the services of a leopard-skin priest he calles out the spear name '*mut Geaka*', 'spear of Gee', a spear-name which combines the representation of the priestly office with that of the Nuer as a whole.

It is essential to note that, with two exceptions, no actual spears of the ancestors of the clans exist, and it is not held by Nuer that they ever did exist, except in the sense that the ancestors had their own spears. The virtue is in the idea of 'the spear of our fathers', not in any material clan relic. Consequently, in invocations any spear will serve the purpose of the rite and represent that of the ancestor of the clan and hence symbolize the clan as a whole. Any spear will do, but, for the reason I have stated, there must be a spear; and when Nuer sitting in my tent recounted to me what is said in invocations they gestured with their right hands as though they held spears in them, for they found it difficult to speak the words without making the gestures, just as in recounting what is said in prayers(*pal*) they found it difficult to do so without moving outstretched hands up and down.

Published literature on the Nuer records information about only two actual spears of clans. The one about which we are told most is the spear, called *wiu*, of the Gaatgankir clan, who are regarded by all, including themselves, as being of Dinka origin; and the spear is a Dinka, and not a Nuer, type of spear. A mysterious origin and power are attributed to it. It is believed to have been held by Kir, the ancestor of the clan, when he was cut out of the gourd in which he was found, and it is also associated with the air-spirit *wiu*, which is regarded as being in some sense immanent in it. When I was in Nuerland it was in the charge of a family of leopard-skin priests of the Tar lineage of the eastern Gaajak tribe. I did not myself see it, but it has been described by Mr. H.C. Jackson, who saw it in 1922 near the Pibor river.[9] He records that it was decorated with cowrie shells and beads and was housed in a special grass hut where visitors treated it with great deference. He says that it was prayed and sacrificed to, especially before raids on the Dinka and Burun peoples;[10] that if two sections of the Nuer wished to engage in fighting among themselves it would be placed between them to prevent an engagement; and that oaths were taken on it. I was told that only old people would look upon it. The importance of this spear to our discussion of clan spear-names is that, as I will explain later, all such spear-names have an association with the spirit *wiu* through the further association of this spirit with lightning and hence with the idea of striking, so that the spear *wiu*, perhaps also because it has a material existence, has become the prototype of clan 'spears'. Of the other spear, that of Thiang clan and tribe, who occupy a territory I have not myself visited, we told by Mr. B.A. Lewis only in whose possession and it is and that it is called *mut bah thiang*.[11] Dr. P. P. Howell who gives its name as *mut bar thiang,* tells me that he has not seen it but Nuer have described it to him as being nearly worn through with much polishing. It is unknown whether any cultic practices like those I have mentioned above are connected with it.

Apart from the Gaatgankir and the Thiang spears the spear-symbols of the Nuer clans and lineages are only names. Through the association of a tribal community with the clan dominant in it the spear-name of this clan is shouted out in invocations when the whole tribe goes to war but, except in this context, which I discuss below, in which a political group is merged conceptually with a clan or lineage, it is only called out in reference to a descent group as an exclusive group. Thus, when I asked a Wot tribesman whether his tribe had a tribal spear he replied: 'We have many spears. One lineage (*gol*) has one spear, another lineage has another spear, a third lineage has a different spear, and so on. 'By 'spear' he meant a spear-name, not an actual spear, Consequently, if two persons have the same spear-name there is likelihood of agnatic relationship, and spear-names are therefore often spoken of in connexion with proposed marriages. One hears Nuer saying in discussions about the permissibility of a proposed marriage 'what about their spears?" they have the same spear, they cannot marry', or 'their spear is different to ours, we can marry their dauthter'.[12] At a wedding the masters of ceremonies on the bride's side and on the bridegroom's side, each acting as representative of his clan, begin their formal announcements that the marriage negotiations have reached a successful conclusion (*twoc ghok*) by shouting out their clan spear-names. The spear-name is also shouted out by the master of ceremonies as the opening words of the sacrificial invocation he makes when a Dinka boy is adopted into the lineage of the man who has given him domicile, the expression for adopting being either *lath buthbni*, to be given shares (in sacrificia meats) and hence to be given agnation, or *lath muot*, to be given a spear (-name), and hence to be made a member of the clan. He also shouts it out in sacrificial invocations at mortuary ceremonies, at settlement of blood-feuds, at initiations, and on other occasions which concern the whole clan. When, as mentioned above, clan tribe are identified politically in war and raiding a representative of the dominant clan of the tribe brandishes a spear and calls out the spear-name of his clan on behalf of the whole tribe. This man, called *ngul*,[13] is usually, perhaps always, a leading man of the senior lineage of the dominant clan, that descended from the eldest son of the ancestor of the clan. Thus in the Lou tribe this rite is performed by a man of Gaaliek lineage of the Jinaca clan. Likewise the Tar lineage who have charge of the *wiu* spear are descendeants of Thiang, the eldest son of the founder of the clan; and the Thiang clan who own the *thiang* spear are descended from Thiang, the eldest son of Gee.

I cannot always explain the meaning of these spear-names or even translate them, and Nuer themselves cannot always say for certain what they mean, for they arose in ancient days. It is clear, however, that they are charged with symbols expressing the unity and continuity of clans and lineages. I give a few examples, choosing those in which the meaning is more or less evident. The Jiruet lineage have *mut tora*, spear of the monorchid. This lineage respects monorchids, whether they be man or beast. The Gaatiek clan have *mut yier*, spear of the stream, because their ancestor came out of a stream. The Gaatnaca clan have *mut ghama*, spear of the thigh. This seems to refer to the loins of the ancestor from whom they sprang. The Gaaliek lineage of this clan have the secondary spear-name *mut tang*, spear of the spear-shaft, because the *ngul*, whom I have referred to above, of the Lou tribe is of this lineage. He uses a spear-shaft in war ritual. The Gaatleak clan have *mut leak*, the word *leak* being simply, it would seem, taken from the clan name itself. Many leopard-skin priests are members of this clan and, as I have explained, they use *mut Geaka*, spear of Gee, as an alternative expression. The Thiang lineage have a secondary spear-name *mut Thiang*, spear of Thiang, which is the name of their ancestor.

When a man calls out his clan spear-name he often does so with embellishments, which are further symbolical representations of the clan. They refer to its ancestor, its spirits, its totems, its ghosts, its cattle, or its origin and traditions. Thus a Gaatgankir clansman in making invocations adds to mut wiu such expressions as *mut kwe, mut jangemo me coali kir*, and *mut gwara. Kwe* is the fish-eagle and also a colour distribution of cattle. The shining of the spear is likened to the white face of the fish-eagle against its black body and to the white splash on the head of a dark coloured cow or ox. *Jaangemo me coali Kir* means 'that Dinka who is called Kir' and refers to the Dinka origin of the clan. Mut *gwara* means 'spear of our fathers'. The spear in the hand of the speaker, the spear *wiu*, the spear used to cut open the gourd in which the ancestor was found, and the spirit wiu all seem to be fused in the representation. In a similar manner the Gaawar clan may add to their spear-name *mut wang*, spear of the eye (I think), such expressions as *mut nhial, mut puara*, and *mut kwoth nyota*. I do not know why the spear is called 'spear of the eye' (if that is the right translation). *Nhial* is the firmament and *puar* is a cloud. Their ancestor fell from the sky and the clan is therefore associated with sky, clouds, and rain. When he fell he had in his hand a sprig of the *nyuot tree*, a tree associated with rain. Hence the *kwoth nyota*, the spirit of the *nyuot tree*.

Thus the spear-name is either that of the ancestor of the lineage or clan or in some way signifies him, and the elaborations of it, such as by reference to a spirit or a totem, are also just different ways of denoting the lineage or clan as a whole; for the name of the ancestor stands for the whole clan, both here and elsewhere. We have noted earlier how in myths a lineage is personified for the purpose of the action of the story, the name of the lineage or of its tribal territory being used to indicate its ancestor. Nuer sometimes even insert the name of a lineage into a genealogy as its founder, though the form of the word shows that it is the name of a group and not of a person; or they give the founder a composite name, appending the name of the lineage to the personal name, for example, Nyang Gaaliek, Nyang being the name of the person and Gaaliek the name of the lineage of his descendants.

I have attempted to show that the spear brandished in sacrificial invocations stands for the person and that when this person speaks as a representative and on behalf of the clan, as he does in collective sacrifices, it stands for the clan. In the one case it is the right hand (vitality) of the individual and in the other the right hand (vitality) of the ancestor (the clan) which is emphasized. In the second case the spear is closely associated with the idea of the clan as a battle host.

When we ask why clans should be symbolized by a spear, or rather by the idea of a spear contained in a spear-name, and not by something else, we cannot give an acceptable answer in terms of the scarcity, and therefore high value, of iron nor in terms of simple utility. The symbol is not *yieth* or *you*, iron.[14] Nor is it the *bidh*, the fishing-spear, which is perhaps even more essential for Nuer than the fighting-spear, for they have no substitute for it and could not survive without a good supply of fish. It is the *mut*, the iron fighting-spear. The fact that the wood, horn, and bone pointed spears do not figure as symbols might suggest that it is because it is made of iron, which lasts longer and makes a more efficient weapon, that the *mut* is the smybol of clans, but it appears to me to be a more satisfactory explanation that it is because the mut not only stands for the right hand and hence vitality but is also the symbol of going to war and of making sacrifice.

The word *mut*, besides meaning a fighting-spear, has a general sense of taking part in war and raiding: '*ce Nath wa mut*', 'the Nuer went raiding'; '*ca mut nang Jaang*', 'war was taken (by the Nuer) to the Dinka'. The idea expressed by the word *mut* in these examples is not so much the general idea of war and raiding as the idea of a collectivity, the clan or lineage in its political or tribal embodiment, going to war or going on a raid. Hence Father Kiggen correctly translates '*te ke mud mediid*' (his spelling) as 'they have a big army'.[15] By syncdoche 'spear stands for 'battle host'.

It is, I believe, in some such sense of the clan militant that we should interpret the spear symbolism of the clans. Nuer always speak of 'spear' where I have used the expression 'spear-name'. However, not only are there in almost all cases no actual spears,but it is not even the idea of any particular spear that they have in mind. What they have in mind is the clan as a whole for which the spear stands as a symbol not just as a spear but as representing the collective strength of the clan in its most conspicuous corporate actitivity, for clans and lineages are most easily and distinctly thought of as collectivities—through their identification with tribes and tribal segments—in relation to war. That the representaton is of the clanas a battle host is shown by the Nuer statement about their clan spears that they only exist in the sense that 'they are in the mouths of men when they go to battle'. Two remarks made by the Nuer give further support to an interpretation along these lines. One man said of all clan spears that '*tuokdien e wiu*', 'their origin is *wiu*', and that *wiu* is the *kwoth*, spirit, of all clan spears. There was some discussion about this remark among Nuer present, and I gathered from it that all clan spears in this wide and symbolic sense of the word *mut* as the battle host signify the clan as a social group in relation to God in the conception of him as Lord of Hosts. The man could not have meant that other clan spears were derived or copied from the spear *wiu*. That would have made no sense, both because there no actual spears and also because the Gaatgankir clan who own the spear *wiu* are regarded by everybody as a Dinka clan of later origin than the truc Nuer clans. That a spiritual conception of *wiu* was meant is further evident from a remark made to me by abnother Nuer, a man of exceptional ability, that when the Gaatgankir clan reach then generations from their ancestor Kir—when they have grown up, so to speak—they will doubtless cease to respect (*thek*) the spear *wiu*, as they do at present, and will respect (the word is here used to balance the statement and not literally) only its name. As we should put it, they will not then feel the need for a material symbol of the spiritual relationship, and a verbal or ideational symbol will suffice. The association of clan spears with the spirit *wiu* is clear to us when we recall that the spirit is also associated with lightning with which, in this hypostasis, God strikes as man strikes with the spear.[16]

In invocations in which clans are involved as such God is appealed to, as I have explained earlier, in some refraction by which he is figured as their patron. This is the '*kwoth gwara*', 'the God of our fathers'. It is on such occasions also that the spear-name of the clan is shouted out as an exordium to the invocation. This is the '*mut gwara*', the spear of our fathers'. I would suggest that we have here in the spear-name a symbolic representation of the clan in its relation to God God is invoked in relation to the clan through the spear of the ancestor held in imagination in the hand of one of his descendants.

If this interpretation is right, then in those sacrifices in which the clan as a whole is concerned the calling out of the clan spear-name by the officiant identifies the whole clan with the intention of the sacrifice as spoken in the invocation. The sacrificial spear in his hand becomes through the exordium the clan sacrificial spear through which in symbol the whole clan offers up the victim to God. The officiant in such sacrifices must therefore be a representative of the clan, what the Nuer call a *gwan buthni*; whereas in personal and piacular sacrifices, in which appeal is made on behalf of an individual or a number of individuals, anyone can officiate and the officiant is usually a senior member of the family or kin of the sacrificer. The intention, and therefore character, of the sacrificial act is different in the two cases. In the first it is of the nature of a validation, in the second of the nature of a piaculum; though in some situations there may be a broad overlap. Religion has always these two sides, the one concerned chiefly with the social life and the other with the relation of the individual soul to its God.

NOTES

1. Being the only thing they have which cuts and is therefore suitable for shaving - their other spears only pierce - the verbal form of the word for fighting spear, *mut*, besides its meaning of 'to spear' means 'to cut' or 'shave hair'. When used in the last sense it often refers to ritual shaving of the head, and it may then be used for the whole ceremony of which shaving of the head forms part, as the final marriage ceremony of consummation and ceremonies in connexion with death.

2. Among many primitive peoples the slight organic asymmetry between the left hand and the right is made the symbol of absolute moral polarity. Robert Hertz has treated the subject systematically in a brilliant essay, 'La preeminence de la main droite', Revue philosophique, xxxiv, 1909 (reprinted in *melanges de sociologie religieuse et de folklore*, 1928).

3. Left and right are of course relative to the orientation of the person. Thus when a man takes his bearings from the entrance to hut or windscreen what is left from the inside will be right from the outside. I do not think, however, that the point of orientation affects the argument, for it is conventional that in reference to any particular matter the one side is left and the other right.

4. All deformed horns in the photographs are left horns. Some branches in them, however, are to the left of windscreens, but

Nuer erect branches for practical purposes as well as for religious reasons, and I do not think it is possible to distinguish between them by sight.

5. I was told that a wife may act as master of ceremonies in her husband's place and shout out the spear-name of his clan at a wedding. This is the *twoc ghok* mentioned later. It is not a sacrifical invocation. It must be a very rate occurrence for a woman to play this role. Probably she can only take the part if she is acting on behalf of the bridegroom's family and hence holds in her hand, not a spear, but the instrument called dang (Fig 4 and also if she is an old woman, of whom Nuer say 'she has become a man'. There is one occasion when women bear spears. Twins go through a fictional wedding before they can go through a real one. In this ceremony men array themselves as women, and women as men.

6. P.P. Howell, 'On the Value of Iron among the Nuer', Man, 1947, No. 144.

7. The Nuer: Age-Sets', *Sudan Notes and Records, 1936.*

8. Among the Shilluk the officiant rubs his spear on the back of the victim, as the Nuer places his right on its back (D.S. Oyler, Sudan Notes and Records, 1920, p.298).

9. H.C. Jackson, op. cit., pp. 168 and 179-81.

10. We are probably to understand, in view of Nuer religious conceptions in general, that Nuer respect (*thek*) the spear and pray and sacrifice to the spirit *wiu*, which is in the sky as well as in the spear. Mr. R.T. Johnston reached the same conclusion with regard to a similar spear among the Bor Dinka. He observes that 'the spear by itself, except by association and as a symbol, is not sacred' (op. cit., p.127). Dr. Lienhardt tells me that when the Government, with remarkable lack of imagination, confiscated and removed this spear lest it should become a focus of opposition to the administration the Dinkas' faith was in no way lessened. The only result was that the spirit associated with the spear, no longer having a recognized material symbol in a single place, manifested itself all over the tribal territory, defying any further intervention.

11. B.A. Lewis, op. cit., p.82.

12. Should the two clans have the same spear-name this is not always a bar in the union, for secondary spear-names may indicate

that they belong to different clans, or other circumstances may be taken into consideration.

13. He is also called *ngul ghok, ngul* of cattle, an expression which probably refers to the taking of enemy cattle on raids, and *gwan muot*, possessor of the spear. As he may break a spear-shaft in two and throw the pieces in the direction of the enemy he is further known as *gwan tung*, possessor of the spear-shaft. I was told that he may also invoke God for success in hunting in time of famine

14. It is true that Nuer lick any metal in taking an oath (p.297), but I regard this as being a derivation from licking a spear, for which any metal stands as a substitute, in the same way as the honorific titles of the Gaatgankir clan, son, and daughter, of iron, derive from the *wiu* spear.The words *yieth*, metaland *yiedh*, to spear or to stab are surely connected.

15. J. Kiggen, op. cit., p.206. One may ask, in the light of this discussion about the *mut*, why it is that the title of spiritual leaders in Dinkaland is taken from the fishing-spear (*bith*) instead of from the fighting-spear. An explanation might be put forward in terms of the analysis I have presented. Whereas among the Nuer the fighting spear is the symbol of the clan because what is being symbolized in exclusiveness and opposition, among the Dinka the fishing-spear is the symbol of spiritual leadership because what is being symbolized is inclusiveness and unity. This is a guess but it receives some support from the fact that among the Nuer, at any rate in western Nuerland, when a leopard-skin priest goes to settle a feud he is accompanied by a kinsman called the *gwan biedh*, the matter of the fishing-spear, which is the title of the Dinka spiritual leaders. However, this may be a loan from the Dinka.

16. Nuer, however, use for God striking a man with lighting the verbs *mar*, to strike, and *pim*, to strike in the sense of 'to hit' or 'to punch', and not *yeidh*, to strike in the sense of to thrust or to stab.

---

* Excerpted from *Nuer Religion* by E.E. Evanspritchard 1956: Oxford